God's Not Done with Me Yet

with Me Yet

(He's Only Just Begun)

*Tiffany My Friend & Gym buddy
Always remember "God's got you"
as long as you let him
Be blessed
Craig*

Craig Walter

(as told to Dr. Bonli)

ISBN 978-1-64349-034-2 (paperback)
ISBN 978-1-64349-035-9 (digital)

Christian Faith Publishing, Inc.
832 Park Avenue
Meadville, PA 16335
www.christianfaithpublishing.com

Printed in the United States of America

To all the children, young adults, and adults
who are still in pain and feel lost.

GOD'S NOT DONE WITH ME YET

Acknowledgments

T o God, I truly give all the glory. Without God, I wouldn't be who I am today.

Thank you, Bonnie, for believing in me and what I write; for your faith and many prayers throughout this project.

Judi and family (Tim, Danny, and Aaron), for being the family for me I desperately needed and your prayers through all the years.

Michelle, Ed, James, Wyatt, Cody, Jonathan, and Billy, for allowing me to be a part of your family; to be a godfather and uncle.

Curtis, for remaining my steadfast friend.

Ken, for your forgiveness and continued undying friendship.

My friend Fred, for always having words of inspiration even in the midst of your own spiritual trials.

Deborra, for encouraging me to write.

Anesha, my friend, you are always bolstering my faith when it starts to falter.

Luke, my friend, you had a faith in me before you knew me. Thank you, to you and your family, for your friendship and constant support.

To everyone who enabled me, when I was younger, or tried to help me, you all played a part in my life that led me to where I am today—right here, right now.

GOD'S NOT DONE WITH ME YET

Foreword

80   cs

Many times, throughout my younger adult life, I have told the stories of my childhood, what it was like growing up in my home. Oftentimes, people would tell me that my story should be in a book. I had always dismissed those ideas because I could talk about it one-on-one with someone but to expose this to the world? This, what I considered a dark secret? I would be too afraid of hurting someone. I may not have cared too much about my family at that time, but I cared enough, as a person, to not want to cause anyone any pain.

I would go through my years of trials, tribulations, chasing my demons, and being chased by demons until finally searching for God and Jesus. It wasn't until a mission trip, when I shared my full life testimony, that I was told by various people, "Do you know how many people you could help with your story? You should really have it in a book." It had been many, many years since anyone had mentioned "my story in a book." I am no one spectacular or particularly special, but when it was brought to my attention about "how many people you could help," that changed my attitude completely and prompted the writing of this book.

I have allowed different individuals, from various walks of life, to read some excerpts of this book as it was being written and got very similar responses from, "My brother needs to read this. He still hasn't been able to deal with—" to, "I have a friend that has spent her whole life struggling with—this would help her so much."

An old friend from high school, Jane—recently finding me and having read some of this—wrote me, saying,

"Craig! What a true witness to the power of faith and finding peace in God's love! Blessings to you and for your mission to serve others with your story."

Holly, who had also been one of Judi's rescue kids and became like a "foster sister" when Judi took me in, recently wrote me:

"I always knew there was something special about you. Your smile could light up the room, but I also saw a painful darkness behind those beautiful eyes. You're a wonderful person, I love what you have written. Can't wait to read the book. I still wish I could go to Honduras with you. You have touched so many hearts there. You're going to the top. Love ya, Holly."

One gentleman went so far as to comment through tears:

"Craig, I know this isn't what you want, but this is going to make you famous by all the people you are going to help."

Fame is definitely not the intention behind this book. As Francesca Battistelli sings in her song, "He Knows My Name":

> "I don't need my name in lights
> I'm famous in my *Father's* eyes
> Make no mistake
> *He* knows my name.
> I'm not living for applause,
> I'm already so adored
> It's all *His* stage
> *He* knows my name."

But the thought of the help—the help this book might bring to someone that reads it. I was feeling deeply inside my heart, my soul, that God was wanting this to be written. He is leading me, that this was yet another reason why He has made sure I have stayed around, to be able to help others in this way.

This is why the book needs to be written now. Years ago, it would have been just another story about abuse and addictions. Today, it's a story of the power of God's healing and forgiving through Jesus Christ.

Timelines may not be exact, and some names may have been altered, but the events are real.

*There was no intent toward malice, by any means, in the writing of this book.

GOD'S NOT DONE WITH ME YET

Prologue

୫ଠ   ଠ୫

This is the story of a little boy who survives a childhood of emotional, mental, and physical abuse—sometimes unimaginable and unspeakable types of cruelty, which no child should have to live through or endure. This little boy tries to run away from home by the time he's thirteen only to be "captured" by the police and returned. As he becomes a young teen, he experiences intense bullying in high school, the divorce of his parents and remarriage of his father, more physical abuse, family strife, his own failed suicide attempt, following his dreams to the theater, being thrown out of the house by his father and stepmother, and landing in jail. His friend's mother takes him in as part of the family. Haunting memories of abuse, strong desires to act, and his desperate need to get away lead to his move to Hollywood.

As a young man, he finds work in the movies and meets or works with many famous people: the likes of Michael Jackson, as an actor in his famous "hair on fire" Pepsi commercial; Robert Downey Jr. and Rodney Dangerfield in the movie *Back to School*; Valerie Bertinelli in *Another High Roller*; Gary Busey in the movie *The Bear*—to name just a few, even dating one of the stars of a popular soap opera. Yet he still cannot escape the memories and feelings of absolute inadequacies, inferiority, and worthlessness subsequently leading to escaping through drug and alcohol abuse.

For many years, he lives a wild, drug and alcohol-infused, sexually sordid, and unsavory lifestyle that lands him in jail a couple of times. His life spirals downward completely culminating in yet another serious but failed suicide attempt—failed because his best friend in Alabama had interfered. This man leaves Hollywood, making a different kind of escape, to Alabama, but the addictions he was trying to escape have followed. He falls in love, but through the course of a sixteen-and-a-half-year relationship and a wonderful dysfunctional extended family of nephews and godsons, his addiction has gotten the best of him. Another suicide attempt, going back to jail, a stint in rehab, relapse, jail again, rehab again, and finally sobriety.

What he did not anticipate was that a few years down the road, he would endure one of his greatest challenges in life—stage 4 cancer—and least of all did he ever believe that this would lead him to the church: coming to Christ, baptism, and mission work. Looking back and seeing his life as a little boy from a painful childhood and the incredible journey toward his life today, he can see that God had always been there.

This boy's story, which you are going to read, is not unlike thousands of other children, teens, and young adults out there who are living through painful, traumatic memories and don't know how to cope with the aftermath of abuse or addictions. Try to remember somehow that you are not alone, that God *is* there. If you are reading this, then that means you haven't given up and God is not done with you yet.

I know this because that little boy is me. I'm Craig Walter. I was born May 16, 1963, and this is my story—my story of struggles, miracles, overcoming, forgiveness, and redemption. By being here and sharing my story with you means I haven't given up either and is just more proof that God's not done with me yet. He's only just begun.

It's not about me. It's not about my story. It's about everyone else who needs to know that there is always hope.

Dredging up the Past

෨   ඬ

I'm twenty-five and sitting in the living room of the tiny duplex I'm renting in North Hollywood, California. I'm renting this place because a acquaintance of mine owns it and I need the lower rent so I can better afford to smoke pot, drink, and go to the clubs. My drinking has slowly evolved into a constant occurrence. I smoke pot every day, all day. Wherever I go, I have my pipe and a bag of weed with me. I'm doing coke and snorting crystal, when it's available, at clubs and other venues—sometimes at work, if a friend has some. Somehow, I'm still managing a good workout at the gym every day, but I have pretty much given up on show business because I need a regular paycheck to support my "needs." I'm still having great difficulties dealing with my everyday existence. My past. My childhood. I have nightmares sometimes about my mother.

I wake up every morning about five o'clock, pack the bowl of my pipe with weed, and start to smoke. I've been in this 5:00-a.m. routine for about two weeks now because this is how I prepare myself mentally for making the cassette tapes that I'm going to send to my family members. This is my way of confronting and dealing with my childhood and what happened in our family. I don't know if I'm going to get any questions answered, but I need to get this out of my head and hopefully stop the dreams. Maybe, I think, just maybe my messed up life will start getting better.

*****

At this point in my life, I would be the last person to believe that twenty-five more years down the road, Jesus Christ would become a major part of my life.

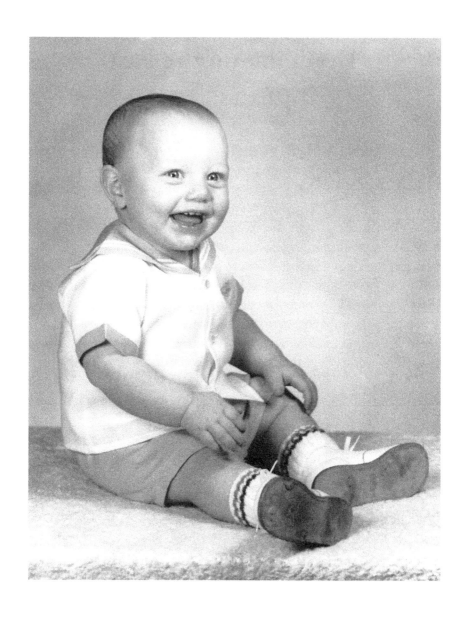

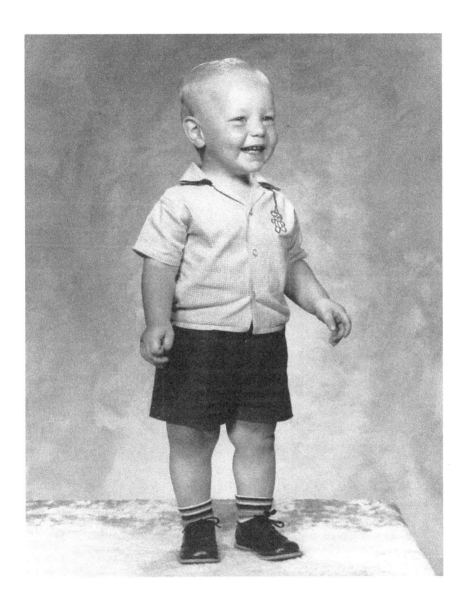

WHEN IT ALL STARTED

GOD'S NOT DONE WITH ME YET

Where Did My Little Brother Go

I was born on May 16, 1963, in Hammond Indiana at St. Margaret's Hospital. To any passerby, we were a typical, middle-class family, living in a house in a suburb of Chicago, but what went on inside that house was anything but typical.

My earliest memory is a traumatic one. It was a clear, pleasant day in the summer of 1966. I remember being in the bathroom on the upstairs level of our four-floor, split level house, where I can see across the hallway to my parents' bedroom. My father had already gone to work, and I saw my mother bouncing a bundle of blankets on the bed. What she was doing and why I wasn't sure, but she seemed to be enjoying herself. I remember being confused by this image that became imprinted on my mind.

It turns out that my little brother—who was born on December 29, 1964, and wasn't much more than a year old at the time—was wrapped up in that bundle of blankets. I was a little over three years old.

An ambulance and a police car came to our house, and my little brother was taken away from us. My older sister and I had to go stay with neighbors. I don't recall for how long, but I didn't understand any of it. My brother was in and out of the hospital and foster homes for a number of years. We would go visit him but always in a staged institutional typesetting, in an area like a waiting room with the cheap wooden chairs with plastic type cushions and some toys in the room. They weren't warm, loving visits you would expect among family, and I don't recall them being very long, nowhere near long enough to actually get to know him as my brother. For a long time, he was practically a stranger to me, a distant relative we saw once in awhile, maybe once a month. It would be years before he came back to live with us.

*****

I find out much later in life when I confronted my father with the tapes I had recorded that they were supervised visits and that my brother had been taken away due to suspected child abuse. I was left behind.

*****

During the years of my brother's absence, abuse at home picked up. My mother was very sadistic and cruel. She took all her anger out on me for reasons that, to this day, I still don't know or understand. I have never dared to approach the subject. She received a copy of my tapes like everyone else, but I don't know if she ever listened to them. They have never been discussed.

Mother loved using the belt, always leaving welts. Sometimes, they were so severe they would bleed in her rages. She also loved to pull my hair to the point that you could hear the crackling noise as the hair came out at the roots. She loved to take the hairbrush and beat me on the head so many times that my head would be nothing but tender painful knots. Many times, she would hit me again before the old wounds had a chance to fully heal, causing more excruciating pain on top of already sensitive bumps and bruises. By the time I was in kindergarten, I was already terrified of her. In fact, I can't remember ever not being afraid. Even during calm times when there was a *hint* of happiness and sanity in our house, there was always a tiny bit of fear in the back of my mind. I was always wary that something, anything I did, could change her mood and trigger that rage.

I won't claim to have been a perfect child. I know I did wrong things like all children do. Children are children. Still, no child deserves the type of torment that I experienced. I learned, at a very early age, that if I told the truth about something I did, my punishment would be as severe as if I had lied and been caught. If I lied,

I stood a fifty-fifty chance of surviving unscathed. The problem is I was always in trouble for something, anything, and everything and—most often—nothing. My older sister, when we were adults, told me of times that I got the blame for things she had done and how fearful she was for the brutal punishments I received. I never saw my sister punished.

*****

While my younger brother is gone, my mother will have another child, the last of my siblings, my baby brother.

*****

Me and my younger brother before he was taken away.
September 1965. He is nine months old.

Me and my younger brother. 1965.

A Church Family

℘   ℭ

We were a churchgoing family. Every Sunday, we dressed up and went to the Methodist church. Then during the week, I would get beat. It was church on Sunday, beating on weekdays; Sunday church, weekday beating. That was the cycle of hypocrisy in my family.

I looked forward to Sunday. It was the one day of the week that I felt relatively safe for at least half the day. Nothing could happen before church, or I would show up with puffy eyes and swollen face from crying. I remember the children would sit with our families in the sanctuary until that part of the service where we would go to our Sunday school classes. I enjoyed those classes because they were calm and I was not afraid. I would listen to our Sunday schoolteacher telling us the wonderful stories from the Bible: Noah's Ark, Daniel in the lion's den, Moses and the Ten Commandments, and Jesus's birth. After church, my mother would usually make fried chicken for dinner. It would generally be a calm day. The problem was that church was once a week. We would go on Sunday, but for the rest of the week, I would spend my days being scared of what might happen next.

Because home was so chaotic, I remember looking forward to kindergarten classes. Unfortunately for me, I enjoyed being around the other kids too much. My teacher would say, "Craig loves to visit." Considering how beaten down I was at home, being at school was a whole different world of freedom and no beatings, but one of my report cards was not so good. Can you believe anyone could get a bad kindergarten report card? It had to do with my "visiting" with the other kids too much. In other words, I like to talk. I wanted to be liked because I was not liked at home. Only in kindergarten and already I felt, at such a young age, that I wasn't liked at home. I was so afraid of what was going to happen at home that when I left school that day, I accidentally dropped my report card in the schoolyard before my mother picked me up. I told her that the wind had blown it away and I couldn't catch it. I got away with it for a couple of days. Unfortunately, a conscientious parent found my report card and called my mother. Thank you, conscientious parent. My mother realized I had lost it on purpose and was so mad that along with all the yelling, she dragged me upstairs to my room by my hair, took my belt off, and gave me a severe whipping that left welts on my skin.

One of my mother's favorite things to do was to take her hands, as if she were holding a pair of cymbals, and bang them on the sides of my head so hard that I would see flashes of bright spots and feel dizzy and disoriented. The more I cried and yelled in pain, the more I got yelled at and hit. It doesn't make sense. She would scream, "There is not a single picture of you with your mouth shut! Every picture we have, your mouth is wide open!" I would hear that repeated many times throughout my childhood.

After kindergarten, I became unsociable and introverted. All through elementary school, I became the outcast and the easy target for early childhood bullying that would extend through my high school years.

Prisoner at Home

ℰ℧   ℭℛ

I don't know exactly when it started, maybe in kindergarten, maybe in first grade. I would get locked in my bedroom every single night for a number of years. On the upper level of our house was a big square foyer outlined by our rooms. Going clockwise, my bedroom was the first on the left, at the top the stairs; straight ahead, next to my room, was our parents' room, then my sister's, and the upstairs bathroom.

Being locked in the bedroom was a form of punishment, I believe, but I have no idea why. I would always be let out in the mornings in time for breakfast and school. My bedroom upstairs didn't actually have a lock, so my mother attached a bell to the top of my door so that if I were to try to get out, it would wake her up. My mother worked the night shift as a prenatal nurse, so this was mostly in effect on her nights off. However, when my baby brother was born, he stayed in their room, so my mother was off work for a period of time. I do remember times that I did wake up in the night to go to the bathroom. That was no excuse for leaving my room. I would be so scared, and no matter how carefully I would try to open the door, that bell would jingle and wake her up. I would then be taken downstairs to the basement so we wouldn't wake anyone, where my mother had a stick that she would crack over my head. I didn't dare holler out in pain. It might wake someone, and that would mean even more cracking over the head.

I thought I had figured out a way to be able to go to the bathroom without leaving my bedroom. There was an old game called "Barrel of Monkeys," where you had to link the monkey's arms one by one until you got them all out of the barrel; I had the miniature version. My plan was to empty the monkeys out, pee in the barrel, close the barrel back up, and hide it behind the books in the bookcase in my bedroom. As a little kid, knowing I was going to get beat if I left my bedroom, this was my solution. My little-boy brain did not think there would be consequences for what I had done, but my mother found that barrel. She took me and the barrel across the hall to the bathroom, stood me at the toilet, and made me drink every drop of my own pee while she yelled at me. When I was done drinking, I immediately vomited in the toilet and on the floor. I remember getting beat with the hairbrush for the mess that I had made and then being made to clean it up. I was always made to go to the bathroom before being shut in my room, but some nights, I would still wake up having to go. So I figured out a different solution. Since my bedroom was on the upper level and my dresser was right underneath the window, I could open it and pee out through the window screen. Mom never found out, so I relieved myself this way until my bedroom was moved downstairs so that my baby brother could have the bedroom upstairs.

My sister used to take dance lessons, and the room on the lower level, just above the basement, in between the TV room and the downstairs bathroom that was still being built, was her dance room. My parents converted this into my new bedroom: my "downstairs dungeon." With mother's bedroom being two floors up, she wouldn't hear a bell attached to my door, so she devised a different way to secure me in my room. In the unfinished bathroom, right next to my bedroom, she hammered a nail into the wall stud so she would be able to tie a rope around my bedroom doorknob and tie it off around the nail every night when I went to bed.

Now I had a problem—a big problem. If I had to go to the bathroom, I was trapped. My bedroom window was now at ground level, which was above my head. Even with the dresser under this window, I could open it, but there was no way possible for me to reach myself to the level of the window to pee through it. My only hope for relief now was my big toy cabinet in the corner of the bedroom. I would squeeze myself as close as I could to the wall in the corner and pee behind my toy cabinet. My urine would run down the paneling and soak into the carpet tiles on the floor underneath my toy cabinet. I got away with this for a long time until one day, my mother couldn't figure out "what the hell" that smell was in my bedroom and "where the hell" it was coming from. You know I was very scared now.

My mother eventually found the source of the smell, moved my toy cabinet out of the way, and saw the urine-stained wall and carpet. Now I am petrified! I remember my mother grabbing me by the hair, yanking me across the room, shoving my face down to the stained carpet like a dog being punished to make sure I got a good smell of what I had done, and yelling at me about how could I possibly live in a stench like this! Then of course, I was forced to get a bucket of soapy water and a scrub brush from the sink in the basement, which was the next floor down, the whole time being hit and yelled at. She yelled even more if I spilled any on the way back from the basement, up the flight of stairs, to my room. It seemed never ending. The more I was yelled at and hit, the more I would spill, and it just wouldn't stop!

These punishments were so exhausting, I can remember feeling as if I was just reeling in an endless state of pure emotional and physical detachment. She would not stop, and I was becoming completely worn out! My father was always at work or not around when these severe punishments took place, but he never did anything about my being locked in my bedroom every night. I did eventually find a solution, a way to get out of this bedroom prison cell undetected.

I found out that when I pulled the door hard enough, the rope would stretch. I can remember it was a thin white rope. If I was careful and stretched it just enough to fit my arm through, I could reach around and feel how it was looped. I had to remember what I was feeling so I could wrap and loop it when I got back in my bedroom. It took a bit of work, but when I was free, I could go into the unfinished bathroom and pee into the drain of the shower. I had to do that because it was too risky to flush the toilet because someone would hear.

This new technique for escape was also good for when I was grounded, which was almost all the time. Grounding rules seemed to have been made for me only. If my little brother ever got grounded, which was very rare, it might last half a day. Before you know it, he would be sitting in mother's lap watching TV. My groundings were at least two weeks to a month at a time. Grounding meant absolutely no TV, no desserts or sweets of any kind, no playing outside, and hard labor, meaning I had to do all the chores and work around the house: washing dishes, taking out the garbage, vacuuming, mopping, laundry, dusting. When the dusting was done, my mother would literally put on a white glove and do the "white glove" test. That was always scary. I know I always tried to do a good job because if I didn't I, would be in trouble. If my mother's swipe of the finger with the white glove came up dirty, I was usually pulled over to that spot by my hair, smacked upside the head, told how worthless I was, and yelled at to dust the whole room over again because if I missed one spot, she was sure I missed many more. There were times when her white glove actually came up clean. You cannot imagine the fear, almost panic, inside anticipating whether or not I was going to "get it." Sometimes, I think it all depended on what mood she was in that day. As often as I was grounded, our house stayed pretty clean.

*****

Me around five or six years old, 1968 or 1969.

The upstairs window on the right was my first bedroom prison.

The bottom window on the right was my downstairs dungeon.

Sugar-Free Torture

ℰℛ

Not being able to have any desserts or sweets meant I always had to sit at the dinner table while my sister, brother, mom, and dad got to eat desserts but I didn't. Since my groundings would last from two weeks to a month and I could easily be grounded again for anything, it was kind of like torture to have to sit at the table and always be left out. If we went out to dinner, there would be no dessert for me there either.

We had a stand-up freezer in the basement that was stocked with meats and such in bulk. One thing my mother loved to stock in the freezer was bags of powdered donuts. Being deprived of desserts gave me cravings for something sweet, so I became sneaky and used my new technique of breaking out of my bedroom prison. In the middle of the nights, usually when I knew my mother was at work, I would open my bedroom door, stretching the rope just enough to slip my arm through and untie it from the nail. I would quietly go down into the basement, get into the freezer, carefully untie the top of the donut bag making sure I knew how to tie it back up, get myself a couple of donuts, and sitting on the basement floor in the middle of the night, I would snack on frozen powdered donuts to satisfy my desire for desserts I was always denied. Since these were bulk bags of donuts, I was very careful not to eat more than two or three from a bag so they would not be noticed. Then I would quietly make my way back to my bedroom, take the loose rope dangling from my doorknob, close the door so just my arm was fitting through, wrap the rope around the nail, and do the little slipknot the way I felt it when I got out. As far as I know, it was never found out because I seriously doubt that my mother would ever have let me get away with such a serious infraction. If she had known that I was able to figure out and beat her little system, it quite possibly would have meant a near-death beating.

There was an incident in first grade. Our teacher had boxes of vanilla wafers to pass out during snack time. But there would be none for me. My mother had instructed my teacher that I was not to have any. She didn't tell the teacher why, at least not the real reason, but it was because, of course, I was grounded. So often, I sat in class watching all the other children get to have treats, just like I would have to watch my brother and sister at home. One day during recess, I had to go in to use the bathroom. I snuck into the classroom, opened the cabinet door where the snacks were kept, and stole some vanilla wafers. I got caught, and my mother was called. If my teacher had any idea what went on at home, I don't think she would have called. When my mother came to pick me up from school, she made me sit on the floor of the car between the back seat and the passenger seat. That way, she could reach around in the back and keeps smacking me and yelling at me on the way home. She had just been grocery shopping, and she made me reach into one of the bags and pull out a bag of dog biscuits that were for our dog Sandy. My mother yelled at me to open that bag, take out a dog biscuit, and eat it. I can remember her yelling, *"You want cookies? You want cookies? Eat these."* I remember forcing the first one into my mouth through all my tears and crying. I can remember gagging and wanting to throw up, but if I did, I would be in even more trouble. I had to keep it down. She only made me eat two.

Grounding also meant no TV. That meant no entertainment at all. However, with my newfound talent for escaping, I was also able to get out very early in the mornings. With everyone in bed upstairs, I could turn the TV on in the TV room right next to my bedroom, keep the volume down very low, and watch whatever was showing just before station sign off. Back in those days (the late sixties), you only got network stations. At the end of a broadcasting day, they would play the national anthem, show a flag blowing in the wind, and then the screen would turn snowy gray until broadcasting resumed early in the morning. Depending on when I woke up, I could catch the last show before sign off or the first shows at the beginning of the day. I remember watching a lot of *McHale's Navy*, *Gilligan's Island*, and—my favorite at the time—reruns of *Bonanza*. I idolized the Cartwrights because they seemed like the perfect family. I loved Little Joe. In a few more years, I would be idolizing Michael Landon as the perfect father in *Little House on the Prairie*. It was during those early mornings by myself with the TV, Little Joe, Gilligan, and the "Skipper too" that I became fascinated with acting and started dreaming of being an actor. I would make sure I was back in my bedroom with the door tied by 5:00 a.m. well before anyone would start to wake up.

We used to go to a pizza place called Shakey's Pizza. I loved their food; they had a buffet with chicken, potato slices, and pizza. The best thing was that they also showed the old, silent, black-and-white *Laurel and Hardy* movies. The only problem was that I had to sit with my back to the movie screen, facing my brother and sister as they watched and I wasn't allowed. I always felt like everyone in there was watching me. Everyone knew I had been bad. There were rare occasions when I would not be grounded and I did get to enjoy being at Shakey's Pizza and watching the old movies, feeling like a normal kid, but those would be rare instances.

It was the same story if we went to the movies at the drive-in theater. Back then, the drive-in movies were very popular. You bring the whole family in the station wagon for a night of movies real cheap. Popcorn, hot dogs, sodas, pillows and blankets…just a real nice warm family outing from the time the sunset until late at night. It would usually be a double feature complete with all the fun cartoons before the main movie. In my case, it wasn't so nice or fun. When grounded, I had to lay down in the back of the station wagon through the entire double feature. The worst part was not so much that I didn't see the movie because I heard it and learned to put pictures in my own mind. Not so much that I didn't get popcorn or sodas. The worst part was that if I fell asleep, my mother would stuff a rag in my mouth to keep me from snoring. I had a problem with my adenoids, so I had a tendency to snore. This wasn't my fault.

I remember one movie in particular that I really, really wanted to see but was not allowed to was *Chitty Chitty Bang Bang*. I had to lay in the back of the station wagon with a rag stuffed in my mouth while the rest of my family enjoyed the movie. Yes, I could listen to the movies and make up pictures in my mind, but I also did a lot of quiet crying in the back of that station wagon. I am sure I was able to watch some movies at sometime, but that would have been so rare that I can't remember. I believe the first time I finally saw *Chitty Chitty Bang Bang* was when it was first aired on television. To this day, *Chitty Chitty Bang Bang* is my absolute favorite kids movie from that era.

1971. Eight yrs. old.

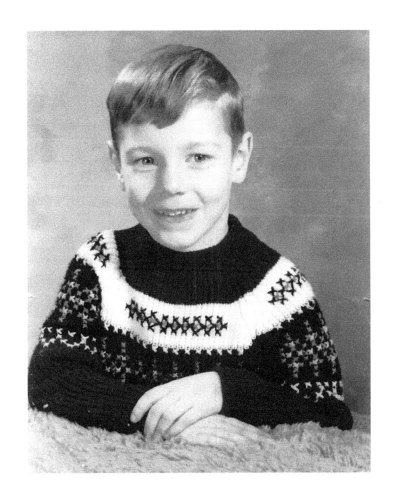

I'm Just Good for Nothing

෮   ෬

My mother had some choice names for me: *"Big butt! Fat ass! Human garbage disposal! Worthless, good for nothing! Will never amount to anything! Ugly! What kind of red-blooded all-American boy are you? Wherever there's Craig, there's trouble."* These were names and remarks that were used on almost a daily basis. *Fat ass* and *Big butt* were the two most common.

I grew up truly believing that I was just an ugly fat ass, big butt, good for nothing. That was the image I had of myself. I had every reason to believe that's how everyone else saw me also.

All these names I ended up believing. To this day, I still have some self-confidence and self-image issues brought about by the barrage of belittling and demeaning remarks that were imprinted on my brain at a very young age. I was brainwashed. I grew up feeling very ashamed of everything about myself. I was a bad boy. I couldn't do anything right. Ugly. Worthless.

I don't know where the name "human garbage disposal" came from because it was my mother that kept forcing food in my mouth. When dinner was done, she would put more food on my plate, make me eat, and berate me the whole time until I finished what was on my plate. The worst was when it was a pot of lima beans. She would actually hold my hand with the spoon in it and force feed me until the plate was empty. Of course, the whole time I was crying, which only made it worse. She wasn't yelling or hitting because my father was there, but she did always make belittling comments that made me feel like I was less than dirt. This happened about once a week or so, and while it was taking place, my sister and brother were off happily watching television or doing something else fun. I was always the one being held back and tormented while I watched them living a pain-free life. I had so much hurt inside, such a deep, internal pain. I would look at my brother and sister and wonder why my mother didn't like me.

Sometimes, Mother would follow me up the stairs at home, reach in between my legs, and start pinching the inside of my thighs, the extremely sensitive area, with her fingernails just enough to bruise but not break the skin and always bringing me to tears. I could never say "stop" for fear of something worse, but I would fill up inside with anger. There was so much anger and hurt and frustration and nothing I could do. This would happen so often that I was always scared to walk in front of my mother. I was always emotionally on guard and in fear.

Other times, she would take the hairs at the base of my neck and start yanking. Little by little, sharp, hard, tiny pulls that would sting and hurt and she would tell me, "This is how a turkey climbs over a barbed wire fence." I never knew what that meant, except that it meant pain. Sometimes, she would say it as a question: "Do you want to know how a turkey climbs over a barbed wire fence?" I felt instant panic because I knew the pain that was about to come. This was one of her torments that she didn't even mind doing in public, like in a grocery store or shopping center. I think because she knew I would fight to hold back the tears of pain for fear of something worse happening when we got home, she could get away with doing this in the open, and nobody would be the wiser. I just screamed inside my head for everything to stop. I would be so angry inside and could do nothing. I always felt that all eyes were on me. Everyone could see that I was this bad, bad, little boy. That's how I felt inside.

I used to love to sit in my bedroom by myself playing with my Tonka toys. There was a lot of comfort in that. Just me in solitude. I had this desire for acting, so I would cut long lengths of fishline from my dad's workbench in the basement and tie the different lengths of line to the front and back of my Tonka trucks and cars. Then I would thread the line around the desk drawer handles in my room. I could sit in one spot on the floor holding the different lines and was able to move my toys around on the floor making them perform little toy skits. I would even rig a flashlight to use as a spotlight. This was one of my favorite ways to occupy and entertain myself when I was feeling really down or lonely.

Small Tastes of Freedom

ℰↃ   ℭ

As horrible as things were most times, I was allowed some freedoms. On those days, it felt like I was a real person. Nothing could go wrong. I had three friends in elementary school: Dale, Brian, and Jim. I remember sometimes going across the backfield to Dale's house. We would play toy soldiers with the little tanks and GI Joe's, just normal kids stuff. Such freedoms and normalcy, though even being with Dale, showed me how different my home was. I remember Dale's mom fussing at him one time. She wasn't yelling at him, just fussing, but I didn't know the difference. Everything was a yell in my house, and it always meant trouble. When she said, *"Dale (middle name) Johnson, I thought I asked you to—before playing,"* I can remember being scared, almost in tears, and it must have shown because his mother would try to assure me that everything was all right. Any time a voice was raised, I would think I was going to be in trouble. It didn't matter that I was at a friend's house, as my mother would tell me many times as a kid, *"Wherever there's Craig, there's trouble."* I didn't know that a kid could just be fussed at and not be in trouble. At my house, I got hit or smacked around for forgetting to do something. That was my normal. I didn't understand that those things didn't happen in other homes. Going to a friend's house was like going to a foreign country for me. I didn't understand the language or know how to act. I always felt a little awkward at other people's homes.

One time, I actually got to spend the night at my friend Brian's house. Other than us playing baseball together, that is about the only memory I have of Brian. It's sad that when there is so much torment and fear growing up, whatever few good memories I have are almost completely overshadowed by the bad.

My friend Jim's parents were so nice, and his mother was always so sweet to me that I was extremely uncomfortable when I would go to his house because those words *"you're worthless"* were always in the back of my mind. That's what I had come to believe. I had no clue how to react to words of genuine kindness. I thought that everyone could see badness in me, that I was a *"good for nothing,"* so how could I be deserving of anything good and kind.

Jim and I also played baseball together, but the biggest common ground we had was our deep desire for show business. We would eventually run away from home together headed for Hollywood, though it wouldn't be until years later that we actually made it. When that finally did happened, the eventual roads taken had become entirely different. So much so that it wasn't until recently that I found out he is out there and is a producer.

The other freedoms that I am most glad about to this day is that during summer vacation from school, my mother would take us to the library. I don't know about my sister and brother, but she made me pick out a book every week, read it, and do a book report for her. I didn't like doing the book reports, but the opportunity for my imagination to soar through the pages of these books was incredible. The majority of books that I read were biographical: Harriet Tubman, John Paul Jones, Nathan Hale, Helen Keller, and so many other American greats. To leave my own tumultuous life every week and live someone else's in my mind was fantastic. I believe it helped fuel the acting part of me that slowly awakened later in my life.

The Most Feared Day

℘   ℭ

My mother was always off work on Tuesdays. It was laundry day, and many times, my mother would keep me home from school. That meant an entire day completely alone with my mother. I cannot even begin to describe the amount of fear that completely saturated every fiber of my little body. My sister would be at school. My little brother had already started school by that time. My father was at work all day. Each time it happened, I knew a day full of being called *"fat ass," "big butt," "worthless good for nothing,"* and anything else she could yell at me was about to begin. The name-calling was minor to the physical abuse that was going to take place. It would be a long, long day.

Since it didn't happen every week, I never knew which Tuesday it was going to be. I think it all depended on her mood and if she was still upset about anything I had done recently.

There was a rule when it came to laundry. Socks had to be safety pinned together in pairs, but the absolute, most important rule was to make sure you did not leave any Kleenex in your pockets.

While I would be upstairs starting to vacuum the house, my mother would be in the basement separating clothes for the wash. That also meant she was checking everyone's pants pockets (or maybe just mine). My dad used handkerchiefs, I know, because she made me iron all of them, so his pants were okay. Nothing was *ever* found in my sister's or brother's pants. I would be upstairs cleaning in fear just waiting for that inevitable *"Craig Allan Walter! Get your fat ass down here right now!"* I don't know how many times I heard that growing up, and I always knew what was coming. I would go downstairs to the basement cringing and terrified inside, almost petrified with fear knowing the pain that was on its way. The thing is I *know* I always checked my pants pockets. Why would I not thoroughly check my pants knowing I risked a severe beating if anything was found?

I would make it to the basement fighting back tears that were desperately wanting to come out already, but that also would mean bigger trouble. Then it would be *"What are you crying for? I haven't even touched you yet?"* I would get to the basement, and she would be holding my pants in one hand and Kleenex and her "stick" in the other. That slender, two-foot wooden dowel she used to push clothes into the water in the washing machine was also my worst enemy.

"What the hell is this? Get your worthless fat ass over here!" Then she would grab me by the hair, bend me over, and start beating me with her stick. Sometimes, it would be the belt. Either one was just as bad as the other. I can't describe the pain. If I moved because it became too much, I would end up getting hit somewhere else on my body, always leaving welts. Many times, I was given notes to take to school that said I could not participate in gym class.

Torments like this would go on all day—smacking me around, hair pulling, the stick, the belt, crying, yelling in pain, and more hitting because I won't stop crying or yelling. These days were very exhausting. I would be completely worn out physically.

Laundry done, house cleaned. I'm sure I was given lunch, then it would be nap time since my mother had worked the night before. She must have been tired also from all the yelling and hitting. I know I was. Now it was nap time and the fear of what happens in the bedroom.

In a way, I looked forward to these naps because it meant calm and rest. On the other hand, it also meant something scary before the nap. I wasn't allowed to wander around the house by myself, so I always had to sleep on the floor next to the bed, never up in the soft big bed where my mom was. I was always on the rug, on the hard floor with a blanket and pillow. I was allowed to read, if I wanted, by the little flicker of light that streamed in through the window above me. But before my mom got into bed, she would turn on the cooler that stood next to me. The loud humming noise it made would drown out any outside noise. I knew what was coming and would start to panic inside and take a deep breath because it made it go faster. She would stand on my chest with just one foot applying pressure. I couldn't breathe. It really didn't take long for everything to start to fade away. The initial panic quickly turned to this wonderful feeling of floating, just floating, and everything becoming quiet. Nothing. Just a nothing peace I can't describe as the room and the world would slowly slip away and then black. Next thing I know, I feel my body shaking. Looking back, I would call them spasms or convulsions, seeing these electrical flashes of sparkle lights in my head and hearing my mom yelling to *"wake up,"* but it was hollow sounding, coming from a distance through a tunnel. Before long, my body and hearing came back to normal, and that wonderful floating feeling was gone—that feeling of just endless peace. I'm back in the room with my mother, and it's time to nap. I think the only reason I never died is because my mom, being a nurse, knew when to step off. Sometimes, I wished she had just let me go. These nap activities took place every Tuesday I had to stay home with my mother.

When we would wake up, my sister and brother were already home, and my dad would soon be home. The torments of the day were over.

*****

I would learn later, as a young adult, abusing drugs and alcohol, how to imitate that euphoric, floating feeling when I discovered self-asphyxiation.

*****

Other Torments

ℰꙨ ℭꙨ

One time, I stole some chocolate when we were at the drugstore. As I said before, I don't claim to be a child that never did anything wrong. Since I was not allowed sweets most of the time, sometimes, the risk was worth it; kids don't always think that far ahead. I had the chocolate hidden in my desk in my bedroom. It tasted funny. Turns out, it was a kind of diabetic chocolate. My mother laughingly told me that while she was yelling at me when she found it. Needless to say, that was a "stay home from school" day. Boy was I in for it. My body never got used to the beatings. However, this time, there wasn't any beating—a lot of yelling and name-calling. But for this offense, she took me to the drugstore to return the uneaten portion and apologize. Though it was embarrassing, that would be a normal thing for a parent to do, but in my case, before we left the store, she bought four bags of regular chocolates to bring home. I had to sit on the floor in the front of the car tucked under the glove compartment while she yelled at me about how embarrassing that was for her. Of course, I'm a worthless, good for nothing. When we got home, I was then force-fed those four bags of chocolate until I was throwing up. The good thing is that I got so sick that I didn't get one of her beatings.

Then there's the push-ups punishment. At times, when she might be in a better mood or not up to beating, she would have me go to the bottom of the stairs that led to my bedroom and do five hundred push-ups. She would then be able to watch me from the kitchen. I also had to count them out as I did them, but I positioned myself so that I could cheat; with half my body in the TV room, I kept my knees on the floor and only used half the effort. It was still tough to do five hundred but not *as* tough. Anytime she left the kitchen, I would completely rest but keep on counting, with my eyes focused upstairs waiting for her return. When I could hear her coming, I would immediately start back into my push-ups, eventually completing the five hundred, or so she thought.

Some other times, I escaped a beating for a more creative punishment when she would make me stay up all night sitting on the bottom step that led to my bedroom. It would be on her nights off so she could keep checking up on me by looking over the railing from the top level where her bedroom was. To make sure I was awake, she would take a cup of cold water and pour it down on my head from over the railing.

My mom had a thing for the cold-water treatment. When I was able to take baths by myself, my mother loved to come into the bathroom with a glass of cold water and pour it on me. When I would see her coming in through the door, I would immediately cringe and tighten up anticipating that cold, cold water about to be poured on me while I'm enjoying a nice warm bath. She would see the look on my face and very sarcastically ask, *"What's your problem?"* Then as she dumped the cold water on me, I would let out little whimpers, the kind that barely sneak out because the cold has tightened up your breathing and you can hardly talk. Then she would tell me, *"Stop your whimpering. That doesn't even hurt."* This would continue into my young years when I would start taking showers. I couldn't see or hear her coming into the bathroom, and I would get a whole pitcher of cold water thrown over the shower curtain. These types of torments and taunts, including the pinching in the thighs and pulling the hairs at the base of my neck, were almost a daily thing. I was always wary, always on my guard, always apprehensive, and always afraid. The terrible thing is that this was a big joke to her and I can't describe the deep, intense hurt, emotional pain, and confusion. I could never understand why she would always do this to me.

My Own Lock Up

ℰ   ℭ

Through constantly being told, I learned and came to believe that I was worthless, good for nothing, ugly, basically just a bad kid all around. I was a very shy and introverted in school, a scared kid, and ashamed. I was embarrassed because I could not participate in gym class many days and would be teased about it. I would get picked on all the time at lunch because I never had anything good like cookies or puddings, dessert type things, and I could never tell anyone why…that I was such a bad kid all the time and I wasn't allowed to have any of those things. I was teased because I had the ugly lunch box that looked like something a coal miner would take to work. I never had the cool Speed Racer, Jetsons, or Flintstones lunch box or even just the brown paper bag. I didn't know why I couldn't because I recall my sister having cool stuff. Cool for a girl, anyway.

I never learned how to stick up for myself because I was too afraid of getting in trouble, which would then mean trouble at home.

During one year at school, I found a way to escape the teasing at lunchtime. When the class would line up to go to lunch, I would make sure I was at the back of the line. As we passed the bathrooms, I snuck inside into a stall until all the other classes went by and then snuck back to my classroom, hid in the closet, and ate my lunch. It was very quiet and peaceful. I didn't do this every day, only the days when I felt more intimidated or already had too much teasing on the playground. I was such an easy target for bullying.

I got away with this most of the year until my teacher finally noticed me missing and came looking for me. I heard her come into the classroom. I stayed so quiet. Talk about scared. No matter what I did, I would always get in trouble. As my mom says, *"Wherever there's Craig, there's trouble.*" She found me in the closet. Amazingly, I didn't get in trouble. My teacher just talked to me. I really couldn't tell her why I was in the closet and then risk getting beat up by someone later for tattling, but I think she knew. She never told my mom. What a relief! She immediately became my favorite elementary schoolteacher. Little did I know that being in the "closet" would later become a relevant part of my teen years and early adult life.

The Neighbor

ℰ ℭ

As my elementary school years went by, kids learned to wait after school to bully me. Our next-door neighbor, Greg, was a big kid around my age and was one of the worst. I was always cautious and wary when school let out because he was one that would taunt and chase me through the field that led home. I had a fear of being beat up. One day, I got so tired and fed up that during the chase, as he was catching up to me, I turned around and swung my ugly lunch box. It hit his head just above his eye. He went down, and I kept running. Now I was doubly scared. What would he do to me to get back? What was going to happen to me at home? I remember going straight to my room to start homework. It wasn't until after my dad got home from work that Greg's dad came over. I could see him talking to my dad through my ground level window. My dad was a violent parent too, in a different way, so I was scared. After they talked, my dad came inside and yelled for me to get upstairs. He wouldn't listen to my story of being chased and trying to protect myself. No one ever listened to my stories. He came at me with his fists, punching my arms and my chest and pounding the top of my head. He cussed and yelled at me because Greg had to go to the hospital for stitches. What I had done made us look really bad. Part of me didn't care because I was so happy that I had finally taken a stance. I could handle my father's fists much better than anything my mother would dish out.

After that, Greg and I got along a little better. When I wasn't in trouble or grounded and could play outside, sometimes, he and his friend John were the only kids to play with. They both liked to be bad, and one of the ways I could fit in and play with them was if I would steal a couple of my mom's cigarettes.

Once in a while, Greg and John had a game they played in the garage that they would have me come over and join in. It was the secret experiment game. It was really just playing doctor. I remember being fascinated. It was exciting to be part of this secret thing even though I thought it could get me into trouble. I felt closer to Greg, my enemy is now my friend, and I liked John.

One time another neighbor, a girl our age, was invited to play. I can remember feeling weird about that. It was not interesting at all. It was more fascinating playing with Greg and John. Sometimes, there was another friend, Michael, from a couple blocks away that would come over and play (Michael's dad and my dad were friends). This was our secret thing. I had no clue what any of it meant or that it was laying some of the groundwork for my future. I just knew that I liked it. We were all only around eight or nine years old, and this would continue, off and on, until I was thirteen. That's when my family moved to Minnesota.

I liked boys. I remember even having a picture of Robert Redford from *Butch Cassidy and the Sundance Kid* in my bedroom. Even at that early age, I thought he was very good-looking. I also liked Michael Landon, who played Little Joe in *Bonanza*. Even the cartoon character "Speed Racer" was good-looking. I was ugly, so I liked any male figure that was attractive and wished I was more like them. I often wondered if somehow that I would get in trouble for these thoughts and feelings if anyone found out. I knew I was different but didn't know why.

The Dreaded Sandwich

෨ ଔ

Since my mother worked the night shift, someone had to be responsible for making her lunches. I just happened to be the chosen one.

My bedtime was generally 9:00 p.m. My mother got up for work by 10:00 p.m., so I had to make sure her lunch was prepared and in the refrigerator before I went to bed. It was always a couple sandwiches and a little baggie of chips. The sandwich had to be made just the way she wanted.

After making her lunch, I went to bed and fell asleep for a little bit but automatically woke up when her alarm clock went off upstairs. Before getting ready for work, I would listen to her footsteps down the stairs to the kitchen to check her lunch and then very anxiously waited to hear if she went back up or came down to me. I was always certain I made her sandwiches correctly, but I lay in bed listening to where her footsteps fell, just waiting. I knew every squeak in the floor above me and how each step sounded on the way down the two flights from the upstairs bedrooms.

About half the time, I would get it right, and she would go get ready for work then come tie my door before she left. The times I got it wrong, in her eyes, I would hear her much heavier steps coming down the flight of stairs to my room. I would lay there scared as she would come into my room, yelling, *"Damn it! How many times do I have to tell you."* She snatched me up by my hair and dragged me up the stairs with my feet and legs trying to keep up with her, hearing some of my hair coming out by the roots. She took me into the kitchen to remake her sandwiches while she got ready for work. Then I would go back to bed laying there crying and hurting while

I listened to her come back down. She would look in and harshly say, *"If you would just get it right the first time, this would never have to happen."* Then she would tie my door and leave for work.

To Lie or Not to Lie

ℰ℧   ℭ℞

That is not really a question. Growing up, I learned that telling the truth meant my punishment was just as severe as if I had lied. If I confessed something I did, I was severely punished. If I denied something I did and got caught in the lie, I was severely punished. If I honestly denied something I didn't do, I was accused of lying, and I still got punished. It was generally a no-win situation for me.

For lies and denials, my mother's favorite punishment was "the soap." No matter what my verbal response was to an accusation, she dragged me into the kitchen by my hair, reached into the cabinet under the sink, grabbed the liquid dish soap, and literally poured it into my mouth, sometimes holding my nose to make sure I swallowed. When I started to get sick, she would yell, *"Don't you dare throw up!"* If it started coming up, I forced myself to swallow it to avoid getting hit. Sometimes, I covered my mouth to try to keep it down but couldn't, and it sprayed out between my fingers. Then she hit me and forced me to the floor to clean it up. If not the liquid soap, she would grab the big block of soap on the sink and, holding my head by my hair, shove it in my tiny mouth, ramming it in and out. I would be crying and gagging. Sometimes, if I wasn't sick right away, she would shove me down the stairs to my room, yelling, *"Get your fat ass in your room, and don't come out until I tell you!"* Then I would throw up into my toy box in my bedroom. Many times, I was not called out of my room and had to go to bed without dinner. Times like that, after I would calm down, I would get my friends, my Tonka toys, and put on a little show for myself.

Chicago Winter

ℰ   ℭ

Nothing about winter in Chicago was pleasant; I hated it. Too cold. Too much snow. Too many clothes. No matter how much you bundle up, you were still freezing. Plus, my mother would lock me out of the house.

In my elementary school, fifth graders were allowed to try out for the band. I wanted to play drums, but they didn't have any drums in the audition room. I chose the saxophone but was told that with my overbite (buck teeth), I would break too many reeds, so somehow, I ended up with the trumpet. That was okay. I knew how to read music because my mother had already made me take piano lessons. Anytime I did something wrong on the piano, I was smacked and forced to play until I got it right, but that's no surprise. At least with the band, it was my own choice. I just had to learn the trumpet.

Usually, I would practice in my bedroom. However, when winter came around, my mother would lock me out of the house after school, generally from around 3:00 p.m. until she got up from her nap, which would be just before my father got home around 5:00 p.m. My sister and little brother were always allowed to be in the house but not me. At least we had the garage.

There was a cardboard box we kept in the garage with an opening cut out for our dog Sandy to get in and out. There was an old blanket in it for her and also a heat lamp to keep her warm. When I would get home from school, I would let myself in the garage, and first thing I would do is sit on the garage floor and stick my feet into Sandy's cardboard box to warm them up from my walk home in the snow. Then I would stick my hands in there for a while. Since I was in the garage, I was protected from the wind, but it was still cold in there.

After I warmed up a little, I got my trumpet out to practice. I had nothing else to do until I was let in the house. However, it didn't take long for my fingers and lips to get cold. This happened every day during the winter. Even on Mom's day off when I knew she was up and around, she would keep me locked out. Even though my mother scared me, I was always so glad when she would open the back door and call me into the warm house. Wouldn't matter if I was in trouble for anything else. At least it was warm. She would always let me back in before my father would get home.

The Paper Route

ℰ   ℛ

D uring the winter, when I was in the sixth grade, my mother made me get a paper route. I delivered two of Chicago's biggest papers. I never asked for that, and I don't know why she insisted upon it. The newspaper bundles were dropped in our driveway early in the mornings, so I had to be up at 2:00 a.m., go get the bundles from the shoveled driveway, and bring them into my bedroom. My mother had stopped locking me in my room for this and expected me to get up and get the job done.

I was in bed by 8:00 p.m. after dinner and the dishes were done and my homework was finished. The alarm was set at 2:00 a.m. I brought in the bundles and started rolling up each paper. On Sundays, the papers were huge. I had at least one hundred people on my route. I had a newspaper route bag that I filled up and carried over my shoulder; plus, I had to load up my red wagon and pull it behind me. This would take about three trips back to the house to reload in order to finish the route by 6:00 a.m. so I could then have breakfast, change clothes, and be off to school by 7:30. I had to do this by myself in the bitter cold Chicago winter mornings whether it was snowing or just bitter cold. It was grueling, incredibly grueling.

I could not keep this up day after day, being up so early in the freezing, freezing cold, carrying that heavy bag over my shoulder, pulling the heavy wagon loaded down with newspapers behind me, house after house after one hundred houses. I was only about ten years old. This started taking such a significant toll on me, but I did not dare say anything. I ended up taking a risk without thinking about the consequences. You would think that by now, age ten, that I would have learned that, but I could only think of the short-term solution for some relief.

I would end up carrying one or two big bundles across the street and dumping them in the far back corner of a neighbor's yard. With Chicago winters the way they were, it did not take long for them to be buried in the snow. Needless to say, I started getting customer complaints. I didn't always skip the same people, but it would generally be the people furthest away so I could finish on time. I only did it on mornings with bad weather or when I didn't feel up to the chore rather than every day because I didn't want it to be *too* obvious. After all, this was an incredible feat for a ten-year-old boy to be accomplishing. Customers who complained got their newspaper delivered by the newspaper office.

I kept this route, somehow without getting caught cheating, until the spring. Unfortunately, the snow melts in the spring. Oh, the surprise our neighbors across the street got when they saw what was being uncovered in the corner of their backyard and, oh, the trouble I got in when everything was uncovered. The neighbors called the newspaper office, and the office called my parents. I did not have that paper route any longer. I never saw any of the money from it anyway. However, later that summer, I was able to ask of my own accord and got another paper route. This one *I* wanted. It was a much smaller local paper and only had about fifty customers, so I could carry them all at one time since they were small. The best thing is that it was an after-school route, the deliveries were made by 5:00 p.m., and it was summer time. I was eleven years old now.

My Trumpet

ဆာ

D uring my last two years of elementary school, band instruments were on loan. As I entered middle school in the seventh grade, my parents had to buy me a trumpet in order to stay in the band. I had one recurring problem with the trumpet. The mouthpiece was always getting stuck. It usually required a certain tool that the band teacher did not have. I don't know how I kept getting it stuck. Sometimes, it seemed that if I just blew in it too hard, it would get stuck.

My father would be able to remove it. He had his workroom space on one side of the basement opposite my mother's space, the laundry area. He had a workbench with all sorts of tools. He would have to rig up something special to remove the mouthpiece without damaging the trumpet. Since it was tedious and he had to be very careful, it always made him mad when he had to do this. It was usually after he came home from a hard day at the office. He would turn completely red, start sweating, and spit while he yelled at me that he didn't have the time to take care of this "shit." *"How many damn times do I have to tell you? How many damn times am I going to have to take care of your damn shit? Get out of my damn way."* Usually, this would be followed by some punching with his fist to my shoulder and the top of my head. If it was too much trouble and he was having a difficult time getting it out, then it would generally be *"Got damn, son of a bitchin', damn, son of a bitchin"* over and over at the top of his lungs. Then I would get his right foot kicked up my backside. Sometimes, he would use the belt, and he really knew how to swing that belt. Either one would generally propel me across the room, and I would go crashing into something. When he would finally get it out, I would hear something like, *"I'm getting damn sick and tired of*

56

having to come home to take care of your careless shit! Go to your damn room!"

My dad's punishments were not as severe as my mom's, but he still scared me. It scared me enough that one time when my mouth-piece got stuck, I knew it would probably be the last straw. I was not looking forward to Dad's beating, so I switched trumpets with another kid in the band. Once again, I was only thinking about the immediate fix and not thinking of future consequences. The world could end tomorrow. I wanted to save my butt literally today.

This actually worked for about a week until this other kid's mom came to school. It seems his name was lightly engraved on his trumpet, which was now in my possession. I couldn't worm my way out of this one since they were checking each trumpet, so I just said I had accidentally taken it. They both were very similar, and we had the same type of cases.

A note was sent home to my parents and had to be signed and returned. What I didn't know was that the other kid's mom had already called my mom before I got home from school, so as soon as I got home, all hell broke loose. My mom was waiting for me at the back door. She dragged me into the living room by my hair yelling and cussing at me and made me strip naked and lay on the couch. She took one of my tennis shoes and started to beat me in my genital area. I was completely overwhelmed with fear and tried to protect myself, but the more I tried, the louder and angrier she got…insane anger. I hurt so bad I could hardly breath. I can remember going to the floor practically choking for air. I was so scared. I don't know what made her stop, but I could hardly move. I know I ended up in my room with a trumpet that had a stuck mouthpiece. That was one of the last really severe punishment I recall receiving from my mother. I was around twelve years old.

Halloween Humiliation

ജ   ൠ

S eventh grade was tough, but then every other grade was too, it seemed. Going into middle school meant there were some of the same kids but also new kids converging from other elementary schools. It was bad enough being with the same kids that had already been taunting me, but new kids were just as bad. I was not comfortable around people to begin with. I was very shy and timid. I didn't dare let other kids see that bad kid inside that I had come to believe I was. Usually, I stayed to myself and, as always, became the easy target because of it.

My sister had been taking ballet classes for a couple of years, and my little brother was placed in early dance classes. My brother didn't even have a desire to perform. That was me. I was the one who wanted to be on stage, but all I could do was go to their recitals. It was all right except that I was very jealous. My mother knew I wanted to perform but would always tell me that I wouldn't amount to anything, that I had no talent.

Of course, my mother would never pass up a good chance to humiliate me. If I wanted to perform so badly, she was going to see to it that I had the opportunity but only how she wanted it.

On Halloween, my first year in middle school, my mother made me dress up in my sister's dance recital costume: a green tutu with a purple-sequined top, nylon fishnet stockings, and a tiara on my head. Of course, there were ballet slippers too. She made me walk to school like that.

There was nothing I could do. I couldn't even cry but had to hold every emotion inside. I can't begin to describe the extreme embarrassment, humiliation, and shame I felt. The laughs and taunts and teasing went on all day long. Teachers, of course, made everyone hush up during class but walking the hallways in between classes? Some kids managed to get rubber bands, and either snapped them on my "stockinged" legs or used them as sling shots to shoot paper clips at me. That stung terribly and made little red marks all over my legs by the end of the day.

I didn't realize it, but there was a Halloween costume contest between all the seventh, eighth, and ninth grade classes. Even though it was extremely embarrassing, I had to get up on stage and walk across to all the laughs, but in the end, I came in second place and got a pumpkin to take home. My mother was not impressed. I don't think my humiliation was supposed to end with me getting a prize, but with all that I went through during the day, I believe I deserved first place.

My Father's Contributions

℅   ℃

To the outside world, my dad was basically "father of the year," but when he was angry, he would cuss up a storm, and if I was in his way or the anger was directed at me, then the fists would fly, and that right foot would be kicking my butt to kingdom come! He was coach of a little league baseball team, where all the parents and kids thought he was great, just the "all-around dad." I was always embarrassed and ashamed of who I was and what happened in our house. It was a huge, degrading secret. Rarely did I ever have a friend over. Not that I had many, but I was usually grounded, and even if I was allowed to have a friend over, I never knew what might happen.

With my father being a coach, I was forced to play ball. I hated it. I could run the bases because I was used to being chased home from school, but when I was at bat, the ball always seemed to be coming straight at me too fast, and it would scare me. The same thing happened when I played outfield and couldn't catch because I was afraid of the ball coming straight down out of the sky and hitting me. Outside of practice when we were at home, my father kicked me around the backyard, saying I never tried hard enough. My mother would always say, *"What kind of red-blooded American boy are you?"*

My father rigged up a baseball on a rope where he could stand in one spot, swing the ball around in a circle, and see if I could hit it. That didn't matter. The ball was still too fast as far as I was concerned; it still looked like it was going to hit me. I would try. I would swing but almost always miss. If I hit it, he was happy. When I would miss, I got yelled at. Out on the field during practice or a game, I don't believe I ever got a hit. I was a disappointment and an embarrassment because I always struck out. He was the manager of the team, but his own son couldn't even hit the ball. My mother was also the team scorekeeper, which made things worse. She continually reminded me that I was *"worthless"* to the team always sarcastically saying, *"What kind of red-blooded American boy are you?"* When we won a game, the whole team was treated to Dairy Queen ice cream. Of course, I always felt that I didn't deserve to be there, so I always stood at the back of the line wishing I was somewhere else. This went on every year from my Pee Wee League in 1969 through my Little League years that ended in 1975. I dreaded each year as summer rolled around.

White Boys Can't Jump

ℰ   ℛ

That's just a play on words from the movie titled *White Men Can't Jump*. And this, this boy, me, couldn't jump. And I will feel my father's fury for not being able to do so.

My sister and I once put on a show in the basement doing a duet of the Tanya Tucker 1972 hit song "Delta Dawn." Not surprisingly, my mother told me I was tone deaf and would never amount to anything. These remarks hurt, but I was used to them by now. Even if I was singing to the radio in the living room, she would belittle me, but despite her comments, I would grow up to do a lot of musical theater.

They knew I did little shows with my Tonka toys, very creative shows. *"Just foolishness"* is what I would hear. They knew what my interests were, but while my sister and little brother (the one who loved sports) got to be on stage and danced in shows, my parents (especially my father) were determined that I was going to play sports. What my father refused to see was that I didn't have the knack or desire to play sports, especially when I was being forced into it, but he still made me try out for the elementary school basketball team in fifth grade.

We had a big patio connected to our driveway with a detached two-car garage. My father mounted a basketball goal to the garage and made me practice for an hour, every day, after school while my mother kept an eye on me through the kitchen window. If I started getting lazy, she would either bang on the window or yell out the back door, asking, *"What did your father say? Your hour is not up yet."*

My father showed me how to do jump shots on the weekends, but I rarely shot the ball high enough to get it through the hoop. I hated those weekend practices. It takes a certain coordination that I didn't have to do a jump shot. I never could do it correctly, yet my father would be out there with me making me do it over and over and over again. Each time I got it wrong, he kicked me around the patio, yelling, *"That's not how I told you to do it. AGAIN! That's still not how I told you to do it…AGAIN! AGAIN! AGAIN!"* I thought, *Can't he see I'm not going to get it?*

Well, tryouts for the basketball team came. Thank goodness (kind of). So many kids tried out, but they could only take a certain number. I was not one of them. It was good because I did not want to play; bad because I was yet another disappointment to my parents. Still not that "red-blooded all-American boy" that seemed so all important to them. I remember when grade six came around. It was the same thing all over again. I was even made to practice during the summer, during the dreaded baseball season, to no avail. I hated it! I hated it! I hated it! I hated basketball as much as I had come to hate baseball every year. Everything just seemed to be all wrong with this creation of a boy.

About the only exciting thing, where baseball was concerned, was the time we went to a Chicago Cubs Game at Wrigley Field. In the early 1970s, "streaking" was popular—stripping nude and running through a public place. There was even a hit song about it. Anyway, during the game we were at, it started to rain, and while they were rolling the tarp over the field, a man had stripped off his clothes, streaked across the infield, being chased by security, and up into the stands right near where we were, where he was finally apprehended. There was something quite fascinating about that to me. And I didn't know or understand why.

Football

೮?   ೧೪

This was very short lived. It would turn out to be my family's last year in Illinois. The fall of my seventh grade year. Yes, the same year as the Halloween fiasco.

I'm not sure who's idea it was for me to play football but I ended up on a city team. Ironically, a nephew of one of the Chicago Bears greats was on my team. Didn't mean much to me because, by now, I really didn't like sports. I had a deep loathing for sports. But somehow I'm on this team.

The only real memory I have is from a day I was in trouble for something. I had my football gear on. My mom was driving me to the park where the practice field was. She's yelling at me the whole time for something. Who knows what. We get to the playing field and park at the curb. My team mates are about a hundred yards away, the length of a football field. All in plain view of what is about to happen.

My mother makes me take off my belt. Makes me drop my pants, both football and underwear. Naked extremities showing to the whole world. She makes me lean over with the palms of my hands on the car and proceeds to whip me. Not long. Just a few quick, hard strikes. Enough to thoroughly humiliate and embarrass me. Enough to make sure everyone sees that I'm a bad, bad kid. I make sure not one tear is shed. That is tough because I hurt. I hurt not only physically but also inside. I'm torn apart trying to figure out why all this happens.

*****

To this day, I could care less about football.

*****

Tennis—My Choice

෨   ෬

I had mentioned that I wasn't always grounded. When I wasn't and could watch television, I found that I liked watching tennis. The three players I liked during the early 1970s were Jimmy Connors, Arthur Ashe, and Bjorn Borg. They were all good-looking and athletic. Remember that I learned at a very early age and on up what was unattractive…me! Looking back, I see that I kind of fixated on people (men) who were attractive, talented, and athletic, things that I was taught to believe that I wasn't—Michael Landon, Robert Redford, Jimmy Connors, Arthur Ashe, Bjorn Borg.

Tennis was a game I could play by myself against only one other person. Although kind of like baseball, there was a little fear of the tennis ball, but there was a net that could stop it sometimes, and a tennis ball didn't hurt near as much as a baseball if it hit you. Also I got a turn at hitting the ball at, well, hitting the ball back to the other person. When I get to serve, it's almost like hitting it at the other person. Tennis was a sport I was actually able to choose on my own. It was surprising that my parents allowed me to do this.

So the last summer before we left Illinois, I was able to take tennis lessons. What a feeling of freedom that was. Like when I got to choose my own little paper route. Freedom to choose was something very rare to me and I loved it. I remember on my birthday my sister gave me five coupons, nicely made out of construction paper, offering to play five games of tennis with me at the city's public tennis court. Sadly, we were never able to.

My Dad, the Mechanic

ℰ   ℜ

My father grew up on a farm. Actually, both parents grew up on farms. However, being the only boy with one sister, my father pretty much had to learn how to help maintain the farm machinery. This, of course, carried over into his adult life. My father took care of everything on our family cars—oil changes, timing, lube jobs, rotate, and balance all the tires. Anything wrong with the engine, my father would fix. I don't think our cars ever ended up in a mechanics shop.

The only problem was that I was always made to help him. I'm about eight or nine when I have to start helping. I might actually have grown up having learned something or even to enjoy working on cars if it hadn't been for my dad's incredible temper and extreme foul language. If things didn't go right, I would become his punching bag, verbally and physically. When my father would tell me on a Saturday morning that we have work to do on the car, I would be dreading every minute leading up to the time we go outside, hoping something else might come up to alter his plans.

We would be in the garage, and my dad would be under the car or have his head under the hood very frustrated because he couldn't get something working. He would start his incessantly loud cussing and yell at me to get him a certain type of wrench (maybe a crescent) or screwdriver (maybe a Phillips). When his temper flared, my brain would get all scrambled with fear, and I could never think straight. I would already be fighting back tears of fear, and my mind would desperately be like, *"Please, please, please, please, please, let me get the right tool. Please, please, please, please."* trembling the whole time. I could never remember, under pressure, what was the crescent wrench or the adjustable wrench or the socket wrench or ratchet wrench. Phillips screwdrivers, standard screwdrivers, what other kind of screwdrivers are there. My brain… my brain is a blank. I'm petrified. My mind is petrified. My dad has me so scared but I have to move quick. I grab the first one I can see, hoping inside. I give it to him and then *"…. Damn it….!!! That's not it!!! I told you…"* then the fist would strike out and he would start punching me in the arm for not using my head and thinking, then I would get the foot upside my backside knocking me halfway across the garage and onto the floor. If, some-how, he pinches or smashes a finger while working then he really goes ballistic with his cussing and punching. Now yelling at me to just get out of his way as he punches and kicks me. I'm begging and pleading inside that this will all end soon. I would feel much better being able to just go to my room and play by myself. Go off into my own make believe world directing little shows with my toys.

Our Poor Dogs

ଛ   ଔ

We had a couple dogs named Sandy and Tipsley. Sandy was a little Beagle. She's the one whose dog house in the garage would warm my feet in the winter. Our dogs would also feel the wrath of my dad's anger.

Growing up would be the same for Sandy as it was for me. Basically, that's saying I got treated like a dog. If things weren't going right for my dad while he was outside, if Sandy just happened to be in the way, she would get kicked around and cussed at just like I got. I hated hearing her little yelps every time she got kicked around. Sometimes, it would just be because she was underfoot and in the way. A good solid kick then the yelp.

By the time we got Tipsley, Sandy was starting to get old. Tipsley was a bigger dog, part Collie and something, but a beautiful dog. My dad had a "run" set up in the fenced backyard. A length of strong wire ran from the garage and tied off to a tree on the other side of the yard about six feet off the ground. Tipsley had a light chain attached to his collar and a link of the chain attached to the wire, and he could run back and forth while the chain would slide along. Tipsley had a big doghouse at the back of the garage he could easily reach. Unfortunately for him, he had nowhere to run to get away from my dad when he got mad. Maybe sometimes, he would bark too much. I don't know, but when my dad got mad at him, it was the same kicking that Sandy and I got. Tipsley would run into the doghouse for safety but only end up being trapped. My dad would get the broom and ram the handle inside the doghouse to beat him with. Poor trapped Tipsley had no way to defend himself. I knew how he felt. I don't know that a dog's fear is any different, that fear of being trapped and getting a brutal beating. I would be hurt and confused and angry when I was the recipient, but when it came to our dogs (my dogs because I fed them and cleaned up after them and consoled them), my feelings were very different. Sometimes, I think I hated my father when he did that, not really hate because I don't believe I have a hateful bone in my body, but a real powerful anger that came very close to hate.

Nine years old (1972). Me and our dog, Tipsley.

My Brother's Return

℘   ℘

I'm trying to remember the timeline. I think I'm around twelve years old because we leave Illinois when I'm thirteen. My younger brother, who had been taken away, has been gone for a number of years now, eight or nine, I believe. Our visitations over the years had dwindled drastically. He's been in and out of Children's Hospital in Chicago a number of times and quite a few foster homes. He has had a life filled with medical issues and surgeries, possibly stemming from the incident many years ago that prompted his being taken away. I never did completely find out about that from my father, but it had always been my belief since my dad did tell me that he had been taken away on suspicion of child abuse.

One of his medical issues was that one of his legs had stopped growing at the normal rate when he was little. My father had told me it was a break in his growth plate, "that one day" was the cause. He would have surgeries placing rods in his leg to slowly lengthen it. It never completely worked, and he would always have one of those shoes with an extra thick sole. He also got teased a lot being called names like "Frankenstein."

I don't know what the circumstances were that allowed him to come back home, but my feelings were very mixed. Of course, looking back, I couldn't imagine what his feelings might have been either. I guess I should have been happy that my brother was coming home, but I was told I would be sharing my bedroom and bed with him. My twelve year old mind was not happy. I'm now being forced to share my prison bedroom, my space, my private domain, my safe place for just me, and my Tonka Toys, with someone who is almost a complete stranger. Then it turns out he snores on top of it. However… I won't be shoving any rags in his mouth, though. We did have some small talks. Sometimes, he would tell me about the different foster homes. That was kind of weird to me, having a brother from foster homes. He would talk about some of the foster parents not being too nice while others were nice. His favorite foster parents were the ones he had just left to come back home. He had many foster brothers and sisters. I think a part of me envied him for not having to live in our house all these years. I do remember I had told my friend, Jim, a few times that I just knew I was adopted. That was a way that I could explain things inside my head.

I have one memory in particular, about my brother being back home, that will always haunt me. I remember my sister telling me, as adults, how she had let me take the blame for some things she had done. I now have that sort of a memory. This was not planned. No intentions of throwing the blame on anyone. I just knew I couldn't face up to what I had done and just allowed him to be blamed while I denied, denied, denied. It would have meant certain death for me.

Mother smoked cigarettes, my father smoked pipes. I had managed to find a book of matches somewhere. I was in the basement playing with them, lighting one, watching it burn, and blowing it out. I did that over and over, then I would toss them over the freezer. We had our artificial Christmas tree box on top of the freezer. One of my parents was calling me upstairs, so I blew out and tossed my last match along with the matchbook and ran upstairs. I don't recall what I was doing upstairs, but I do remember some time later, my father smelling smoke. Frantically trying to find the source, it led him to the basement where the Christmas tree box had caught fire. His workshop was in half of the basement, and he always had a fire extinguisher by the workbench and was able to quickly put it out. The beams on the ceiling, the floor to the living room above, were only singed. My father was relieved nothing serious came of it, but he had found the book of matches and now was extremely mad, basically yelling at everyone wanting to know who had been playing with matches. This wasn't one of his regular rabid mads. This was more mad mixed with a lot of fear and deep concern. Not a "beating" mad, but I still wasn't going to fess up to anything. I've had a whole life to know it would be extremely bad for me if I did! I know my mother was around somewhere, but she was letting my dad handle this one.

Somehow, and I really don't know how, but my younger brother, who really hasn't been home for a long time yet, managed to get the blame. I think it was because we all kept denying and he was the easy scapegoat and just went along. I remember feeling guilty right away. My dad got really mad and was yelling at my brother but a yelling that was filled with caring concern. My mother, however, didn't seem to be too satisfied with how my father handled the situation. The next day, my father was gone. I don't know where my sister and youngest brother were, but my other brother and I were home. She brought him into the living room to teach him a lesson in what happens when you play with matches. She lit two small candles on the coffee table, firmly grabbed each one of his hands, and held them both over the flames until he started screaming. I was horrified and filled with extreme guilt and terror but also knowing that, if it had been me, it probably would have been ten times worse.

*****

My past has been dealt with through forgiveness, but I was also just a child, and that horrendous memory still haunts me to this day!

*****

The Runaways
(My Escape)

ℰ   ℭ

J im and I had been friends for a few years. He was probably my best friend. In a way, I had a small crush on him, just a small schoolboy crush. I think mostly because I wanted to be him. He was good-looking and had the perfect parents. I never told him. Well, you didn't tell things like that. Besides, he was my best friend. Even years later when I tracked him down and he came to L.A. to visit, it remained a secret…until now. He was good-looking. Good in baseball, he was on my dad's team also. My mom would sometimes say, *"Why can't you be more like your friend Jim."* She would talk in general, but I think mostly she meant when it came to baseball. *"He's a real red-blooded all-American boy,"* she would tell me. Maybe I was just a little envious because he was everything I wasn't and had wonderful parents and a great life at home.

Jim and I both had dreams of Hollywood. The movies. I was definitely going to be an actor one day. I always knew that. I also knew that one day, I was going to win one of those gold statues called an Oscar. I was going to be famous. I was going to live all these different lives on that big movie screen. I was going to be important. I was going to be someone. What was also in the back of my mind was that this was going to be my escape from this home.

We had been planning this for a couple weeks. It was late spring around the beginning of May. I remember because it was only a couple weeks before my thirteenth birthday. I was going to take the ten-speed bicycle that was locked up in the garage with a chain and padlock. I knew where the key was kept. I didn't know it at the time, but my parents were planning on giving me that bicycle for my birthday. I had thought it was for my sister because I didn't get stuff like that.

We had a road map of the United States. From Chicago, the map showed one thick long line (it was an interstate) that went straight to Los Angeles. It looked real easy. Of course, at almost thirteen years old, we didn't figure in miles and how long it would actually take. Didn't realize there was an obstacle called the Rocky Mountains or that there was going to be a big desert. We just saw that one thick line that ran straight from Chicago to Los Angeles. It seemed so simple. How hard could it be. Besides, if worse came to worse, the weather was warm, and we could always sleep outside on the beach if needed. Remember, "It never rains in southern California," or so went the line in the song. We were going to Hollywood.

I believe it was on a Saturday when we left. Baseball season had started because we were supposed to have practice that evening. The team would come to our house, and we would practice in the field behind our backyard. We were going to be long gone by then. I was nervous and scared. I had a big paper bag filled with stuff we could sell if needed, some rocks and fossils that my grandma had given me that I thought might be worth something. Grandma was a collector of rocks, fossils, minerals, and gems (a rock hound). I also had a little food in the bag. Just some things I grabbed out of the kitchen cupboards. And I had snuck open my dad's wallet that morning before he had showered and dressed and grabbed some money. My heart was pounding while I was doing that, but I was going to get out of this house and out of this town as far away as possible and that meant Hollywood.

I think it was early afternoon when Jim finally got to my house. I had already snuck the key out and unlocked the bike. My packed bag was waiting next to it. I had played it cool all day so far, and no one seemed the wiser at all. When the coast seemed clear, we got on our bikes and headed out of our suburb of Chicago, passing all the familiar places one last time, the Dairy Queen where we got treats after ball games. There goes the Shakey's Pizza. Goodbye to what I had come to hate and hello to a brand new life—a whole new world.

I was finally free and on the road with my best friend Jim headed to Hollywood. I was never coming back.

We had only been on the road for maybe an hour when we decided to stop and buy a candy bar or something and look at the map. We were enjoying this freedom. Plus, we were about to get on the interstate, that long thick line on the map.

We got back on our bikes and started on our way again. The interstate was much busier than the city streets and much bigger, but we got on and started pedaling away on the shoulder of the road alongside the traffic that was much faster than us. I remember the wind in my face and how exciting this was.

I don't know how long we had been on the interstate, but we came upon a tollbooth. We were ready to pay our toll, but the guy in the booth said we had to exit the interstate at the off ramp ahead. Seems it is illegal to ride bikes on the interstate. We said *"okay"* and exited at the off ramp. When we were out of sight of the tollbooth, we hopped the guardrails and onto the onramp back to the interstate. The wind in our faces once again, pedaling our (my) way to freedom. Kind of like a modern-day Tom Sawyer and Huckleberry Finn. Then our dreams got shattered. My hopes…blown to smithereens. My heart stopped beating. A real cold chill went through my body. A wave of fear set in. Certain death filled my brain. Two police cars came up behind us with their lights flashing and a quick burst of the siren. A voice came over their car speaker to stop. We talked with them. Told them we were headed to Hollywood. I didn't dare tell them my *real* story. I didn't trust adults, and I certainly wasn't going to tell the police what was going to happen if they made me go back. They would tell my parents what I said, and there would be more trouble. I never told anyone these things.

The officers loaded our bikes up in the trunks of their cars and drove us back to the tollbooths. There was a main booth with phones. That's where they called our parents.

You know you see on TV how parents are so glad when their children are found and returned? Well, that was definitely not the case with my parents. But then I already knew it would be like that.

Our parents had to come get us. My father was the one to get me. I didn't know when I would see Jim again.

Not a word was spoken in the car all the way home. There was a feeling of impending doom. When I got home, the rest of the baseball team was there for practice. I was told to go straight into the house. That's where my mother was waiting. I remember her closing the curtains to the window that looked into the backyard where everyone was. I truly felt that this time, I might not get out alive. She started yelling and screaming obscenities at me. I was certain the team could hear. I was so humiliated. With my running away, I was sure everyone knew the dark secrets about what took place inside this house, that I was this awful, bad kid.

The team went out to the backfield before my mom started smacking me around. It was then that I found out, during all her yelling, that the ten-speed was going to be my birthday present. She said *"There is no way in hell you are getting that bicycle for your birthday now!"* I didn't participate in practice that day, but I do believe Jim was able to show up. I know he didn't receive the type of "welcome home" that I got.

Years later, Jim and I would both make it to Hollywood. Our roads there would be vastly different, at different times and with very different outcomes, but we did make it.

*****

I have recently searched for Jim on the Internet and found that he is an accomplished producer in Hollywood. From what I have read about Jim, I am really proud and happy for him.

*****

Grandma and Grandpa (I Adored You Both)

ഔ   ൽ

I can't leave this early chapter of my life without talking about my maternal grandparents. They were farmers and lived in Kansas. Both my parents come from farm families in Kansas.

There wasn't a closeness with my dad's side of the family as there was with my mom's side. We just didn't see them as much. I adored my grandma and grandpa, my mom's parents.

My grandpa internalized feelings (I'm like that also), but you still knew he loved you deeply. Anytime we went to Kansas to visit, there would always be a ride on the tractor with Grandpa at the old farm, but Grandpa would always have a tear run down his cheek, and his voice would crack when it was time for goodbyes. Grandma was always full of hugs and holding my hand a lot, always liked holding me close to her, and she was always so full of kisses when the goodbyes came.

It seems just about every summer we would go on a family vacation together. We would leave Chicago in the station wagon with Mom, Dad, my sister, me, and little brother pulling our camper behind us. My grandparents would leave Kansas, and we would meet up at a predestined point, depending on where we were going that year. We travelled through just about every national park in this country: Grand Canyon, Yellowstone, Glacier National Park, Petrified Forest, Painted Desert, Mesa Verde, Great Smoky Mountains, Grand Tetons, and the Rocky Mountains, to name a few.

My grandma was a "rock hound." She knew a lot about geology. She collected all sorts of rocks, gems, petrified things such as dinosaur bones, parts of petrified trees, and many types of crystals such as geodes. Wherever we went, she would take me wading through the streams and rivers teaching me about fossils, geology, and rocks in general. Grandma would *always* find fascinating fossils and things wherever we went. She had a strong desire to share all her knowledge with me and explain things in a way a child would understand.

Grandma would also teach me the history behind the parts of the country we were in. In Mesa Verde, it would be about the Pueblo Indians or the Cherokees of the Southwest, the Cheyenne Indians in the Wyoming area or even the Comanche and the Pawnee from their state of Kansas. How our family came from Germany and settled in the Kansas territory in the mid-1800s in its early statehood. How we would help Indians in the area when they would come to our door in need of food. My grandma was full of history, and I loved listening to her.

I was still a bit wary of my parents when on vacation, but any chance of severe punishment for anything was extremely slim. Rarely would my mom do anything around her parents. If anything, she would take me to the side and give me stern threats. My dad, on the other hand, I remember one time in the Rockies, it's summertime but we're up where there's still snow. It was so neat. We were all in shorts and having a playful snowball fight, my brother, sister, me, and our dad. I threw a snowball and accidentally hit my dad in the groin area. I'm a little kid so how hard can I really throw. Well, my dad got so mad, and I got my butt kicked pretty good for that in front of my grandparents.

I recall a time when my dad actually had to "lay into" my grandpa.

Each time we got to a new campground we would set up camp, everyone would pile into the station wagon, and we would go on a day filled with sightseeing. On many of our vacations, there would be moose, elk, and bear sightings either in the campground or along the road. It was on one of these road trips that we pulled off to the side with other vacationers to take pictures, from our cars, of all the bears that were just wandering around. At one point, a bear came right up to the front passenger door of our car and had its nose pressed against the window. I remember finding this exciting and was in awe to see a bear so close until I heard my dad start to yell and cuss at Grandpa. Well, it seems Grandpa was about to roll down the window a little to feed the bear some cookies we had. Yes, it would have been a dangerous thing, but looking back, I find it a bit amusing.

Aside from that, vacationing with Grandma and Grandpa were the happiest times of my childhood. Actually, as hard as I try to remember, those are the only really happy times I can clearly recall. So many *wonderful* stories with Grandma and Grandpa that I could go on forever. But those stories in the making would be no more when we move to Minnesota. Grandma and Grandpa, I did adore you!

The Job Transfer

ℰℴ ℭℛ

S ome time by the end of summer 1976, we would be leaving Illinois. I vaguely remember the talk at home of my father being transferred for his job. I recall him having a choice of at least a couple places: Minnesota and California. I can remember that much because I was so hoping that we would be moving to California. After all, it was just a few months ago I had ran away, and now we might be moving there. No such luck. We were going to Minnesota, a small town outside of Rochester. It turned out his job had him there before when my sister was just a baby. We were moving further north to an even colder, snowier part of the country. I am so thrilled. Little did I know that my mother's reign of terror was about to end.

I know there must have been some happy times, but as hard as I try, I can't find them. Everything is overshadowed by all the memories of fear and pain. I do remember my sister trying to teach me to ice skate backward on a little rink my dad made in the backyard one winter. I ended up falling and cracking my chin open and getting stitches. The only birthday I remember was when my baby brother got sick and vomited on the cake. I can't recall a single Christmas that wasn't plagued with a little fear. I really don't have any good memories to take with me when we move, except for some memories of my few friends

Jim and Brian I would lose touch with. Dale ended up being killed in a car accident shortly after we moved.

*****

It would still be decades before I realize that God has something wonderful in store for me.

*****

Minnesota
(A New Beginning?)

ℝ ℞

I don't remember much about the actual move except for all the packing, the long drive, all the unpacking, and everything being very hectic. We did have to put our dog Sandy to sleep the day before we left. My parents decided she was too old to go through a Minnesota winter. That was very sad, but with all the commotion and chaos due to the move, it was a short-lived sadness. We still had our newer dog, our German Shepherd, Brandy. I can't recall what became of Tipsley.

My mother's demeanor seemed to change a little after the move. Maybe it's because I was too old to strip naked and beat. Although, there was the time she had me in my bedroom. Once again, I don't recall what I had done, but my mother had grabbed me by my forearm and started slamming my hand down on the top edge of the desk. After a few times, there was a tiny cracking sound as my index finger snapped and broke. I was yelling when she slammed it again. It swelled up immediately. Mother took me to the hospital, and I remember getting really angry inside when she flat out lied and told the doctor I fell. That was the last physical punishment I would receive from her. It wasn't long after that when I was given the ten-speed bike that I was told I would never get.

I was given my own bedroom, and my two brothers had to share a room. That was nice.

We now lived in the "Land of 10,000 Lakes," so my father had to buy a boat, one that we could water ski with or just go fishing. We would spend a good amount of time on the Mississippi.

I wasn't good at a lot of sports, but after a few tries, I actually learned how to get up on a pair of water skis behind the boat. It was fun for a while zipping back and forth jumping the wakes in the water that the boat left behind, but you can only jump the wakes of a boat so many times before it starts to get boring. However, I think my dad was kind of proud that I could do it, that I could do something.

We also did a lot of fishing. Fishing was all right, but any time I would get my line snagged, which was quite often, my dad would get mad at me. He would hit me on top of the head, like a hammer with his closed fist, and cuss me out. It's not like I intentionally did it, but he sure acted as if I had. I think my fear of his anger was partly the cause of my doing things wrong. My fear made me panic. I would worry too much inside and just mess up. But once again, if I caught something then, he was kind of proud. I hated cleaning the fish afterward. It was slimy and gross, the gutting and filleting, and being told to *"quit being such a baby."* It's not like any of this was my idea to begin with.

I dreaded when our day on the river would end. My dad would drive the boat up to the dock and slow it down. I was to be positioned on the bow of the boat, and as we got close to the dock, it was up to me to jump onto the dock with the rope and hold the boat steady. From where I was, it was a long jump onto the dock, and I was afraid of missing and falling in between the boat and dock. There was always a little panic racing through me. There was always the fear of hurting myself versus the fear of my dad's temper if I didn't do it and get it right.

One day, I didn't get it right. With my heart pounding, I made that big jump but wasn't able to stop the boat from hitting the dock. The front of the boat went under, and a metal strut tore a deep gash in the bow. My father was absolutely furious! He didn't care who was around. He laid into me verbally and physically, kicking my butt from the end of the dock all the way onto land. That was probably a good thirty yards. Boaters waiting to launch their boats, people just sitting around on the shore, all witnesses as to how horrible of a kid I was. I am humiliated to the core once again. I am seathing inside with anger. I am so fed up with the treatment I get! I want to explode, but I can't. I end up sitting inside the car sulking but fuming inside. I grow to hate every weekend that my dad wants to go to the river.

My Mother Unveiled

ℰ   ℭ

My mother and I seem to be getting along a little better. She's actually being nice to me. I'm still cautious but not as fearful as I used to be. Not too long after we moved to Minnesota, she has already taken a flight back to Chicago for about a week to visit.

I had always thought it would be exciting to fly in a plane.

I used to have those "flying dreams" that seemed so real. In my dreams, I could run and jump off a building and just soar through the air. Run real fast down a sidewalk and just take off. I could also fly around my bedroom. When I would wake up, it had all seemed so real, and I would feel out of breath and exhilarated.

When my mom would come back from her trips, I ask if I could go on the plane with her some time. She said the next time she went to Chicago, I could go with. Well, when the next time came, I couldn't go along. There was a reason, and by the time I found out why, it left me confused but happy.

For about the last year or so, before we moved from Chicago, my mom would have a small group of nursing friends from the hospital over on a regular basis to play cards. It seems one of the ladies, Lois, was who my mom was going back to visit. This time, my mom would not be coming home. She was bringing Lois back with her and moving into an apartment she already had set up in Rochester.

My mom was leaving my dad, and us, for another woman. I remember her last time in the house. She and Dad were in the garage talking. She left and I caught a glimpse of my father coming into the house wiping his eyes.

I was happy because for a long time, I had secretly wished/prayed for a divorce, or something, anything to happen. I knew I stood a better chance with only one parent and hoped it would be my father. His fists and foot were a lot easier to take than my mother's cruelty. He already had a temper, but after my mom leaving, he became an even angrier man. I would end up feeling the brunt of the consequences for my years of wishful thinking.

I was familiar with Lois from the card games and liked her well enough. They had the apartment set up as two separate bedrooms for appearances. My mother never actually "came out" to me, but it didn't take me long to figure out what the real situation was. It didn't matter to me because I was living with Dad about fifteen miles away. Besides, I was trying to figure myself out and why I had an attraction to other guys. Maybe this was the reason.

The New School

ℰℛ

New schools are tough to begin with, but I was raised with absolutely no social skills. I didn't know how to interact so I didn't make friends easily. There were feelings of incredibly low self-worth and self-loathing. I'm a fat ass, big butt, good for nothing, worthless, will never amount to anything young teenager. I'm a troublemaker. I can never do anything right. Everybody can see right through me and know all this about me. I was embarrassed about myself, my family. I'm shy and timid, practically afraid of my own shadow. Definitely afraid of other people and what they think about me. Why would anyone in their right mind want anything to do with me. Those were basically my feelings going into school in this new small town. I'm thirteen, emotionally scarred and scared.

The school held all junior and senior high grades seven through twelve—scary. There were only around one hundred kids in my class going into eighth grade. With classes being this small, everyone knew each other and already had their little cliques formed. The jocks, the nerds/geeks, I didn't fit into any of these. I felt inferior to everyone including the punks/smokers/potheads. I would prefer to forget about most of my high school years.

My father, now divorced, became a more bitter angrier man and would project that even more on me. I would do what I could to stay away from home, so I forced myself into sports. They didn't have tennis. Junior high football was all that was available. I wasn't good at it, but it kept me away from home and my dad. I would eventually break my collarbone; that was an easy way out of football. I would ultimately get on the cross-country running team. In the spring, I would even give the track team a shot.

I stayed with the trumpet and joined the band. I also got involved in the choir. I realized that I *can* sing, what do you say now Mom. However, she is still in the back of my mind. Whenever I am singled out to sing by myself, I get panicky inside, I get hot and flushed, and I can feel my face get burning red with embarrassment because that "Mom" voice keeps telling me I'm no good. I do fine in a group but panic when singled out. It's the same in the band.

English literature class is no different either, any class for that matter. I'm good with my studies, I get good grades, but don't call me to the front of the class. I know you are all looking at me with judgmental faces and thoughts. How I see myself is exactly how I just know you see me, and that is extremely painful. I get so anxious inside, my neck muscles tighten up so much that my head would literally start nervously shaking.

There's a real tiny part of me that wants to burst out, saying, *"I am good,"* but that much bigger part of me that is brainwashed and reminds me of all the bad things about me always wins over and I remain this shy little timid, afraid-of-my-own-shadow kid. I'm the kid that's so easy to pick on and bully.

I became that kid who always got slammed into the lockers, tripped or shoved to the floor, or had his books knocked out of his hands and strewn all over the ground for everyone to laugh at. Bullies became more vocal and would intimidate with nicknames, the favorite being "faggot." I wasn't in any way an effeminate teenager, shy but not effeminate. Aside from the fact that I knew early on that my interests were toward guys and I didn't understand it and nobody knew, but faggot happens to be about the most hurtful name to be called at that age. I would endure anyone, or multiples of, this type of taunting harassment almost on a daily basis throughout high school. It was always a relief when the day would finally be over.

Teachers always saw what was going on, but they never got involved. I couldn't go home and tell Dad. What would he do? Nothing. So one time in tenth grade, I finally got so fed up with one of the guys who was constantly shoving me around. I was so angry inside that I just snapped. I became enraged. Infuriated. To my own surprise, I actually took him and threw him down to the ground. I don't like to hurt people, so I didn't throw any punches. I just pinned him to the ground and kept yelling at him. *"I'm tired of this and you! This is gonna stop! You're not gonna do this anymore!"* I grew up with a lot of cussing, so in my anger, I threw a lot of cuss words around myself—a lot.

A teacher finally came and broke it up. I was the one sent to the principal's office. The principal reprimanded me. When he asked me what I had to say, I was still so angry that I remember telling him very loudly, *"None of you do anything about all the shoving around and bullying! I am so fed up that if I had a knife, I would have used it!"* This is in the late seventies before weapons were ever a "thing" in schools. That's how sick and tired and fed up I was. I stood up to the principal. This coward briefly broke out of his shell. I got detention and a letter sent home to my father.

Guess who got in trouble that night. Of course, my dad wasn't going to hear my explanation in my defense. However, the minute he started raising his hand to me, I got up the nerve and ran to my bedroom, slammed the door, and locked it. I'm getting about fed up with my father also. He came after me and started banging on the door demanding I open it. I start making sure my room is straightened up as he yells, *"I'M GOING TO COUNT TO TEN AND THIS #%@!#@ DOOR BETTER BE OPEN!!!"* I was scared because I had never run from or defied my dad like this, but I was ready. Just as he got to ten, I opened the door. That also seemed to have given him enough time to calm down a bit. His fists weren't swinging anymore. Just yelling and cussing about how I'm too much damn trouble. I never stood up to my father before, but I would learn something from this. There would be other times when I would get the nerve to run away.

My Teacher 'The Perv'

℘　℅

P hysical education (PE) classes were always rough, the one class I would get bad grades in. That did not make my dad happy. How could anybody get bad grades in PE? I was usually one of the last guys to be chosen for any teams so participation was never a huge thrill.

The locker room was always distressing. It was easy to change into shorts at the beginning of class, but afterward, it was a rule that you had to shower. I'm uncomfortable and ashamed to get undressed in front of other people. Even though I'm a teenager now, I still believe that I'm that ugly, fat assed, big butt person I was raised to see myself as. It's bad enough being that atrocious person fully dressed, but completely naked? In front of everyone?

The shower was one big open area with showerheads sticking out of the walls. Everyone showered together. Half the guys in class were on the football team and were in good shape and good-looking, everything I wasn't. At least I didn't think I was. I was ashamed of my body and ashamed of who I was, and I wasn't going to shower with everyone. I would get myself a corner locker and, for a while, got away without showering. Someone in class had caught on to me and finally snitched on me. I tried to worm my way out of the situation. Everyone else was dressed and ready to go to the next class, but our PE teacher made me strip while everyone laughed. The bell rang for the next class, and everyone left, but I had to stay and shower while the teacher stood and watched. I know I struggle with this attraction I have toward guys. I don't understand it, don't know why, but him watching me and staring at my private area while showering and dressing made me very uncomfortable. This would happen every time we had PE. Me staying after to shower while teacher watched until I finally started showering with everyone else. There would still be times I would try to skip showers with everyone, but usually, one of the "I'm all that" jocks would yell out, get me busted, and I would have to stay after class and shower. This is why I got bad grades in PE. My father would be furious with me. I never told my father about this until I came home, when I was twenty-five, to discuss the tapes I made. Even with cross-country and track, I wouldn't shower. That was easy because practices were after school and I could go home and shower.

Intro to Acting

ℰᴑ   ℭℜ

My favorite teacher was Mrs. A. She was part of the English department focusing more on speech and drama. I was always petrified to get up in front of the class to do a report or speech, always afraid of being judged harshly and laughed at in front of everyone. I was very self-conscious of how I looked. When I got to the front of the class, my neck muscles would tighten up so badly and quiver that my head would slightly shake. It's when my face would turn a burning red with embarrassment that some in the class would start laughing.

Mrs. A would sometimes ask me to come see her after school. Growing up in my house and being in trouble so much made me ultra paranoid that I would always fearfully ask if I had done something wrong. She would always assure me that I had done nothing wrong. When I would come to her class after school, her first question would be, "So how was the rest of your day?" and then "Is everything all right at home?" I would get a little worried inside because I was sure I never let anything slip. Stuff at home is the family's dark secret, or at least it's my dark secret of shame, and you just don't talk about it.

Mrs. A's reasons for having me stop by was to introduce me to script reading. I would be nervous and read them as if I was doing a report in class. She taught me how to forget about being me and become the person that was on the pages I was reading. It was incredible! I didn't like me. Didn't like anything about me. I was raised believing I was nothing. This was so freeing to become someone else and feel comfortable inside. Unfortunately, it didn't do much for me when I came back to being me. She would suggest I try to become someone else when I was doing a report, but I couldn't figure out how. After all, the report is *mine* and it's *me* reading it. There was no other character to play that I could see—just *me*. I am doomed to a life of nothingness as long as I am nothing.

The school did two huge stage productions a year: a fall play and a spring musical. Mrs. A always directed the fall play and convinced me to audition. The show was *The Miracle Worker*. Wow! I had read all about Helen Keller in Illinois when we would do our summer library trips. She had a fascinating and incredible life. I had also seen the movie with Patty Duke playing Helen Keller. It was a very moving portrayal. She won an Oscar for her performance.

I'm cast in the minor role of Percy the son of the servant to the Keller family. Weeks of rehearsal and set building keeps me away from home. My dad is not too thrilled but I am having the time of my life. I don't feel like an outsider. Being in a cast is like being part of a different type of family. A good family. I feel like I finally have something in common with other people.

Opening week rolls around. We do a matinee performance for the school then weekend performances. Opening night is incredible. A different kind of nervous like I have never felt before. The proverbial butterflies in the stomach. The second I step foot on stage in front of an audience for the first time, under the lights, the nerves go away. I'm in another world, another time, and I become Percy. The most exhilarating part is the end of the show during curtain call. The thunderous applause. The standing ovation. A glance out to the audience and I can see many wiping tears from their eyes. I have been a small part of a whole cast that moved an audience to tears. It is unbelievable. Even though I have wanted to be an actor since I was little, I have now officially caught the acting bug. It is incredible. I even get a new respect at school. People giving congratulations on a good show. Although it doesn't take long for that to fade away. After the show finishes it's run, things return to 'my normal'. Neither my father nor my mother came to the show.

Mrs. A also gets me into the Declamation Club, basically a speech club. There are various numbers of categories such as Original Comedy, some type of debating. The category I choose to compete in is Serious Pro's, an oral interpretation of a dramatic reading. I was always more attracted to the serious performances I would see on tv. The kind that really pulls at the emotions. I dabble with some excerpts from a few different books and finally settle on a reading from the book "A Day No Pigs Would Die" Robert Newton Peck's autobiographical novel. Mrs. A and I spend a lot of time putting the most heartfelt excerpts from the book together. A speech can be no longer than three minutes. In that period of time I have to fully immerse myself into the character and completely pull my audience into the story. A lot of serious rehearsals preparing and on to competition. I have totally become that thirteen year old boy on the day he has to help his father slaughter his beloved pet pig, Pinky, because the family is dealing with the rough economic times of the 1920's. I bring myself to tears as I describe, in emotionally graphic detail, about having to hold Pinky down while father clubs her to death. I have my audience moved to tears also. All this I do within a three-minute time limit. To find these emotions in me I would have to recall how my own father used to beat our dogs. As strong as my performance was, I would bring home a trophy at the Conference level and another one at the District competition but never did place at Regionals. Not at this school.

*****

When I'm twenty-five and come back for that short visit confronting my family, I stop by the school and meet with Mrs. A for a bit for old time's sake. She told me that she always had a feeling that something was not quite right at home because I often displayed a small amount of fear of people. She knew there was more inside me wanting to get out and the best way she knew how to help was through other characters.

I would continue with Declamation always trying to improve on that one story. I also stayed with acting and would eventually start getting better roles.

*****

94

Move Over Gene Kelly

ℰℴ ℭℛ

Not quite "Singin' in the Rain" but I'm cast in a supporting role in my first musical, *Brigadoon*, another Gene Kelly film (and my mother said I was tone deaf and couldn't carry a tune).

Andrew McLaren is the character I get to portray. I get to sing, I get to dance, a whole number of my own, in fact. I get to learn to tap dance. Many, many nights of rigorous tap dance rehearsals. It is exhausting. Our choreographer, Ronny, was a professional dance instructor direct from the Civic Center in the big city of Rochester. She will also become instrumental in introducing me to the director of theater at the Civic Center.

I will continue to play other roles throughout high school. I was student/assistant director and portrayed Mr Witherspoon in "Arsenic and Old Lace", co-starring as Jacquot in the musical production of "Carnival", the lead role of Billy Crocker in the musical "Anything Goes". It's amazing how good of an acting job I can do when I have to kiss the character Reno Sweeney when, off stage, that actress and I are bitter enemies. Her boyfriend is the one I said I would have taken a knife to. He would continually stalk and harass me.

Despite his terrorizing, everytime I'm on stage, becoming someone else, entertaining an audience, transporting them to another time, another place, I experience such a natural high it's unbelievable. The intense excitement. The adrenaline rush from the audience's applause at the end of an act or musical number. I am never so happy as when I'm on stage. I'm not me anymore. I still have dreams of making it to Hollywood one day.

However, with every high comes a crashing low. During the two months of rehearsals for "Anything Goes" the 'boyfriend' and his little gang of buddies would find my car, no matter where I parked. They would unscrew the valve stem from one of my tires just enough to release all the air so my tire would go flat. Many nights I would be changing a tire just so I could get home. Sometimes they would actually remove the valve stem. No matter what, I would have to tell my father because he will want to know why I'm getting home so late. I would also need his help to get new valve stems and get tire filled with air. Each time this happens he would always get mad, start cussing me out and blaming me and telling me I'm not worth all this trouble. Never once would he try to help with a solution to all the harassment.

I still continue with the theater. Choreographer, Ronnie, tells me about an upcoming audition at the Civic Center for the musical "South Pacific". This is a huge step up from big high school productions and I'm pretty excited. An audition is an audition but now I'm also in a theater filled with adults auditioning. This is a whole new, different level. It seems a lot closer to professional type work. I have never seen a stage so big or a theater hall that can seat so many. It must hold around five hundred. Just the thought of performing to such a huge audience is exhilarating.

I meet Bob, the director and producer. He takes us all through some simple tap dance moves. Thank goodness for "Brigadoon" and all the tap I learned from Ronnie. Then a few hours are spent with cold readings. I make it through the auditions and land a minor speaking role as Yeoman Herbert Quale. This character is not in the movie, just the stage version. It's a very large cast. A lot of people auditioned and I'm very thankful that Bob cast me in my first Civic Theater production that people from all over the city and surrounding areas will see. I only have a couple of lines but I get to sing and dance in some of the big musical numbers. We have a heavy rehearsal schedule but it is so worth it.

Opening night rolls around and it turns out that our two week run is sold out. There is an actual Green Room, a roomy area with couches where we hang out when not on stage. Flowers being delivered to some of the leading actors. Real dressing rooms. I know it's not Broadway or Hollywood but the feeling and excitement is as if I were there. Curtain rises and a couple of our first boisterous opening numbers are "Bloody Mary" and "There Is Nothing Like A Dame" The thunderous applause every night is just incredible. I am lifted into another world when I'm on stage. I feel like the luckiest teenager in the world to be a part of this.

By the time "South Pacific" ends it's run there are already auditions for the next show at the Civic Center "A Midsummer Night's Dream". A Shakespeare play. I have always had trouble understanding Shakespeare but decide I am going to audition anyway. As long as I can be on stage, if I can make the audition cut again. The Civic Theater has a much, much larger turnout of actors competing for roles.

I go into auditions wanting one of the leads, Lysander or Demetrius. I figure, why not aim for the top. Reach for the stars. As always, auditions are fraught with nerves but I also feel so alive. This is where I belong. Where I fit in. I don't know how I made it through the readings, faking my way around Shakespeare language, but I did, figuring I flubbed up pretty well. A few days after auditions everyone gets a phone call. The cast list is also posted at the theater. *I'M IN!!* I'm very excited and a little disappointed that I'm not one of the leads but I do get a very good role. Francis Flute, the bellows-mender. In the play the craftsmen put on a play to celebrate the wedding of Theseus and Francis Flute is forced to play the hilarious role of the girl Thisbe who is in love with Pyramus.

We are set to go into rehearsals the evening after the closing cast party for "South Pacific". Rush, rush, rush. Excitement, excitement, excitement. This has got to be close to what it feels like to be on Broadway. That's how my teenage mind is thinking. Interesting because I never had a desire for Broadway. It gets too cold in New York. But I do love the stage.

Bob has us spend the first two nights reading through the play paraphrasing every line so we know what we are saying when we go into all the "thee's" and "thou's" and "where for art's" it helped me to be able to understand Shakespeare much better.

I have a blast with my character especially when I become Thisbe speaking in falsetto. She has a very melodramatic death scene.

I'm using nerf footballs cut in half as breasts under my robes. When a sword gets plunged through my chest I do an overly dramatized death twirl where one of my nerf breasts flies out into the audience. There is an uproar of laughter reverberating through the theater hall every night. I get audience members coming to the Green Room after the shows to compliment me.

I also get a very nice mention in the theater review section in the paper after opening night. I am just loving life.

Downside to all the excitement is that every time I'm in a show I'm usually also involved with something school related that keeps me busy right after school. Declamation or cross country, then rehearsals at night. My father thinks I should be spending more time at home doing things around the house. This causes a lot of friction. If everything isn't done as he likes, by the time he gets home from work, then tempers flare. When tempers flare, the fists fly and the fowl language begins. "A Midsummer Night's Dream" will be the last show I do at the Civic Center.

Dreams and Screwups

₭ ℛ

I also resent my littlest brother. I have for as long as I can remember. He was allowed to do anything. He didn't have to do anything and got away with everything. My sister, I was always kind of jealous/proud of her because she was popular and excelled in all areas. My younger brother, I felt sorry for and was embarrassed for him. He had all sorts of medical issues, one leg shorter than the other and had to wear a "Frankenstein" shoe. I despise my father. I can't stand anything about him. I'm not sure how I feel about my mother these days.

I spend weekends with my mom and Emily(Lois has legally changed her name) on occasion. That's all good because she doesn't hurt me anymore. At least not physically. I don't think she dares, or can, since she doesn't have custody. She does, however, always manage to get her small insulting put downs and quips and jabs in. Interestingly enough, after all the years of her insults of me not being able to sing, she did eventually see me in a performance of "Anything Goes" and told me after the show she was proud of me. I really wasn't sure how to feel about that. She had never said anything like that to me before.

*****

These days, actually for a few years now, my favorite TV show is "Little House On The Prairie". I still love Michael Landon but his portrayal of the father, Charles Ingalls is always so moving. A father full of love for his family no matter what. Many episodes leave me in tears. I have often said that just watching Laura Ingalls milk a cow would probably make me cry. Oddly, to me, despite my attraction

99

to guys, I do have a small crush on Melissa Gilbert (Laura Ingalls) I think it's her buck teeth, like I have, and her tom boyish way in the show. I love "Laverne and Shirley" and "Happy Days". Who doesn't love Scott Baio. The drama of "Hill Street Blues" and the prime time soap "Dynasty" first airs my senior year. The Carrington family of "Dynasty" is such a wealthy and handsome family that when I make it to Hollywood I want to change my name to Stephen Carrington after the "Dynasty" character (Steven). He was very good looking and one of the first gay main characters on TV. Also because I never liked my name. It's a constant reminder that I'm part of this family that I despise.

Some of my favorite movies through high school and into my early twenties would be "Dirty Dancing", Patrick Swayze, Hot, but the music and the dancing are phenomenal. "Grease", the music. the singing, the dancing. "Friday The 13th", "Halloween", "Nightmare On Elm Street" I love a really good scare. The "Alien" movies. All the "Star Wars". To be on that big screen playing any one of those characters in a good sci-fi is a dream beyond dreams. Besides, Harrison Ford and Mark Hamill… very good looking!! The "Indiana Jones" movies. The action and suspense of any "Bond" movie. "Ice Castles" with Robby benson To be able to move audiences like that, to make them laugh or cry, is a dream that won't go away. This was partially shot up in the Twin Cities. I would hear about it on the radio and I had wanted so badly to be able to go up there and try to be in it but I was clueless as to how. It doesn't matter because I will get to Hollywood one day.

*****

I am socially awkward and inept but I do have three close male friends through my high school years. Ken, my best friend, Jeff and Ted. Ken, Jeff and I are in band, we play trumpet, choir, cross country and track together. I don't last long in track but Ken and Jeff letter in both cross country and track. Ken and Jeff also play in the orchestra when we do musicals. I don't recall how Ted fit in. I think he joined the choir at some point. Mostly, Ted was comic relief. He was always joking around. The class clown. Ted co-starred with me in "Anything Goes" as the hilarious Moonface Martin. He would win the best actor award while I got best supporting actor.

Most of our hanging out was at school or at school functions, practices and competitions. I never brought my friends over to my house because I never knew what might happen. We have a beautiful house but I'm ashamed of my family. I don't tell Ken this until much later in life but I had a small crush on him, my best friend.

I am not a perfect teenager. I work hard to maintain good grades because it's required in my family…or else. I just don't excel academically. I do screw up in other areas of life. One major mess, in particular, was a week after I got my driver's license. I was driving my dad's big Chevy Suburban with both my brother's and two of their friends from down the street in the car. We were on a country gravel road and I decided to be a show-off. I was going too fast, lost control of the car. When I over corrected we hit the ditch and rolled three times. It's true when they say your life flashes before you. Not only flashes but in slow motion. We landed upright next to a cornfield and facing the road. My younger brother, seated just behind me, was the only one in a seat belt. The rest of us were thrown from the car. One of their friends was tangled in a barbed wire fence.

I was about to head to the nearest farm house when a car stopped. It was a doctor going on vacation with his family. They saw us flipping from the highway on the other side of the cornfield and came to our rescue. We all ended up in the hospital with cuts and bruises. The friend that ended up in the barbed wire fence had to have forty stitches. I was devastated inside as to what I had caused. I was only sixteen and full of fear about what my dad might do when he shows up. The police came in and I told them a lie because I was afraid of going to jail. When my father showed up, he was just glad everyone was alive. He never punished me saying that what had happened was traumatic enough. I didn't understand his reaction. My mother, on the other hand… when she had me over to her house the next time… I thought it was going to be a regular weekend but she took me to a barber shop and had my head shaved as punishment for the accident. She made sure I knew that it was because my youngest brother (her special) had been with me. She couldn't physically hit me so that was the best she could do. Make sure I would be publicly humiliated for a good long time.

I was fearful of driving now and it took me six months to start feeling secure enough to drive again. My dad had bought a new van and would take me out to practice. It was scary being back behind the wheel but I did learn to become a safer, more careful driver. Eventually I will buy a cheap, very cheap, car of my own.

Other Teenage Indiscretions

ℬ ℛ

No. My lifetime of beatings did not make me become the perfect teenager. I actually became somewhat rebellious and slightly mischievous. Yes, me, the one afraid of his own shadow.

There was a time in school, in science class, when I organized a classroom strike. Our science teacher was kind of like me but much older, of course. He was quiet and unassuming, the weak one that all the kids made fun of during his classes. I would join in just to feel 'part of'… just one of the guys. I would get some attention. I never called him names out loud like others, but I would partake in the "spit wads" thrown at the chalkboard when his back was turned. One time I had all his pens and pencils super glued, sticking straight up, on his desk by the time he came into the class. The class thought it was funny. I was just looking to be accepted in some way, any way I could.

One day, I thought it would be cool if we all went on strike. I got it passed around the class to bring straws back from lunch to use to make little picket signs. When our teacher came into class, we all held up our "On Strike" straw picket signs and refused to do any work. For a minute, I felt important because I had organized this, but it soon got out of control. Everyone started moving their desks to the front of the class surrounding his big lab table with him trapped behind it. Then they started kicking the table, pummeling it with their feet. I looked at his face, and I believe I saw an expression of fear. I was flooded with feelings of guilt. This was not what I had intended. I had only planned on a quiet little strike. Luckily, our assistant principal was walking by in the hall and witnessed what was taking place. The second he came into the room, the class quieted down. Some loud, stern instructions from him and our class quickly came to order, everyone back in their proper places and then a lecture.

I had become a bully myself just to try to get attention and fit in, but I didn't like how I felt. After school that day, I went to my science teacher's room and apologized for being a part of what happened. I didn't tell him I had initiated the strike, but I was truly sorry for what had happened.

*****

I experimented with alcohol for the first time when I was fifteen. I used to help mow the yards of our next-door neighbor. A married couple, Jim and Kathy (they didn't like the titles "Mr. and Mrs."), were friends of my dad. Since they were friends, my dad and Jim, on occasion, would take turns barbecuing. This was before my dad started to date again. Between mowing their yards and barbeque dinners in their backyard, at times, I had become familiar with their house. They liked to drink, and I was aware of which cupboard in the kitchen they kept their alcohol. On one Saturday of barbecuing at their house, I was taking some dirty dishes into their kitchen. Everyone else was outside on the deck laughing and carrying on; the adults had their drinks. A spur of the moment idea raced through my mind, and when I knew it was safe (I was shaking inside) and no one was looking, I opened their liquor cupboard door, reached for the nearest, smallest bottle I saw, pulled it out, slipped it into my pants, and went back outside. I excused myself to go back to our house.

When I got home, I went straight into my bedroom and pulled out the bottle. It was a half pint of blackberry brandy. I was still shaking just a little bit. I unscrewed the cap on the bottle and sniffed the opening. It smelled good. Not sure what to expect, I tentatively took a little sip. It burned a little bit going down my throat, and I immediately felt warm all over, but I really liked the taste of it. I took another tiny little sip, screwed the cap back on the bottle, hid it under the mattress on my bed, and went back to our neighbor's house. They were playing yard darts. We stayed until it got dark then went home.

I went straight to my bedroom again. When I heard my dad go to bed, I pulled the bottle out and started taking sips. It took me until around midnight, but I drank the whole half pint. It didn't take long for my throat to not feel the burn anymore. I kind of liked the way it made me feel tingly all over, but mostly, I loved the blackberry flavor.

We had to go to church in the morning, and when my alarm rang to get up, I really didn't want to get out of bed. I didn't get sick, I just felt really groggy. My father never found out. That's okay because I won't be going to church much longer. The Methodist church we go to got a female pastor. My father was so much against it that he became Lutheran, started going to that church, and insisted the rest of the family does the same. I defied him and told him I wouldn't follow. Major argument. Not pretty, I got shoved around but stood my ground against my father. The final call is that he decides to leave it up to me. I don't go to church anymore.

*****

I didn't start becoming a drinker. I didn't like it that much. However, one time I wanted to be a big shot and got arrested for shoplifting. It was just prior to the cast party for *South Pacific*. It was mostly an adult party, but some of us younger cast members were going to go. We all wanted to be cool. A little more grown up and wanted to have something of our own to drink. I told them that I would bring something for us. I knew my dad kept alcohol in the house, but it was mostly wine and a little bit of whiskey, so I couldn't touch any of that without it being noticed.

One evening, close to the cast party date, I drive by a liquor store and decide to stop. It's winter time so I'm wearing my parka that has pockets on the inside. I go in, act natural and walk around until I see the flavored liquors. I eye the peppermint schnapps. It sounds like it would taste good. I take a nice sized bottle and tuck it in one of the pockets inside my coat and casually walk outside. As soon as I got through the door I was stopped by the manager. I was busted. He brought me into the back office where I took the bottle out of my inside pocket and returned it. He showed me the hidden window in the office looking out into the store, it was right behind the peppermint schnapps. They had a front row, center stage seat to witness my crime.

I was arrested and taken to jail. My father was called, and he came down to get me out. Luckily for me, the juvenile detective was an acquaintance of my father and no charges were filed. When we got outside and in the car, the first thing my father said to me was, *"Do you really think you're worth all this f_ _ _ing trouble!!"* The rest of the drive home was quiet, and I was afraid of what would happen when we got there. Once we got inside the house, I thought I was going to get hit, but the only thing my dad said in an extremely firm, angry voice was, *"What do you have to say for yourself?"* The only thing I could think to say was, *"If you're going to beat me, can you wait. We're closing one show and going right into rehearsals for the next, and I really don't want to have any bruises."* My dad just looked at me then said, *"I think your being in jail was enough punishment."* He didn't do anything else. Shocking to me because my whole life, I got beaten for ridiculous reasons or for no real reason and here I'd done something major and he surprised me with some sort of understanding? Compassion, maybe?

Another alcohol-related incident that my father never found out about was a Saturday night when Ken, Jeff, and I went out. We didn't get to do that often. Ken was driving. We had gone to a movie, and afterward, we thought we would be cool and see if we could get into a bar. The thing was none of us really drank. I had never seen them drink. We were just out having fun and wanting to be cool.

We decided upon a bar called "Golden George's" for no particular reason. I don't smoke, never tried, but I managed to get a cigarette from someone before we went in. I thought it would help make me look older. After all, I was the actor and the cigarette was just a prop. Not realizing that Ken and Jeff were wearing their letter jackets, how much older could I really look. Ken almost went along with me on the smoking but decided against it. Lucky for him because within a few minutes of entering the bar, we just happened to run into our assistant principal Mr. Harris. We didn't even have time to see if we could order a drink. The look of shock we must have had on our faces when he looked at us and said, *"Good evening, gentlemen."* with a little *"you're busted"* smile on his face. Needless to say, we didn't stay in the bar for long, but we sure laughed our pants off all the way home.

Unfortunately, that Monday, we were called to the office. It seems that being under age in the bar was not breaking any school rules, but the fact that I had a cigarette was against, even after school, rules. Ken and Jeff didn't receive any punishment, but I received six weeks suspension from any afterschool activities which meant, at that time, declamation competitions. I did still manage to make it to Regional's that year. A registered letter was sent to my house for my father that I was miraculously able to intercept and save myself from a beating.

No, I was not the perfect teenager. These are just a few of my transgressions. There were other little things also, but for the most part, I was a good kid. I did like to get into a little mischief when I was out from under my father's, sometimes brutal, thumb/fist.

Who Am I

ஐ   ௸

I don't know. I'm confused. I'm angry. I'm sad. I'm lost. I'm alone. I don't fit in. I'm different.

Before my father switches churches, and I stop going, I take confirmation classes at the Methodist church we were going to and I get confirmed there. This is something I'm supposed to do but don't really know why. I learn more about the Bible during classes. Among many, many things, like having to memorize and recite the Apostle's Creed, I have also learned, according to the Bible, that homosexuality is a sin. This is one of my biggest confusions right now.

At my age, I know but don't really know what homosexuality is. I don't think many other kids really did either. The terms "faggot" and "gay" were used freely and frequently in school, generally aimed at the guys, such as myself, who were the easy targets for bullying. I was in no way effeminate; I was just the weak one. The easily intimidated one and "faggot" and "gay" were the two names that were certain to inflict nonphysical pain. It always worked. The thing that bothered me the most was that it had to be true. I've always been attracted to other guys. I don't know why, but I know nobody else knew this secret.

I did eventually meet someone else in my class who was like me. Blaine and I met during set building for one of the shows. He lived only a couple blocks away, and he would come over sometimes when my father would be gone. While other "normal" kids in school were dating, we were having our own "secret" dates. During school, I would steer clear of Blaine because he was somewhat effeminate and I couldn't take that risk of anyone finding out or just being curious and escalating the bullying. This will stay a secret throughout my time at school.

I do try to be like the other guys. There are a lot of pretty girls in my class, mostly the cheerleaders, the ones that only date the jocks. I know what *pretty* is and *sexy*, but I'm just not attracted to girls "that" way, the way guys are supposed to be. I don't understand their "locker room talk" about girls. I can't figure out those desires. I don't get it. However, there is one girl, Pauline, that I think is very cute. Her older brother is a jock, which means, in my class, that's the clique she belongs to. She's not a cheerleader, but she hangs out with them.

After fighting a lot of nerves and fears of ridicule, I instigate the passing of notes in class to show my interest. For a period of time, that's how we communicate. Can't talk to her in the halls in between classes because she's always with her friends and I would be made fun of. As long as she keeps passing notes back, I maintain a positive attitude. I'm getting close to wanting to ask her out. I have no idea what I would do if she said yes, but I want to be like a "normal" guy. My last note to her, I asked when her birthday is. Her note back to me said February 30. It's nice to know a little something personal like that. I'm thinking I'm going to ask her out. Then I run into that wall of humiliation. Another girl in class that sits near Pauline and her friends could overhear the jokes they were making about me. She reminded me that February doesn't have thirty days. I was all hung up on thinking Pauline might like me. How stupid I was to think that it could be true. Instead, I was just the *big butt* of their jokes and ridicule.

This brought back a memory from just before we left Illinois. There was one girl in my seventh grade class, Delynn, that I thought was cute also. I was going to my friend Dale's house but went down the street to Delynn's house instead. It was going to be my first kiss with a girl. When I got to her house, we went into the garage, and just when I thought we were going to kiss, two of her friends came out of hiding and started laughing and making fun of me. My attractions aren't really in that direction anyway. I guess I really can't be like a normal guy. I'm really not comfortable with who I think I am, but it seems girls really aren't worth it.

Dad's Dating

My father eventually joined a single parents club. I believe it was called "Parents Without Partners". Kind of a catchy name. They would all get together one night a week. That was nice because I would try to stay away from home after school and my dad would spend evenings out, either at their meetings or he would be on a date. I generally liked the ladies he dated. They were alright, mostly because he never showed his true self when he would bring them home. I remember one time I didn't get the house vacuumed by the time he got home from work, he started his cussing and hitting and I gave him a hard furious glare, yelled back at him with everything I had *"WHAT WOULD YOUR GIRLFRIEND THINK IF SHE SAW YOU ACTING LIKE THIS!!"* I remember he stopped yelling and had a look as if I had just slapped him in the face. He then yells at me to go to my room and I'm not to come out until he tells me to.

I'm getting very fed up with my dad and close to the breaking point with his temper. I'm risking further bodily harm by standing up to him but I'm tired of being hit.

I'm fifteen, my sister has already gone off to college and all the housework is left to me. Making sure laundry is done, house clean, dinner ready. My younger brothers aren't held responsible for anything. The youngest is ten and still the spoiled one, my brother just behind me still has a lot of medical issues.

One time my father comes home from work to find I don't have dinner ready. It's summer break. I had spent most of the day trying to clean the house and do laundry but my little brother kept bringing friends over messing up the house complicating the situation. I only had TV dinners on the menu for supper and had just placed them in the oven when he got home. He goes into his yelling and cussing *"What the hell have you been doing all day"*. I'm already mad at my brother. Years of my dad are wearing on me. I take all the anger that is building up and festering inside of me and focus it into my fist. As much as I would like to use it on my father the only semi-sane thing I can think to do is to slam my fist onto the kitchen counter in angry frustrated protest. Shatter resistant plates are a relatively new product and my clenched fist comes down on one of them so hard with such angry force that it actually shatters cutting my hand up. I see all the blood and furiously storm past my father, go into the bathroom and lock the door. My dad, after seeing all the blood, stops yelling and comes to the bathroom door acting all concerned asking to come in and see if I'm ok. By the time I get myself cleaned up and bandaged I come out of the bathroom. My dad's mood has changed and he's pulling the finished TV dinners out of the oven. He tries to talk to me but I ignore him all through dinner.

In the past, when my spoiled, bratty little brother would bring friends over I would end up having to lock him out of the house if I was going to get anything done so I wouldn't get in trouble. He would either threaten to tell on me or call dad at work. If he called him at work then my dad would quietly threaten me over the phone letting me know that I had better not be locking anyone out of the house if I knew what was good for me. As always my dad doesn't listen to me when I try to explain that I can't get a single thing done with my brother and his friends messing up the house. My brother knows exactly how to handle my dad and the situation so that he doesn't get into any trouble. Scenarios such as these are common place in the evenings.

One time I was so furious with my brother messing things up when I was cleaning the kitchen that I grabbed the first thing within reach and threw it at him. It happened to be a butter knife and it hit him square in the mouth splitting open his lip. I didn't mean for that to happen. It was an accident, but I was very angry!! I was sorry that happened… but also not sorry at the same time, and very scared about what might happen later. Needless to say I got the devil beat out of me when my dad got home. Since he was my mother's little baby, she banned me from spending any weekends for two months.

Whether it's summer break or even during school, it was always a relief when my father would go out on a date or have his group meetings, especially when I didn't have any extracurricular activities of my own going on after school. I would get a nice quiet evening at home without dad and I would usually be in bed by the time he got home. I'm so tired and worn out from all his yelling, cussing, hitting, and demands.

*****

In 1979 my dad starts dating a woman with two kids. They get married in the Spring of 1980. Among all the existing turmoil I now have a step-mother, step-brother and step-sister. And I'm thrown out of the house, for the first time, the beginning of that summer.

*****

The Stepfamily

☙   ❧

I don't recall when in 1979 they started dating, and I don't recall much about their dating. It all seemed to happen fairly quickly. She had two kids of her own: a son, two years younger than me but the same age as my younger brother; and a daughter, maybe six years younger than me, younger than my youngest brother. This was already such a broken and volatile family situation, I'm sure she had no idea what she was walking into.

It seems we were just thrown together. There weren't any 'family' dinners or any 'get togethers' in order to get to know one another. Her son played hockey and one day, out of the blue, my dad tells me I need to go into Rochester to the recreation center and pick him up from hockey practice. I have never met this kid before. My dad and his mom are going out to dinner and I have to go pick up this kid, this complete stranger, and bring him back to my house until our parents get back. I was not happy about this but did what I was told. When I got there it was very uncomfortable asking around for this kid and very awkward on the drive back home. We barely spoke to each other. What was there to say. That was my introduction to my future step-brother.

I just keep myself busy with the theater and work. I have a part time job at a well known fast food franchise. Before I know it my father is building a bedroom in the basement for her son, about the same time they announce their engagement. The care he takes in making sure the room is just perfect for him. The daughter will have the fourth bedroom upstairs, two doors down from mine.

During their engagement there were some 'family' outings for dinner or just get togethers at home. I tried to make myself scarce but it didn't always work. Sometimes my dad would threaten me to make sure I would be around and on my best behavior. I couldn't believe how different my father was when they were around, acting like the perfect guy and stepdad to be. He would go above and beyond to make sure everything was perfect for them. I would fume inside my head, saying, *"You are so full of _ _ it!!"* I would be so angry I would just want to yell at to him to *"STOP IT!!"* Then go on a rant about, *"You want to know what he's really like? You want to know what his fists feel like? You want to see him mad?"* That would have made me feel soo good to blow his cover. I was filled with such disdain for him but, out of fear, I would keep my mouth shut. I really don't have anything against these 'other people' personally but the side of my dad they don't get to see is that angry brutal side. All winter, prior to the spring wedding, my father would seriously kick my butt inside out every time I would 'ditch' my car in the snow at the end of our driveway. Our driveway is on a slope and always slick in the winter and I could only get halfway up before sliding back down and into the ditch. My father would raise total hell, when he got home, every time he had to get my car out.

Eventually Spring 1980 rolls around and the wedding day is upon us. I'm certain I went. I doubt my father would have let me get out of going but I have pretty much blanked out that period in time. I didn't want to be a part of my own family for most of my life and I certainly wasn't ready to be blended with another. But... I don't have a choice.

I also don't remember when everyone moved in but, before I know it, we are all one family under the same roof. I get along fairly well with my step-sister but my step-brother and I are at extreme odds. He's a smoker and a pot head. When I would get home from school in the afternoons, if I didn't have any activities, he would have his stereo blaring from in the basement and you couldn't hear anything upstairs if the TV was on. Some days there was a slight scent of pot smoke coming from the basement. I would stomp my foot on the floor and yell at him to turn the music down. This was pretty much a daily routine and would be extremely aggravating.

Between my step-sister and step-brother, word would get to my father about what I was doing. I would either be taken to my room or out to the garage to get yelled at for *"intentionally trying to make his records skip and get scratched. If I knew what was good for me I had better learn to get along with him!!"* I have learned to stand up to my father a little bit so I yelled back… *"with his bedroom in the basement there is no way my stomping is going to skip his records since he's on a carpeted concrete slab and besides…can't you even smell that he's been smoking pot??"* Does my dad listen to me?? NO!! Of course not!! I get punched and shoved up against a wall and, again, told that I *"had better learn to get along if I know what's good for me!!"* I am so, so, fed up with my dad!! Many days my step brother would come home and you could see by looking at his face that he was stoned.

When I am home I spend a lot of time in my bedroom and get in trouble for not being sociable. One time, in my room, he takes me by the shoulders, violently shaking me and yelling *"You will become a contributing member of this family!!"* And, as usual, ends it with *"If you know what's good for you!!"* I give him a blank look of, *I could really care less,* then he starts pounding me on top of my head with his fist and yells at me *"You make me so damn mad!!"* I'm filled with so much frustration and contempt. I look at him and, with every bit of anger centered on keeping a firm and focused voice, I tell him *"don't you ever hit me again!!"*

Emotionally I'm drained. My father really doesn't give a crap. He can have this other family. I'm through. I just don't want to be around anymore. He leaves my bedroom and I get ready to go to work. Before I leave I go into the bathroom and stare at myself in the mirror. I don't really see anything. I see a face with no future. I don't want to come back here anymore but I don't know what to do.

I'm not sure what I'm doing but I open the medicine cabinet and look around. I don't see much of anything but I take the practically full bottle of aspirin out and look at it. I'm not sure what I'm thinking but I want a way out. I open the bottle and take little handfuls of pills. I pop each handful in my mouth and stick my face under the sink faucet and suck water into my mouth and swallow. I do this until the bottle is empty. I look at myself in the mirror again. I'm not sure what this is going to do but I'm hoping this will be it and I think *"it's done"* Before I leave for work I call my best friend, Ken. I tell him what I did, say my goodbye and leave for work.

Halfway through my shift Ken calls me to see how I am. Unfortunately nothing is happening. I'm not even getting sick and I'm going to have to go back home (I had no idea at the time but I guess God wasn't done with me yet). The next day Ken, Jeff and Ted come over to my house to see how I'm doing. This was awkward because my dad was home and friends had never come over before. We went into my bedroom to talk for a while and I assure them I'm ok. It's nice to know I have friends that care but I'm still stuck in this house.

Don't Come Home

୫ ଓ

There are good days, and there are bad days. Unfortunately, the bad ones outnumber the good. I have not had any real issues with my stepsister, aside from my belief that she's telling on me when I stomp on the floor to get her brother to turn the volume down on his stereo. She does know how to play the game as my little brother does. She can manipulate her mom and has my dad tied around her little finger. She knows how easy it is to get me in trouble.

It's about the end of May. I've recently turned seventeen, she's probably eleven. School is out and summer vacation starting. I have earned enough money to buy myself a nicer car, an early seventies Camaro. I actually financed it on my own, no cosigner, because the bank president's daughter was in my class. I buy my own gas and pay my dad for insurance. One day, before I have to go to work, my stepsister and I are innocently horsing around. We're running around the house through the family room, down through the sunken living room, up through the dining room, through the kitchen, back through the family room, sunken living room, etc. She's laughing, carrying on, round and round. Just innocent horseplay. Until one time through the sunken living room, she slips on the carpet and slides like a ball player into home plate, into the leg of the coffee table hitting the heel of her foot real hard. She starts screaming bloody murder in pain. My immediate reaction is of concern, and I try to find out if she's okay. She won't stop screaming as I keep asking, *"Are you okay? Are you okay?"* I try to get her to let me look at her foot, but she just keeps screaming bloody murder and crying, yelling at me to leave her alone.

She finally gets up, yelling at me, *"I'M CALLING MY MOM!!!"* I can see she's walking so not really hurt, just a good painful bang. My concern for her instantly turns to mortal fear, and I practically beg her not to call her mom. I know what that outcome will be. *"Don't call your mom. We were just playing. You know that."* Back and forth, we went a few times.

"I'M CALLING MY MOM!!"

"Please don't call your mom!"

I'm begging my little eleven year old step-sister, who's hardly been a member of this "family". Begging because I know I'm treated "less than" and I know that whatever story she concocts will be the one believed. Out of sheer frustration, after her last *"I'M CALLING MY MOM!!"* I yell back at her *"GO AHEAD AND CALL YOUR F_ _ _ING MOM!!"* Words like that rarely come out of my mouth, even around friends. I went into my room, grabbed my work shirt, that I would change into at work, and left the house.

Sometime later that evening, while I was working the cash register, my manager came to me and said that I had a phone call in his office. I went in, picked up the phone *"Hello?"* the reply back was *"THIS IS YOUR F_ _ _ING STEP-MOTHER!! DON'T BOTHER COMING HOME!!!"* Then I hear a click on the other end as she hangs up. I'm speechless. I'm not sure what just happened. My world has just collapsed. I'm dumbfounded. I have no idea what I'm going to do. I finish out the night in a daze. A part of me wishing that day I had taken all those aspirin had worked the way I wanted. I may not know what I'm going to do, but at least I have my car. I guess that's a plus. By the time we close up, I'm not so much in shock anymore, I'm just really pissed. I do have a couple work friends, Tim and Steve, but I don't tell them. They're just work friends, both a year younger than me, and I don't need people at work knowing the crap that goes on in my home life.

I generally work the closing shift, so it's about ten o'clock. I sit in my car in the parking lot for a little while thinking about what to do. I can't really think, so I drive up and down Broadway, the main street. A few blocks from work, on a side street, there's a popular movie theater. Shows are done for the night, so I turn into the alley and park in the parking lot behind the theater. I'm tired so I recline my seat, curl up a little, and try to get some sleep.

Before too long, there is a bright light shining into my car. I rise up to see a police car had pulled up next to me. They motion me to roll down my window. My mind is racing trying to come up with a story. They ask me if I'm okay and what am I doing. I tell them I was really tired from work and didn't want to drive the ten miles back home. I just needed a little rest. They informed me that I wasn't allowed to be sleeping in my car. It's against the law. I apologized and told them I would be leaving.

They watch me drive off, and at a stoplight, I see them pull out of the alley and drive off also. I drive around for a little bit, and when I think it's safe, I drive back to the theater parking lot and park. It's close to midnight. I get out of my car and start walking down the alley and around onto Broadway. It's a Friday night, so most of the shops are closed, but there's quite a bit of traffic since there are bars up and down Broadway. There also happens to be an adult bookstore that I am walking by. I'm very curious, and well, I have no place to go. I know I'm not old enough, but I take my chances, open the door, and walk in as if I've been in one before. There's an older man, probably around my father's age, forty or something, behind the counter. There are aisles of magazines on one side of the store, and in a big room to the left were many little rooms for watching movies. I walk over to the magazines and just start browsing. The man behind the counter is watching me but not saying anything.

Lots of magazines with naked women and men together. I've never seen anything like this. I look at a few and keep walking around. Suddenly, I'm on an aisle of magazines with nothing but naked men on the covers. My interest is really piqued now. I start looking at a few. I'm curiously fascinated. I spend more time in this section than I did on any other aisle. The man behind the counter notices and tries to start up a conversation with me. He says I look old enough to be in the store (eighteen is the legal age) but doesn't think I am. However, that's all right with him because he runs the store and his apartment is just above the store along with a handful of other apartments. He said, *"If you want, I can let you have a couple magazines for free."* I'm thinking, *Wow, how cool.* So I hesitantly said, *"Yeah, sure."* He actually came out from behind the counter over to me and picked out some male magazines he thought I should have. He picked out five and gave them to me. Awkwardly, I said, *"Thanks."*

He said, *"You're a very good-looking, sexy guy. What are you doing out by yourself?"* No one had ever complimented me like that. It made it a little easier to talk. It also made me curiously cautious. I told him about what had happened with my stepmom. He mentioned, *"If you need a place for the night, you can stay in my apartment upstairs."*

I was still a little curious, but it also felt weird. I remained wary and told him, *"That would be nice, but I'll figure something out. I should get going."*

He then told me, *"I have a couple guys, college friends, just a couple years older than you, that come down from the Twin Cities and stay with me for the weekend sometimes. They would love to meet you. I think you would like them also."*

I told him, *"Maybe but I should really get going."*

He led me to the back door that led to the alley and showed me the stairs outside that led up to the apartments. He said, *"If you ever need, anything just stop by anytime. Never a problem."* He said his name was Harry. I told him my name and said thanks again for the magazines. He said, *"If you ever need any extra cash, I could always use a little help with odd jobs around here."*

I told him *"Okay"* and started outside down the alley toward the parking lot where my car was parked. I wait until he's back inside before I go to the parking lot. It's about one-thirty now, so I get in my car, shove the magazines under the passenger seat, and curl up in the front seat again.

I have dozed off, but I'm startled awake by a "whoop, whoop" and a bright light shining in my car again. I'm panicked now because it's the police again. I don't have another story. I look at my watch real quick and see that it's about two o'clock. They get out of their car. One of them comes over to the driver's side of my car and tells me to get out. They wanted to know why, after telling me I couldn't sleep in my car, I'm back in the alley parking lot. I didn't see any other choice but to tell them the truth. I was kicked out of the house. Told not to come home. In doing so, I'm not only embarrassed for airing ugly family secrets but also embarrassed because I feel like I'm the bad child.

The officers tell me that I cannot stay in my car and they have no choice but to take me to jail for breaking the law after they had already warned me. I'm scared and feeling like this night, this nightmare, is never going to end. They don't handcuff me, but they do put me in the back of their squad car and off to the police station we go. They ask a lot of questions about my situation, but I don't talk much because I don't want anyone knowing everything. I do have to tell them my father's name.

When we get to the police station, I'm placed in a jail cell. Back when I got arrested for shoplifting, I was just put in a room with a detective. This time, it's an actual cell, bars and all. The officers ask, and I give them my dad's phone number. They leave me in the cell alone to go call him.

It seems like forever before my dad gets to the police station. It doesn't really matter because I'm rather emotionless about this whole situation, kind of just numb inside my head. They let my dad come back to the cell by himself to talk to me. He stands there looking at me for a moment. I stare back with a detached look on my face. I have nothing to say. The first words out of his mouth are, *"I've said this before. Do you really think you're worth all this f_ _ _ing trouble!!"* Not a question. More like a *"I'm through with you"* statement. One of the officers comes back, unlocks the cell, and we go up front. I wasn't charged with anything, but my father has to sign some papers, and we leave. I glance up at the clock on the way out. It's only three o'clock. It's only been an hour since they picked me up.

In the car, my dad asks, *"Where does your mother work?"* My mother works the night shift in a nursing home, but I don't tell him where. My reply is, *"Take me to my car!"* That only makes him mad. He goes on a rant about, *"I'm fed up with your damn shit all the time!"* criticizing me about how I *"have no consideration for anyone else in this family!"* I'm blown away, stunned, and stupefied. My mind is saying, with an angry force I don't dare let out, *Consideration? My whole f_ _ _ing life you and mom have beaten me, whipped me, abused in so many ways.* But all I say is, *"Take - me - to - my - car!"*

My dad drives around the city stopping at various nursing homes, asking, *"Is this it?"* I either don't reply, or I stick with my same answer, *"Take me to my car!"* He finally relents and says, *"If I take you to your car, will you drive to your mother's work while I follow?"* I said I would. I just wanted back in my car and away from him. We drove to the nursing home where my mom worked and went to the front desk. The nurse paged my mom, she came to the front, and my dad and her had a talk then he left without looking back.

It was about five o'clock. I'm very tired. It's been a long night. My mom gets off work at six o'clock. I will just wait in the lobby until then. I can tell she's not pleased with this, but it turns out she's not happy with my dad for bothering her at work with this.

When she gets off work, we go to pick up Emily, who works the night shift at another facility, and we head back to their home. I explain what happened, that I'm not allowed to come back home. This is messing up their schedule, which is only aggravating them. My mom lets me know that I can't stay with them. Doesn't surprise me.

I have no home.

My mother ends up calling my grandparents in Kansas. They agree, and are overjoyed to take me for the summer, at least. I feel bad that it has come to this. I'm glad they are happy to take me because I adore my grandparents, but I feel bad because I'm the "bad child" and my "badness" must be creating a burden on them and they are just too nice to say no. My mom makes the flight arrangements. I'm allowed to go home to pack suitcases under my dad's supervision. Not a word is spoken between us. The bank is only open until noon on Saturdays, so I make a quick stop there. I take out a couple hundred dollars, in case I need spending money, and make a couple car payments in advance. I've always wanted to fly on a plane, but these were not the circumstances I thought would lead to my first flight. I always thought it would be to California, but come Monday, my first flight is taking me to Kansas.

I'm Off to See the Wizard

ℰℴ ℭℛ

Grandma and Grandpa meet me at the airport in Wichita, Kansas. Our destination…their house in Rozel. A tiny, tiny little town in the middle of America's heartland. Population around one hundred, literally, surrounded by miles and miles of wheat fields and soybeans. There's a small high school, a church, And a little post office. Everybody in town walked there to get their mail. I would go with Grandpa first thing every morning after breakfast. This is where I will spend my summer and maybe longer. Everything is kind of up in the air right now. In limbo. I just know that I love and adore my grandparents and I feel safe.

This is an old house, and I will stay in the attic bedroom, which was really cool. A long narrow staircase in between the walls of the kitchen and Grandma and Grandpa's bedroom led up to the room. At the top of the stairs, there was a cubby hole to the left and right for storage. The bedroom had sloped attic ceilings and windows at floor level that jutted out from the roof. In the middle of the floor was a square ventilation grate that allowed the warm air from downstairs up to heat the room. As small children, when we would visit and cousins were over, we all loved to crowd around that grate and "spy" on the adults below. Now the room is my safe haven with big grandma soft beds and fluffy grandma soft pillows.

I'm an early riser like Grandma and Grandpa. They're up around 5:00 a.m., me about 6:00. Besides, the smell of Grandma's coffee and the sound of the coffee percolator make their way up that narrow staircase every morning into the bedroom. It's better than any alarm clock, especially if Grandma's cooking something for breakfast, which she would usually do on Sunday's before church (I will be going back to church). That's where Grandma likes to show me off and brag that her grandson is staying for the summer.

I go downstairs, take a shower, and have a bowl of cereal with Grandpa. I don't like coffee. One time, mother made me drink coffee when I was little, and I threw up in the kitchen. I clean our bowls for Grandma. Grandpa and I then head down to the post office, collect the mail, and head next door to the soda shop/pool hall. Grandpa now gets to show off and brag that his grandson is staying for the summer. This is our routine every morning. I love the time spent with Grandpa.

My grandmother is a retired nurse, and my grandfather has been a wheat farmer his whole life. He grows winter wheat that gets harvested in the summer. Some of the weekdays, Grandpa takes me to the old farm with him. As a kid, Grandpa would take me for rides around the field on the tractor. The only real happy memories I have as a child. I'm a bit old for that now, but he takes me out to assist him with anything he may need help with. The old farmhouse is so dilapidated. Very small. Three or four rooms and an outhouse that's barely standing. It was pretty much lost to a tornado in the early 1950s, that's why they have the house in town. Even if Grandpa wants to just come out to show me the wheat fields and look at it growing, he's so proud of it, I love being with him. Someone else will actually harvest the wheat for him this summer, but I will help him burn the wheat stubble afterward.

On other days, Grandma will take me on sightseeing trips to places I've seen as a child but can appreciate the history more now that I'm nearly a young adult, places like Pawnee Rock where the famous Santa Fe Trail, the wagon train superhighway of the old west, runs nearby. Pawnee, Cheyenne, and other Indian tribes used Pawnee Rock as a lookout for wagon trains that they would raid. The Santa Fe Trail was so well ridden that there are still wagon ruts permanently imprinted in the ground. Grandma loved history, and she loved sharing it. One day, she took me to the old homestead of her family when she was a child in the early 1900s. Her childhood home was still barely standing covered in vines and shrubbery. She told me how my ancestors, on her side of our family, immigrated from

Germany to America, in the mid-1800s, and settled in the Kansas Territory. We would help hungry, displaced Indians when they came to the homestead looking for food.

Grandma would also take me to the Pawnee River and go wading through the water and do some rock hunting. Grandma was practically an expert "rock hound," and as a child, she taught me so much about fossils, geology, and minerals. In the Pawnee River, if you know what to look for, you can still find Indian arrowheads, shards of petrified dinosaur bones, maybe some fragments of old Indian pottery.

Grandpa didn't care much for these short trips, wading, or rock hunting. He would rather stay home and nap if there was nothing to do at the farm. The bigger sightseeing trip to Dodge City, Grandpa was eager to join. Even though there are museums, Grandma is like a history book and, many times, more interesting to listen to. Dodge City was a huge part of the Old West. Wyatt Earp and Doc Holliday lived there. Famous Boot Hill Cemetery is there. Grandma loved sharing, not only hers but also knowledge in general, with me. My grandma and grandpa love me. I know that. And that's a good thing to know.

One of my mom's brothers and his family of four, my cousins, live in Kansas, so they're able to see Grandma and Grandpa often during the year. They come to visit but don't know why I'm there. Only my aunt and uncle know. We have a great time. I love seeing my cousins. I think they were told the reason on their way home. Years later, at a family reunion, my cousins will tell me how jealous they were that I got to spend that entire summer with Grandma and Grandpa.

I was an avid reader and made sure I packed a few books for the summer. I was a huge Stephen King and Peter Staub fan. The two biggest horror writers of the time. After dinner and some TV together, Grandma would do her crossword puzzles, Grandpa wasn't picky about what we watched. However, at ten o'clock, the channel would always get changed so Grandpa could watch the Johnny Carson Show. He never missed it. I liked Johnny Carson but wanted to get to my books, so I would kiss Grandma good night, give

Grandpa a quick hug and a rub on his bald head, and make my way up to my cool attic room. I would turn out the lights, except for the reading light on the nightstand, crawl into my grandma soft bed, pull the covers up tightly, and dig into my scary novel. I would read and be scared 'til the early hours of the morning, usually around one o'clock. I'm caught up in fear in Peter Staub's *Ghost Story*. It gives me some really cool scary dreams. The book has my heart pounding with each chapter, and I think this would make a great movie.

Considering I want to be in the entertainment industry, an actor, I think that maybe I can write also. When I finish the book, I decide I'm going to write the screenplay. It takes me about two weeks, writing in pencil and filling a whole spiral notebook. The kind you use in school. I'm pretty proud of it. It reads scary to me. There's an address inside the cover of the book. It might just be the publishing company, but I don't know where else to send it, so it's worth a try. I get a manila envelope, pack it in with a handwritten cover letter, and mail it off. I never heard anything back, but a year later, in 1981, the movie *Ghost Story* comes out in theaters. I didn't think it was as scary as my script, but it was fun writing it.

The summer goes by fairly quickly, a little too fast for me. I've thoroughly, completely enjoyed the time spent with Grandma and Grandpa. Aside from all the fun, there have also been some serious conversations and phone calls. My mother has called to check on me a few times. Grandma and Grandpa sit down with me for a talk. I find out they are extremely angry with my father for what has happened, his total abandonment of me. Grandma also tells me about all the times they had witnessed him hit me or verbally abuse me. Grandpa, not being a talker but being the emotional man he is, wipes away some tears as Grandma brings back memories. I'm like Grandpa. It's difficult to verbally share my emotions, but they surely do come out in tears. Grandma tells me they never knew what to do because you just didn't get involved in your children's family affairs. Boy, if they only knew all the things my mother did.

It was a long, emotional conversation but summer's almost over and we have to discuss what I want to do. They tell me how much they love me and that I am more than welcome to stay with them and finish school in Rozel, if I want. I tell them how much I love them, but I really want to finish school and graduate with my friends back home. They completely understand, but we have to figure out where I'm going to live.

My options are extremely limited. My mother is out of the question. I don't want to burden any of my friends' families and bring them into this complicated, humiliating situation. The only person I can really think of is Bob, the director from the Civic Theater. After two shows with him, he knows me fairly well. I know he's single, and…I think he's gay, which might make it a little easier. I call him and awkwardly explain my situation. It's just as awkward listening to his response. Without going into any specific details, he tells me that I'm a great "kid," and considering his "life," it just wouldn't be appropriate for me to stay there. I could read between the lines and understood what he was saying.

That was really my only option. Now I have no choice but to humble myself, tuck my tail between my legs, and ask my dad if I can come home. Grandma and Grandpa talk it over with me. They want to make sure I'm going to be "okay" with my decision. I tell them there is nothing else I can do.

This has been the best summer of my life. No fears. No getting hit. No being cussed out. No being afraid of my own shadow. Lots of love. My whole being was relaxed. Aside from our little trips and helping Grandpa in the fields, I also did the yard work and dishes for Grandma, and we went to church together every Sunday. But now it's time to call my father, and fear sets in again.

I'm sitting at the kitchen table with Grandma and Grandpa, and I call my dad's number. My hands are clammy holding the phone, and I'm very nervous waiting for him to answer. Someone else answers, and it's a voice I didn't really want to hear. It was the voice that told me, *"Don't bother coming home,"* my stepmom. I ask to speak to my dad, and I wait some more. My heart is really pounding now. My dad gets on the line. I bury everything inside me and ask him if I can come home. I tell him I really want to graduate with my friends. There's a moment of awkward silence then my dad proceeds to tell me how *"happy and peaceful, for the first time"* the house has been since I've been gone.

I'm hurt and angered by that remark. It's as if in the very few short months that we all have been a *"FAMILY"* I, somehow, am responsible for single handedly turning everyone's world upside down. My father had no part in it?? My step-brother had no part?? My step-sister?? My step-mom?? Everything was me?? REALLY DAD?? These are my angered feelings. I can feel my face getting all warm as it turns red with emotion. I restrain myself and keep my mouth shut to let my dad talk. My grandma has her hand on one of mine in loving assurance.

In a stern, cold callous voice, my dad tells me that if I'm going to come home, there will be rules that I will have to follow:

"You will show respect to everyone in the family."

"You will not be harassing your stepsister and causing turmoil by chasing her around the house."

"You will make sure you are home more often to help with work around the house."

"You will eat with everyone as a family at the dinner table when you are home."

"You will be home more often."

"You will not harass your stepbrother by stomping on the floor trying to make his records skip."

And on and on.

I'm fighting back tears of frustration and anger. I'm not going to cry in front of Grandma and Grandpa. I'm angry because my dad doesn't get it. I never harassed my stepsister. We were playing, and she knows it. He's dead set on believing that I'm trying to make my stepbrother's records skip when it's impossible to do it by stomping on the floor above his basement room. But yet it's okay for him to come home stoned showing no respect or consideration and just start blasting his music so you hear it all through the house.

Yes, I'm mad because everything is always my fault in my father's eyes, but I want to graduate with my friends, so I swallow what little pride I might have and agree to abide by all his rules for me. He then says I can come home. By the end of the following week, it's a tearful goodbye at the airport. Lots of kisses and "we love you" from Grandma and strong hugs from Grandpa. I board the plane and head "home."

All Quiet on the Home Front

෩ ௲

There definitely weren't any "welcome home" banners for me. My dad picked me up at the airport, and the drive home was quiet. No warm greetings at home either. Immediately, I feel like I'm walking on eggshells. Have to be on my guard to make sure I don't do or say anything wrong. It's the weekend, and school won't start until Monday, so I have time to go into Rochester and try to get my job back. My old manager told me that when I just didn't show up for work, he called my house and was told I didn't live there anymore. I told him that there were some family issues and I had to leave urgently to stay with my grandparents in Kansas and now I'm back to finish my senior year. He said that since I had always been reliable, he would hire me back. Whew…!!! What a relief!! Money is very low in my bank account since I have not worked all summer, and I'm behind a month on my car payment. I also find out Tim and Steve are still working there.

When school started I felt like all eyes were on me. Small town. Small class. Word gets around. That paranoid, very insecure part of me believed that everyone had to know I had been kicked out of the house, just reinforcing that long instilled belief that "I'm a bad kid." There were whispers, but no one really said anything directly to me. I talk about it with Ken, Jeff, and Ted since I wasn't able to let them know at the time. They had been concerned when they had called the house, one time over the summer, and found out I wasn't there anymore. I didn't get involved in any theater-related activities, school, or civic, but I did stay on the speech team. I couldn't give that up. I stay with the same recitation *A Day No Pigs Would Die* since it is so emotionally powerful. Some after-school rehearsing and occasional Saturday competitions. Other than that, it was home after school to show that I am a good, participating member of this family, like I promised, or I would be at work.

Life at home had not changed. Stepbrother still gets stoned and blares his music to an extreme annoyance while stepsister reminds me that I can't stomp on the floor. I have to hold my tongue. Have to be careful where I sit in the living room because stepsister is all about, *"I was sitting there,"* even if she wasn't. Have to bite my tongue. She also has the monopoly on the television. Not that anything is worth watching with that music blaring from downstairs. I end up going to my room until either my dad gets home or I have to go to work. This is my new daily routine. Toto… we're not in Kansas anymore.

If I'm not working, I have to be out of my room before my dad gets home so it looks like I'm being sociable. I would rather be working. Dinners are usually quiet, at least for me. Stepbrother's coming down from a high (nobody shows any concern there), so he's hungry and chatty. The others chitchat about their day, all trying to act like we are a normal family. Maybe this amount of extreme dysfunction in a house is normal. If conversation comes around to me, I bury my distaste for this place and everything about it, so I usually don't say much of anything. Just enough for the illusion of being sociable, a functioning member of this "family." I really don't care to talk about my day with anyone. I really don't care to be here anyway, just trying to graduate. Besides, I'd rather be at work. I can be more myself outside of this wretched house. My younger brother, with the medical issues, lets me know that he understands where I'm coming from but worries that something bad is going to happen. My little brother, the spoiled one, lets me know that he thinks I'm just being a jerk. He has no clue. I'm just trying to graduate and… I'd rather be at work.

I can't stand being at home anymore, so I find a solution to my emotional dilemma. Since I really don't have to rely on my dad for spending money, I try to get as many hours as I can in the evenings at work to keep me away from home. If I can't get the hours and since I'm not doing any shows, I'm left with nothing to do. Some evenings, I'll pretend I'm at work but will actually spend the evenings walking around the mall from 5:00 until 9:00 p.m. when the mall closes. I normally get off work at 10:00 p.m., so I'm left trying to fill that last hour.

I spend time cruising up and down Broadway. There's nothing much else for me to do before I need to head home. I keep passing that adult bookstore. I'm still intrigued and find myself with an even more curious fascination than I had that first time I was in there before I got arrested. In fact, those "magazines" were still under my car seat when I got back from Kansas. I hid them in my bedroom closet after I got home.

One week night, to kill that time, I drive into the alley and park. I make sure I'm not in the movie theater lot. I go to the back entrance of the bookstore from the alley. I feel like a thief in the night because I'm nervously looking both ways, before I enter, to make sure no one sees me. I'm also very cautious when I enter because I don't know who's going to be inside. When I get inside, I'm a little relieved because it's the guy, Harry, who runs the store, sitting behind the counter. He seems happy to see me and tells me to come to the front, to the counter. I feel a little more relaxed. He asks why he hadn't seen me anymore. He thought for sure I would come back.

I filled him in on what happened that night after I left his bookstore and where I spent the summer. I also mentioned that things were still not too great at home. He tells me he's glad I'm back and that I decided to come visit him. (It's not so much that I was there to visit him. I figured if he was there, it would be cool, but I was more curious about the store.) He hands me some tokens and tells me to go ahead and go into the next room and I can watch some movies. He even tells me which booths I should go into.

I go into the next room. It is very dimly lit in here. There's probably about ten booths, and you can hear the whirring sound of, what seems to be, film projectors. There are other people back here. I follow his suggestion, go into a booth he mentioned, close the door behind me, and lock it. This is kind of weird because I have never done anything like this, but it was also exhilarating at the same time. My heart is beating very fast. I sit down on the little bench in front of a window screen that's maybe one foot by one foot. The booth itself is probably no larger than four feet wide by five feet long. There are token slots in the wall under the screen. The kind of slots you put money into on an arcade machine.

I stick a token in one of the slots, and immediately, I hear the sound of a film projector, and the screen lights up in front of me. I have never seen a porno flick before, and I was mesmerized. There are two guys in this film. I'm hypnotized watching them. Before I know it, the projector shuts off. Seems a token only lasts a minute. I hastily grab another token and put it in the slot to continue the film. I am captivated watching this. Another minute, another token, and another minute and another token. This continues until I use the last token. He had given me eight.

I left the booth and walked back out to the main area. Harry asked me if I enjoyed watching the films. I was obviously embarrassed when I said yes because I could feel my face getting warm as it turns red. He told me not to be embarrassed because it was okay. I looked at my watch and told him I needed to get going. He said that he's almost always there at night and I could stop in anytime. He reminded me that his apartment was upstairs and that he had movies up there also. When his young college friends come down from the Twin Cities, they watch them, and I am more than welcome to come by, he says. I kind of smile and say *"maybe"* and start to head to the back door. Before I leave, he comes to the door and gives me two more magazines and says, *"I'll see you soon."* I leave and head home.

Calm before the Storm

ဆာ ಣ

I t's about mid-October, and I've been home for a couple months now. Long enough to, at least, have my senior pictures taken. I'm careful about spending too many evenings pretending I'm at work, but I detest being at home. When I am home, I play my part, be obedient, and stay out of everyone's way, but with my step's, I'm always having to be cautious about anything I say or do. That's a very uneasy feeling, having to walk around on eggshells all the time, trying not to rock the boat. Have I done anything that anybody can use against me? I don't feel like anybody really wants me back home, and I think my dad and I are barely putting up with each other.

I like the weekends when there's a speech competition, away from home and out of town for the day. I feel much more at ease and calm, especially when I'm competing and in the character of my story from *A Day No Pigs Would Die*. When I see an audience member wiping away tears or a look of shock and dismay, I know I'm doing well. I feel good. But that's only because I'm in my character.

At work, I'm becoming better friends with Tim and Steve. I have told them both about why I was gone all summer. Tim tells me he has some issues at home with his dad. I actually have a little crush on Tim but will never tell him. I don't make friends easily because I don't trust people, but he's a really nice guy, kind of a free spirit I wish I had. He knew how to be himself and not care what other people thought. I spent my whole life worrying about what people thought. He was also good with the girls. I am kind of jealous because I don't have that kind of attraction and it's not easy talking "guy" stuff with your buddies when you don't feel it, but I fake it.

One Saturday night, after work, I try to "prove" myself. We decide we're just going to hang out nearby. Tim has his girlfriend,

Michelle. Steve has his girlfriend, Jenny, and I so desperately want to be like a normal guy, like my friends, but I don't have anyone. There's this girl at work, Julia, who, by rumor only, has a reputation. I get brave and ask her if she wants to come with us. She says, *"Okay."* I'm a bit nervous because this is new territory for me and nobody knows this.

Aside from stealing a bottle from my neighbors that one time, I have not been a drinker, but this night, I drink again. Somehow, I know it's going to give me courage. I will need it because I'm going completely outside of my comfort zone. Besides, this is totally playing with fire where my father is concerned, but a part of me says *"I don't care."* We change out of our work shirts and throw on our regular shirts and coats and make a run by a liquor store. We manage to buy. Drinking age is eighteen. I'm almost there, but they don't check our ID's. The only alcohol I'm familiar with is blackberry brandy, so I buy a pint bottle. I think Tim and Steve just buy some beer.

We head to a nearby park. They are both smokers, and one of them also has "something else" to smoke, but I decline, I don't do either. They joke around and tell me, *"One day, you will."*

"Nah, not me," I tell them. That's just not me. Besides, I don't even really drink. Julia declines also. After a little hanging out and drinking, Tim, Michelle, Steve, and Jenny head off. Julia and I stay behind.

We're both a little tipsy, which gives me a little more courage. I don't feel that "thing" I'm supposed to feel with a girl, but I start to kiss her thinking I can force that feeling. It's chilly out, so we get in her car, a Buick, which is roomier than my Camaro, and start to make out. The alcohol buzz is helping me some, but this all feels foreign and unnatural to me. We keep going further, and I'm thinking that if we just "do it," that feeling will suddenly, spontaneously manifest itself, and I will be "normal" just like any other guy, just like all my friends. Well, my few friends anyway. We never get to that point. A couple pieces of clothing off but the alcohol has gotten to her, and she has to say no. I'm actually kind of relieved, but I still don't get it, why I can't feel that "feeling." We dress and sit in her car for a few minutes. I ask her if she's okay, she says she is. It's around midnight, and we both realize we need to be getting home. I work Sunday evening, and we both work Monday evening, so we ended with *"See ya' at work Monday,"* and we leave.

I make it home safely. All the lights are out. Everyone's already in bed. I quietly walk through the house, very careful not to wake anyone, especially my dad. I make it to my room and go to bed. Laying there somewhat inebriated, I wonder again, *Why am I not like the other guys? Why am I the way I am?*

I'm awakened in the morning by my dad's loud knocking on the door telling me to get up. He opens the door and pokes his head in to tell me, *"You're going to church with us this morning."* He said that everyone else has been going and it's about time I started going. I haven't gone to church since he "went Lutheran," with his permission, and I don't intend to go now. I've always considered my father to be a hypocrite, going to church on Sundays, pretending to be the perfect father and then me being his punching bag during the week. Now that we're this "family," I am certainly not going to sit in church pretending I'm part of this "clan" being all about God, singing hymns and hallelujahs. I told him flat out, *"I will not."* I still stand my ground on this. A part of me is thinking, *Church was not part of the rules.* Besides, I'm still feeling a little sluggish from last night. I don't think my dad knows. He gives me a hard look and says *"Okay"* in a tone that means, *"We will discuss this later."*

I stay in my room listening to all the 'rushed Sunday morning off to church chatter' such as…Step-sister—*"Mom I can't find…"* Brother—*"dad do you know…"* Step-mom—*"come on guys, hurry so we're not late. Did you brush your teeth?"* Dad - *"Okay, everyone, let's go. We'll go out for breakfast after church".* Something I am so completely not a part of. I watch out my big french window as they leave, all six of them. Dad, step-mom, step-sister, step-brother and both brother's.

I have the house to myself now. I turn the TV on to something good that I want to watch. Nine o'clock service and breakfast after means they won't be home until noon, at least. What I do know is my father's tone of voice. Even though I keep a clean bedroom (a rule since birth), I had better make sure it's tidied up and, if there's anything around the house that can be done, dishes or more tidying, I should do to try and keep the waters calm.

It's been a rather enjoyable morning for me, with all of them gone.

The Storm

₧⍺

They get home some time past noon. They had stopped to get some groceries, after their breakfast out, so I help bring them in. Our house is usually kept pretty clean, but with seven people in the house, there's always some little things needing to be done. I did make sure the kitchen was tidied up along with the living room. No one ever uses the sunken living room. It's more for show.

The afternoon is relatively quiet. They're watching some football game on TV. I pretty much detest football, so I go to my room. I have to be at work in a couple of hours, four o'clock on Sunday, so I get my work clothes ready then lay down to read. I'm actually in the middle of Stephen King's *The Shining*. The movie came out earlier this year, in May, but I was kind of "in the middle of stuff" and haven't been able to see it yet. I can't wait because the book is really scary.

After a while, my dad comes down the hall, opens my door, and—with an angered and agitated voice—tells me, *"We need to talk!"* I sit up on my bed, and he tells me, *"If you're going to shut your-self up in your bedroom because you can't sit your ass out in the living room with the rest of us and act like you're part of this family, then you're going to keep your door open, or I'm going to take the damn thing off!"* As he's saying all this, I'm feeling thoughts and emotions that have been festering inside me for some time start to heat up. In my defense, as if that were ever any good, I angrily talked back, *"But it's all right for him..."* I stand up and thrust my arm out pointing to the other end of the house indicating my step-brother *"...to hide out downstairs in his room doing who knows what!! Are you clueless about anything else going on or only what concerns me! Is this all just because I didn't go to church with you this morning?"*

138

My father does not like my talking back to him. His face starts to turn red with anger, but I keep going. The momentum has already started and won't stop, as if I had opened Pandora's box and nothing will stop all the evil angry feelings and words about to come out. It's like the floodgates, controlling the overflow of emotions for so long, have suddenly burst open. He shoves me back on the bed and tells me, *"You will not talk to me like that!! I'm about f_ _ _ing fed up with your attitude, insolence, and lack of respect for everyone around here!"*

I fire back yelling at him, *"I've been following all your damn rules for me while he (stepbrother) gets stoned, smokes cigarettes, does whatever the hell he wants. I'm tired of having to constantly be careful of every f_ _ _ing thing I do!!!"* I have never sworn at my father before. By now, my stepmom has come to my room and is standing in the doorway and starting to yell at me. How dare her! I've never really had anything against her. She married into an already volatile situation. My anger with my father goes back years, and this is none of her damn business. This is between me and him!

Words come spewing out of our mouths at each other. I yell at him about how I've been pretending to go to work half the time because I can't stand being in this hell house anymore. Every bit of my pent up anger and frustration from all these years, as far back as I can remember, comes out of my mouth and is unleashed on my father.

He has me on my back, on the bed, hovering over me. His arms flailing through the air now as his fists pummel my arms and my chest. I'm trying to fend them off blocking with my arms and yelling at the same time. My dad yelling and cussing at me, spittle flying out of his mouth with his anger. My stepmom in the background screaming at me to get out of this house. Everything I've ever harbored inside of me, against my father and my mother, just explodes and erupts out of me like a volcano that's been dormant for centuries. My parents have taught me well. My amount of rage and cussing almost surpasses anything they ever showed toward me. We are like two huge storm fronts that have collided with such massive force.

In a flash, a vision flies through my mind. A scene from a Hollywood movie yet to be made. In a split second, I see myself dramatically diving through my French window, rolling down the front yard to safety. Instead, while my father is still pounding me with his fists, I pull my knees up to my chest and plant my feet squarely on his chest and push him off of me with such force it slams him into the wall. I jump off the bed, put him in a headlock, and punch him, yelling, *"You will never... ever... ever... hit me again!!!"* I remember three punches. One for never (punch) and ever (punch) and ever (punch). My stepmom is *screaming* at me to *"get out of this house!"* I notice that I have busted my dad's glasses and one of his eyes is cut open and bleeding pretty badly. I let him go, grab my car keys and work clothes, and rush out of the room with my stepmom still screaming at me, *"Get out of this house and don't ever come back!"*

I jump in my car and race out of the driveway onto the backcountry road that leads into Rochester. I don't know how fast I'm going, but it's well over the speed limit. All my anger is now in my foot on the gas pedal. I cannot believe the chaos that just took place. I can't believe my own self and my actions. My world is totally and completely upside down right now. My mind is flooded with thoughts and emotions. I fly through an intersection where, to the left, is a huge rock wall that had been blasted years ago to make room for this road. In another flash, my mind wants to jump the ditch and crash into the rock wall and just end it for good, but that split second thought also tells me I probably won't die but will just be severely injured.

I continue at my high speed the ten miles into Rochester and to work. I don't know what else to do at the moment but think I can figure something out at work. I'm about an hour early. My arms are sore from the punchings. I sit in my car, in the back of the parking lot at work, just thinking. I cry a little bit out of anger, frustration, and fear of not knowing what I'm going to do, but then I straighten up and tell myself, *"NO!!! I am not giving up!!!"*

*****

It will be another three decades, thirty more years, before I realize that God will never give up on me.

*****

My senior picture taken fall 1980

What Do I Do

❧   ☙

There's a pay phone at the corner of the parking lot. I'm certain it will be fruitless because she wouldn't take me for the summer, but I'm going to call my mom. Mom and Emily work nights, so I know they'll still be sleeping and I'll be waking them up. I'm afraid I'm going to make them mad, but I have to try anyway.

Emily answers the phone. I explain to her what happened. She seems a bit irritated by this but says she'll get my mom. I get the same thing from my mother. I hear agitation in her voice when she tells me, *"You know you can't stay here."* The thing is… I know I can't because of their "secret relationship." That's more important. I'm just an inconvenience. That bad kid. The bad son. Not wanted. Story of my life. I'm feeling angered. Confused. Lost. A multitude of emotions. Most of all, I feel completely alone.

I go into work and try to focus on my job, at the same time, trying to figure out what I'm going to do. I don't have a clue, and I have school in the morning. People at work don't know about my family life, not even Tim or Steve. I finish my shift without a solution to my predicament. We close up the store, and after everyone leaves, I sit in my car in the parking lot trying to think of something. I keep glancing down the street, Broadway. The bookstore's just a couple blocks away. I'm not going to risk trying to spend the night in my car and get arrested again. Besides, it's late fall and also a little too cold. Right now, the man that runs the bookstore, Harry, seems like my only alternative.

I drive into the alley, park, and go to the back door. I'm a little scared because I don't really know the guy and I've always figured that he has ulterior motives where I'm concerned, but I'm a little desperate right now and have no one else to turn to. That's one thing that *is* safe about him is that I don't really know him. I can tell him all this personal stuff without the risk of being made fun of, ridiculed, or talked about behind my back. And I think he kind of "gets me" as far as my sexual confusion goes.

I look around to make sure no one is watching and go in the back door. Harry is at the front counter. He sees me and waves me on in and tells me to come up front. He has a big smile and says he's happy to see me. I'm nervous but I just spit it out and tell him every-thing that has happened, that *"I have no place to stay tonight, and I have to get to school in the morning."* He tells me everything's going to be okay and I can spend the night upstairs in his apartment. I'm very apologetic about bringing my problem to him, but he is extremely gracious. He tells me it's *"no problem whatsoever."* He even gives me the key to his apartment and tells me I can go on up. He says it's just a one bedroom and I can sleep in the bed or on the couch, whichever I want. He says he's closing in about an hour at midnight, since it's Sunday, then he'll be right up. There's an entrance from the front of the building right next to the bookstore, but he tells me to use the back fire escape to the second floor. His door is the first one. I tell him, *"Thank you very much, and I'm really sorry."* He tells me again that it's not a problem and he's happy to help. I ask him if he can *"please, please, please make sure I'm up by seven so I can get to school."* That also is not a problem.

I go up the back fire escape to his door. I'm very uncomfortable about this whole situation, but I have a place for the night, regard-less. I unlock the door. There's light shining in from the alley, so it's easy to find a light switch. I turn the lights on and look around. I've entered into the kitchen. It's kind of messy but not too bad. I walk around. There are some male magazines strewn about his apartment. I would have figured. I peek into the bedroom. I don't know why because I know I'm not sleeping in there. There's a small lamp on an end table next to the couch. I turn it on then turn the main ceiling light off. I'm really tired, emotionally drained. I lay down on the couch. Knowing he will be up before too long, I try to fall asleep. Thoughts are racing through my mind—what happened at home, my mother not taking me, where I'm at now, what am I going to do.

I have actually dozed off when I hear Harry coming in the back door. I stay lying there with my eyes closed as if I were asleep. He comes into the living area and quietly asks if I'm awake. I mumble that I am but keep my eyes closed. He sits on the couch, pats me on the upper part of my leg near my hip, and reassures me that everything will be fine. I keep my eyes closed and say, *"Thank you."* He starts to rub my leg then tells me to lay on my stomach so he can give me a back rub to *"relax me"* and *"help me get to sleep."* I'm feeling really creepy about this but not completely surprised. I comply. He gives me a back rub then has me turn over, and he starts massaging me in other areas. I tell him, *"I really need to sleep because I have to get to school in the morning."*

He's very nice and calming about it and says, *"This won't take long."*

My mind keeps saying, *I need a place to stay. I need a place to stay. I need a place to stay,* as I allow him to have his way with me orally.

The Day After

S omehow, I managed to sleep a little. When I woke up, I looked at my watch, and it was only six-thirty. I laid there thinking about last night, or should I say, early, early this morning. I know I like guys, I don't know why, but that was really weird, and I still feel a little creeped out about it. He's my father's age probably. Would he be considered a "dirty old man?" He's nice enough, and I'm sure he doesn't mean me any harm. I justified my actions, inside my head, by telling myself, *"I did what I had to do. I needed a place to stay. I will just go on from here."*

I hear his alarm clock ringing, I look at my watch, it's quarter to seven. He comes out to wake me up but sees that I already am. He goes into the kitchen to make some coffee and asks if I want any. I tell him I'm okay. He asks if I want something to eat. I say, *"I'm okay there also."* He gets his coffee, comes back into the living area, sits at the end of the couch, pats my leg, and asks if I'm okay with last night. I told him, *"Thank you for letting me sleep here."* He said he was talking about *"everything else."* I knew what he meant and told him, *"It's all cool, I'm good."* Then I asked him if I could take a shower. He lets me shower, uninterrupted.

I don't have a toothbrush so can't brush my teeth, but he does have some mouthwash, so I can at least rinse. I get dressed in yesterday's clothes, come out, and tell him, *"I need to get going."* He asks what I'm going to do tonight. I tell him I have to work but beyond that, *"I don't know yet."* I tell him I'm going to talk to a counselor at school and see if that might help. As I get ready to leave, I thank him again. That's when he stops me and hands me a twenty-dollar bill.

"This is to help you with gas or anything else." I know what he really means. He also gives me his phone number and tells me, *"If things don't work out, the couch is always here."*

I say thanks and head out the door. I have to get to school. For some reason, with all that is happening, I know I need to finish school. That is not an option. I am too close, and I know, I just know, I have to.

I get to school and tell my homeroom teacher that I need to see a guidance counselor. She gives me a pass to go. There are only a couple, and I get our male counselor. Male adult figures are more threatening and intimidating to me for some reason, and in a situation like this, I'm more comfortable talking to a female. I always connected better with my female teachers.

He has me sit on the other side of his desk from him. He's all serious looking as he places his arms on the desk, folding his hands together, asking me, *"What can I do for you so early in the morning?"* I'm really uncomfortable and embarrassed airing "dirty laundry" like this, but I give him an overview of what has happened at home. No great details were given about my bruised arms or my dad's bloody eye. Basically, I laid it out that I've been thrown out. I want to graduate from Byron High, but I have no place to live.

I emphasized the *"no place to live"* hoping for some help. Some *guidance.* When he asked where I spent last night, I told him, *"At a friend's. I might be staying in Rochester, I don't know."* All I got in response was, *"Rochester is outside the school district. If you don't live within the school district, you can't go to school here. If you can find a place to live in Byron, you can stay in school here."*

That was it? No help at all? I *am* completely on my own. I just tell him, *"Okay. I'll try to do something."* I leave his office feeling empty again. Lost. Dumbfounded. I thought for sure someone with the school could help. Then I harden myself inside again. There is a rebellious attitude of determination inside me. *Screw my family. Screw this school. After all these years of crap, I Am Going To Make It!*

By the end of the school day, I'm not any closer to a solution, but I have told Ken and Jeff, my immediate inner circle. I do have a few female friends—Denette, Karen, and Jane—but I never shared any of this with them. Ken and Jeff are concerned. I don't ask them for help, even though I'm desperate to stay in high school. That's a burden I couldn't place on a friend. It's not their problem. I just wanted them to know just in case, especially since I left them uninformed and completely in the dark all summer long when I was in Kansas.

After school, I realize I really need to get some clothes and my toothbrush. I hate the thought of going by the house. It scares me. A part of me thinks there will be police watching the house, waiting to arrest me. After all, I'm the bad kid. I practically beat up my father.

I drive out to the house. I drive by it about three or four times. It's right off a county back road, so I don't have to turn onto our street to see it. It appears safe enough. My dad's car is not there, neither is my stepmom's, and there's no SWAT team waiting.

I pull into the driveway and go up to the front door. I'm very nervous. It feels like I'm returning to the scene of a crime. The front door is locked, so I use my key to let myself in. It seems the school bus has already dropped my stepsister off because the second I'm inside, she's telling me, in a know-it-all way, *"You're not supposed to be here. I'm calling your dad."* I told her I was just getting some clothes. I grabbed the suitcase in my closet from my summer trip and hurriedly packed it with some clothes. I went to the bathroom grabbed my toothbrush, took the toothpaste, shampoo, and hair dryer and grabbed a towel—just because.

There is one last thing I want. I have a small coin collection. It is nothing spectacular: old Indian Head pennies, Mercury dimes, and Kennedy silver half dollars. I've packed also because I may need to sell them. But the one thing that is on my mind is the Gold Five Dollar Indian Head coin, early 1900s that my dad has always kept in a small jewelry box, with his tie clips and miscellaneous stuff, on his dresser. I knew it was wrong, but I went into his bedroom anyway and took it, making sure my stepsister was not around to witness this theft. After all, I need to watch out for myself right now, and if worse comes to worse, I need to make sure I have a little financial cushion. I don't have a lot built back up in the bank yet, not as much as I want.

Just as I'm getting ready to leave, my stepsister tells me, *"I just called your dad."* She actually calls him by his first name. *"He told me I'm supposed to call him if you showed up."*

I told her, *"Fine. I am leaving anyway and don't plan on coming back again."* I drop the house key on a table and leave. Now I have to figure out what I'm going to do for the night. I have to work again, so that takes up some of the time, but do I spend the night at Harry's above the bookstore again? At least I know it will probably make me an easy twenty dollars. It's not like it was the end of the world. I didn't get struck by lightning. I didn't feel great about it. It was just weird. But hey, I did what I had to do. When I get to work, I give him a courtesy call from the pay phone in the parking lot and let him know the day went okay, but I got no help. I'm just wanting to leave this option with him open. I tell him I'll call after we close and let him know. I change into my work shirt in the car, go inside, and clock in for my shift.

What the Night Brings

৪৩   ৫৪

A t least I don't have to worry about dinner. We get a free meal with each shift: just a small burger, fries, and drink. Plus, whenever someone works the special sandwich table, that person usually hides extra chicken patties in the spare steamer drawer to snack on. That's not something officially taught in training. I'm working that table tonight. I will be snacking before and after my dinner break. I won't leave work hungry tonight.

Julia is working and we end up taking break at the same time. She apologizes for the other night. I tell her it's okay and that we probably shouldn't have had anything to drink. I tell her I'm not really a drinker. She says she's not either but she would like to see me again. Panic in my brain. I just don't have that attraction "thing." Luckily, I have a way out. I'm embarrassed but reluctantly I tell her about what's going on with me, what all happened after "the other night." I don't tell her about Harry, of course, but I let her know I don't have a home anymore.

While we're on break, another girl, Janet, comes in the break area. She's first year student at the community college here. We're vaguely familiar with each other. She overheard us talking and mentioned that she just has a one-bedroom apartment but she could put me up for a few days if I don't mind the couch. Boy, do I not mind the couch. And a few days gives me a little more time to figure things out. I hardly know her, so I shyly tell her, *"Yes. Thank you, thank you."* We are both closing so that makes it easy. I'm uncomfortable about this because I don't like feeling as if I'm being a burden, but I am so relieved.

After work, I make a quick stop at the pay phone to call Harry and let him know I have things taken care of for a few days. He makes sure I understand that I am always welcome to stop by his apartment or the bookstore if I need to. I'm certain I know what he means, and I tell him, *"I'll keep it in mind."* I may not be comfortable with it, but I've learned that I can "stoop" to almost any level and do what I need to if I have to. I'm certain I will be back at the bookstore and seeing him again some time.

I follow Janet to her apartment, only a couple miles from work and in the direction I need to go for school. It will make for a slightly shorter drive in the morning. It's a small one-bedroom apartment, and she says she's only home to sleep otherwise she's at school or work. She politely lets me know I can only stay for about a week because her boyfriend is coming to town next week. I am very grateful for the week and hope I can figure something out before my time is up.

I drive the distance from Rochester to Byron every day for school knowing I really won't find a solution to my living problem, but I just keep going. I even stay after school one day to discuss the situation with my favorite teacher, Mrs. A. I'm humiliated at having to bring this up with her, but I'm desperate. She said she had noticed that something was wrong with me, but there is nothing she can really do to help. I get the feeling she wants to but can't. I think that anybody who works for the school is not allowed to help in these kind of matters. She gives me a hug and tells me to please keep her informed of my situation. I tell her, *"Thank you,"* and leave. I'm starting to think things are hopeless, but I still hold out hope that something will just magically happen, that a new home will all of a sudden materialize.

I'm not on the schedule to work until Friday, so I have three evenings off. I don't have anything to do after school and feel uncomfortable going to Janet's apartment by myself and just sitting there. I debate it in my head, shove all the negatives aside, and head to the bookstore apartment. I'm a little uneasy about it, but I know I'm welcome there. I also know why, hence the reason I shove the negatives aside. I also know there's a good chance I will make some money, and right now, I'm willing to go to certain extremes to make up for not working these three evenings. I'm really afraid of having nothing.

When I get there, it turns out that Harry has another young "friend" over. His name is Paul, and he's a year younger than me, sixteen. It seems Paul has a distressed family life also and met Harry similar to how I did, through the bookstore. After hanging out for a little while, Harry makes a proposition to me and Paul and that would be the two of us together, while Harry is there, and we each get twenty dollars. That's a little more than I would normally make at work in an evening. Sometimes, Harry would film these get-togethers for a little extra money. It's a little awkward and uncomfortable, but I learn to push those feelings aside, and it's better than having Harry directly involved. Besides, I don't know what the future holds, but I do know I need to have the money. I also agree to come over, after school, the three evenings I'm off since Paul has agreed also. A part of me doesn't feel real good about myself, but then I haven't felt good about myself my whole life. The other part of me says *"sixty dollars,"* more if he's filming. Then it's much easier to put feelings of self-worth aside. Done it my whole life.

These are long drives back and forth to school every day. I could sure use the gas money, and I don't have to do much of anything except have fun with another guy who's good-looking and my age and pretend Harry's not there.

I get back to Janet's apartment each night around the same time that she does. She has either been at work or the library. I always tell her I've been with friends since school let out. She always asks if I've eaten. I tell her I ate at a friend's house—a lie. I use some of the money I made to buy food at a tiny little taco place down the street from where we work. We have time for little chit chats before bed, and she asks each night if I'm making any headway on a place to live. I tell her no, but I'm sure something will happen and I will be out by the end of the weekend, and I thank her again for a place to sleep and the time she's giving me. Friday night, Janet tells me her boyfriend has had a change in plans and it will be yet another couple weeks before he gets here and that I am welcome to stay the extra time, if needed. I am so relieved, still concerned about being a burden, but relieved. I have a little extra time and a little less stress. However, I do know that if "worse comes to absolute worse," there is one place I can stay reluctantly and for a price—me.

There's Gonna Be a Party

ଐ   ଔ

My first week comes and goes with no real hope of a home. I request extra hours at work, but I'm not getting put on the schedule as much as I would like because *"everyone else needs hours also"* is what I'm told. The apartment above the bookstore remains my second part-time job. Better money and I'm given the courtesy to believe I'm someone worthwhile and desirable. I'm not seeing any more options for a home, so the way things are looking, this apartment above the bookstore may become my home after all only so I can finish high school.

Another Friday rolls around. I'm now coming up on the end of my third week. Only this weekend left. I really don't see any hope. I'm feeling kind of "down" this morning. My time is definitely running out now, and I'm just no closer to finding a good place to live. There's nothing anyone is willing to do except Harry. I am making extra money. This all has me feeling kind of "down" this morning, but I get up and get ready for school as usual. I work tonight, and I know Janet does also. As I'm leaving, I tell her I'll see her at work tonight. I get in my car and head off toward Byron. Driving down the highway, a million thoughts seem to be flooding my mind all at once, reflecting on everything that has happened in these two short weeks, that have already seemed like a lifetime. A lifetime of pent up anger and frustrations unleashed on my father. Thrown out. Trying to find a place to live. Doing things I never thought I'd do for extra money and a place to sleep. People in positions to help, can't or won't. Options and time are running out. Things are looking dim, but I keep myself hardened inside and a focus in front of me to whatever—I don't know.

I am feeling emotionally drained, exhausted. Halfway to school, I turn onto a back road, pull onto the gravel shoulder, and stop. I sit there and think for a little bit. I see a school bus go by heading toward town in the direction of the high school. Skipping school was not something I made a habit of, but I decide I'm going to skip school today. I turn around and head back into Rochester. I haven't been eating breakfast these last couple weeks, and I know where there's a donut shop. I stop in and get six donuts. It's cold out, and I hate coffee, so I get a hot chocolate and a little carton of milk in case the hot chocolate is too hot. I also just love milk.

I take a seat at a back corner table. Six donuts is a lot for me, but I figure I can eat a couple and save the rest for later. I take my time eating so I can figure out what I'm going to do. I decide, no bookstore apartment today. Instead, I'll go to the pawnshop down the street from the bookstore and sell my coins. I've had my dad's coin in my pocket, and my small collection is in the trunk of my car with my belongings. For the rest of the day...? The movie *Private Benjamin* just came out a week or so ago. I love Goldie Hawn. The commercials on TV, for the movie, look really funny, and I could sure use a good laugh.

I finish eating, go out to my car, toss the bag with the rest of the donuts on the floor of the passenger side, and drive off toward the pawnshop. It's about nine o'clock, so it should be open. I have to park in the alley that runs behind the bookstore and the movie theater, which is good because I can check the marquis in front of the theater for the movie time. I get into my trunk and pull out the small collection I have then walk around to the sidewalk in front of the stores and go into the pawnshop. I'm a little nervous because I've never sold anything in a pawnshop, but I've overheard stories of others that have. I'm mostly nervous because the one coin, the five-dollar gold piece, is actually stolen and I'm a bit afraid.

When I get inside, the lady behind the counter asks if she can help me. I tell her I just want to sell some coins. She asks to see them. I place them on her counter. The Mercury dimes and Indian head pennies are in coin books. I have a Susan B. Anthony dollar, uncirculated, gold plated, in a frame with a certificate of authenticity that I ordered from a catalogue, and I lay the five-dollar gold coin down also.

She looks at them and tells me the Susan B. she can give me two dollars for. I paid more than that from the catalogue. She looks over the Mercury dimes and Indian heads, and based on their condition, she can give me forty dollars. The gold coin she takes longer looking at, and I can feel my heart pounding, just knowing that I'm going to go to jail for good and there's no way out of this one. She asks me where I got these. I told her I had ordered most of them at one time and the gold coin was a gift from my father for my senior year. Then she asks why I want to sell them. I can't think up a lie fast enough and make it look good, so I pretty much tell her half the truth, that there was a big fight at home last week. I got thrown out, but I'm staying with a friend's family and finishing my senior year on my own and wanted to sell them for extra money. Even though I have a job, I want to have extra in the bank to make sure my car payments are covered. She seemed to buy it because then she told me she could give me two hundred dollars for the gold coin, in total two hundred forty-two dollars for everything. All she needed was my driver's license for the paperwork. My brain was like *"WOW!!!"* Two hundred forty-two dollars right now. I'm feeling euphoric. That's a lot of money. She paid me in cash. I have never held this much money of my own in my hands before. I tell her, *"Thank you,"* and head back out to my car.

On the way to my car, I walk in front of the movie theater and check the marquis. It turns out I can catch an early afternoon movie and have plenty of time to get to work. I know I have to be real careful with this money and quickly decide to drive back out to Byron, be smart, and deposit it in my bank account right away. When I get to the bank, I'm a little worried, with Byron being such a small town, that someone might see me that knows my dad and tell him I'm not in school, but I don't run across anyone. I deposit the money, get my balance, and, even though I have all these problems right now, I'm feeling pretty good and pretty rich for seventeen. I go back to Rochester and hang out at the mall until movie time.

The movie *Private Benjamin* was absolutely hilarious!!! Exactly what I needed. Money in the bank and two hours of laughing. Now I'm back to the real world again and my dilemma. I have about an hour until work, which is just a couple blocks away, so I sit in my car, change into my work shirt, and munch on a couple donuts to kill time.

This day has put me in a pretty good mood, regardless. When I get to work, I'm glad to see that Tim is also working tonight. I have a buddy to hang out with. I fill him in on what has happened at home. He said he had heard something from people at work. Because I've been staying at Janet's and also with Julia knowing, word has gotten around about my situation. I'm embarrassed but try to brush it off, act all big, and just tell people everything's all right. No big deal. Although deep inside, I know the clock is ticking. The sand in my hourglass is running out.

About halfway through the shift, another one of the college girls at work tells me she and her boyfriend are having a party at her place after work and that I should come by if I want. There will be a big keg of beer, so I don't need to bring anything unless I want something else. Other people from work will be there. Tim tells me he's going. I figure, what the heck. I have nothing else in the whole world to do. Why not. I have never been to a party before. Kids at school would have keggers when their parents were gone, but I was never invited to one. I'm a little anxious because outside of work or the theater, I'm not comfortable in groups of people, where I have to socialize. I'm socially inept, especially if I'm not familiar with the people. I'm not very trusting of others. People are too quick to judge you, but I'm going anyway.

At the end of our shift, I wash up in the bathroom and change into my regular shirt. I know where the party is and tell Tim I'll see him there. When I arrive, there are quite a few people in the apartment already, and I'm pretty hesitant because, well, I'm not comfortable around strangers. Someone pretty friendly shows me where the keg is, so I get myself some beer. Someone else shows me the table that has some of the harder stuff. I'm not too big on beer, so I drink this cup down pretty fast, but I don't really feel the affect as suddenly as I did with the brandy, so I hit the hard liquor table. I'm not really familiar with anything on there, so I pour about a half cup of "something" and fill the rest with soda and drink that down quickly. A warm feeling instantly hits my gut, and a slight dizzy feeling comes over me in just a couple minutes. I definitely like that feeling and make myself another drink. And then another. And I'm feeling loosened up but don't want to stop.

I believe this pattern carries on to the point of my drinking myself almost to oblivion because I don't remember much of anything. What I do recall is that at some point of the night, I'm in the parking lot, there is snow on the ground, and I can't find my car. My next recollection is sitting on a curb and Tim laughing because I'm so drunk, telling me I can't drive and he's going to take me to his house. At some point, during the drive to his house, he has to pull to the side of the road so I can open the door and throw up onto a snow drift. I don't remember anything else from that night of my first party and my first real drunk. I don't even remember getting to Tim's house.

What Just Happened

⁊ ⳇ

I wake up, I guess it's morning, and through the extreme fog of my mind and the excruciating pain in my head, I see a kid peeking in a door and yelling out to someone unknown, *"He's awake."*

I look around. I'm in a downstairs bedroom because I can see a window up near the ceiling. I remember being in Tim's car, so I must be at his house, and this must be his bedroom. I'm lying in a bean bag chair in my underpants. Someone has undressed me. The only thing I'm really sure of is that I got totally drunk last night, completely smashed. I don't know what embarrassing things I might have done at the party last night, but I'm waking up in a bedroom somewhere, on a bean bag chair, almost naked. I could swear someone must have slipped something into one of my drinks. Couldn't have been my fault.

Tim comes into the room and hands me my clothes. He tells me I threw up all over myself and in the wash tub in the laundry room. He and his mom had undressed me, and she washed my clothes. I get dressed and stagger up the stairs into the kitchen. My mouth tastes horrible, I really need a shower, and all my things are at Janet's or in the trunk of my car, wherever my car is. Sitting at the kitchen table, with a cup of coffee and a cigarette, is Tim's mother.

Laughing at me, she introduces herself in a real sweet voice, *"Good morning. I'm Judi, Tim's mom, but even in your state of mind, I'm sure you figured that out."* She laughs some more, not a mean laugh either, more a sympathetic one. *"I figured you might need some coffee to help you out, there's some on the stove over there. Help yourself. There's a cup on the counter."*

I have to politely decline. *"Thank you but coffee will make me sick."*

With another laugh, she replies, *"You don't think you got it all out of you last night?"*

I am so embarrassed. Humiliated. Meeting my friend's mother, for the first time in this condition and knowing she had undressed me because I had thrown up all over myself the night before. I tell her how sorry I am and that I don't remember anything.

She says, with a singsongy laugh, *"I'm quite sure you don't."*

Judi tells me to come on over and sit down, asks me if there's anything she can get for me. All I could really use is a glass of water, and she gets me some. There is a younger boy sitting at the table also. *"This is Tim's younger brother Danny. He's the one that was checking in on you."* Danny, who is ten years old, very polite and quiet, sits silently observing. *"And in the living room watching you is Aaron, Tim's youngest brother."*

Aaron, who is five years old and looks different from his brothers, asks, *"Are you sick?"*

Judi says, *"Aaron,"* in a laughing reprimand then to me, *"Don't mind him. He just heard us talking about you before you came up."*

Their dad comes in from outside, sees me, and starts to laugh. *"So you made it through the night,"* which makes Judi laugh some more.

"This is my husband, David, the boys' dad."

David comes over and shakes my hand and says, with another light laugh, *"Rough night last night?"*

I'm glad he's laughing because David is kind of scary looking. Picture Genghis Khan. David is Korean. I will be told later that Judi already had Tim and Danny when she and David met. David adopted Tim and Danny then they had Aaron. Now I see why he looks different. Beautiful little boy.

Judi tells me that if I would like to, I can take a shower. She has some extra toothbrushes (the kind the dentist hands out) because she's sure I would like to get completely freshened up. This feels so strange. I grew up feeling unworthy of anyone's kindness yet here is a complete stranger, my friend's mother, being so nice to me after the way I came into her home. I tell her that would be so nice. She shows me the bathroom, where the towels are, and leaves a new toothbrush with me. She then tells me that Tim has filled her in on a few things about my situation and, after I'm all cleaned up and feeling better, she would like to have a talk with me.

I don't think a shower *ever* felt so good! I'm in a cozy little home with a very warm-hearted family. I'm not sure how to act. I've spent the night at someone's house only once in my life as a little kid, and I certainly wasn't in this condition. I have a lifetime of family secrets, and she wants to talk to me. She seems really nice. So does her husband, even though he's a little scary looking. Should I be on my guard? My whole life I've been very cautious and wary about letting anyone in.

I finish showering and dressing. I feel so good and refreshed. Being courteous and polite, I make sure I leave the bathroom neat and ask Judi what I should do with the towel. She matter-of-factly tells me to just leave it on the edge of the tub. *"I'll get it when I go to finish the laundry I had to take out to wash your clothes,"* she says that in a good naturedly tone. She asks me to come over to the kitchen table to sit down.

Judi is the type of person that immediately makes you feel comfortable and at ease. She exudes the feelings of warmth, concern, caring, and compassion. As cautious as I am about trusting anyone with my feelings and emotions, Judi is able to put those fears to rest rather quickly. She calmly and caringly tells me that Tim has already filled her in a little bit about my predicament, that I have no place to live due to a fight with my father. She's curious as to what happened. I'm still a little bit uncomfortable because it's not my place to burden someone else with my problems, but she insists that it's completely okay to tell her.

I tell her all about the fight, but in doing so, I have to take her back through the history of my family. The deep shame I feel from my upbringing. I take her back to my brother being taken away, My being locked up at nights. Drinking my own urine. Being locked out in freezing winters. My mother's brutal beatings. The near suffocations. The verbal abuses. Being my father's punching bag. Being thrown out before. Jail. We talk for a long time. She listens intently with looks of stunned disbelief, shock and horror, at times asking *"Good gosh!! What were your parents thinking!!?? What was your mother thinking!!??"* She has many questions with a lot of "why's" that I can't answer. She asks if I still see my mom and I tell her that I do occasionally, on weekends, which prompts another *"Why"* that I don't know how to answer other than with a perplexed question, *"I don't know. Because she's my mom?"* Judi doesn't understand, but then neither do I.

It actually feels good to get all that out, although it was very uncomfortable. The shame I've lived with all my life. The shame doesn't get washed away, it's just out there now. I open up about almost everything. Judi is very easy to talk to. She would tell me, *"The shame is not yours to bear. I can tell you're not a bad person. I know you're not a bad person."* My whole life, I've always believed I was that "bad kid." Nobody's ever told me I'm not a bad person. I don't know what to say to that. I can look in the mirror and see an "okay" person, but inside, I've never felt good about myself. I know I don't dare tell about the man above the bookstore. I do tell Judi that my biggest concern is to finish high school.

Judi calls Tim and tells us we should probably go get my car and bring it back here. I'm a little confused. I don't know why we're coming back here. I really need to get to Janet's and let her know I'm okay, just to be courteous, then Judi says, *"I'm certain you'll be ready for a little something to eat by the time you get back, so I'm going to make some soup and grilled cheese sandwiches for you guys. Does that sound all right?"* I'm not certain how to reply to this niceness.

I look at Tim, and he tells his mom, in a laughing way, *"Yea, he'll be ready. His stomach's been empty a while, and you talked his head off."* Then he motions to me and tells me to *"come on."*

We go to get my car and come back. The drive seemed to take forever. I had to follow Tim, or I would have been lost. The party had been on the extreme northwest side of the city, and Tim's family lives on the very southeast side. I'm sure glad Tim brought me home last night. I can't imagine what would have become of me in the condition I had been in. Judi had soup already heated up and was waiting for us to get back to make the grill cheese sandwiches, a light meal that was very soothing on my stomach. It is probably the best soup and grilled cheese sandwiches I had ever had up until then.

Danny and Aaron joined us. David was in bed sleeping because he has a night job and has to go into work later. While we eat, Judi mentions that she and David had a talk while we were gone. She told me they had decided that if I wanted, I could stay with them. Tim already has an extra bed in his room, for whenever one of his friends would spend the night, and Tim and I would share his room. Tim was cool with that. Danny and Aaron thought that was really cool also. It seems I'm not the first injured bird or lost puppy to be brought home. I will eventually meet Holly, now an adult with a little girl of her own, who, as a teenager, had a troubled family life and lived with them also. She becomes like a foster sister to me. I'm relieved and grateful inside but, again, feeling uncomfortable because I grew up being a "nothing", "undeserving" and I really shouldn't be a burden to others. They don't even know me and are willing to take me in. This has my insides all confused. I'm not familiar with this kind of generosity. Judi assures me this is what they want. Of course, she will have to get in touch with my father. That is a real scary thought. I have no idea what that will entail. After all, my dad *is* the perfect father.

On Sunday, I go to Janet's to get my things. She's glad I have a place to live, and I'm so thankful to her. Back at Tim's house, Judi and Tim make me feel at home immediately. I get settled into Tim's room, then they, along with Danny and Aaron, take me around the property. They live in the lower hills on the outskirts of the city, their property extending into the forest. Danny and Aaron are eager to tell me that they get deer coming into the backyard during the winter. Then Danny and Aaron drag me to the large dog run where I meet there Great Dane Sundance, aka Dancer. I love dogs but I have never seen a dog so huge. Dancer was the size of a small horse; beautiful dog, though. By dinnertime, Danny and Aaron are wanting me to sit next to one of them. Tim is telling his little brothers to, *"Settle down you guys. Craig can sit where he wants."*

Judi is saying, *"Sheez, you two. Craig, why don't you sit here in between them."* You would think that I had always been a part of the family. Maybe in some cosmic, spiritual way, I had.

*****

Many years later, about the time of the writing of this book, Judi will tell me,

"It is almost as if, with everything that led you to us, your time living with us was really where your life actually began. Nice to know the Lord had it all planned from the beginning."

Only today can I see the truth in that.

*****

A New Family

℘   ℭ

I will live with Judi and her family from November 1980 until January 1982. Aside from the summer with my grandparents, these fourteen months will be the safest and most love felt and cared about times of my life to date. At some point, I had to get in touch with my dad so I could get the rest of my things. We arranged a day for me to come by. When I got there, everything that was mine (even the magazines hidden in the closet) was dumped in a pile on the driveway for all the world to see. I was horrified!

All the neighbors must be thinking "that 'bad kid' (since that's how I viewed myself I figured everyone else must also) was finally so bad he had to be thrown out." No one came out of the house. I was in the driveway by myself loading my belongings into my car as neighbors drove by. My emotions just turned cold. I have not a single feeling left for my family.

*****

In the beginning, I was so uneasy and uncomfortable with the kindness and caring shown toward me that Judi many times would have to tell me, *"This is your home now also. Stop being so timid and meek."* I would often help clean the kitchen after meals to make sure I was "pulling my weight," proving I'm not a "bad kid." She would tell me, always with a smile and light laugh, *"Thank you but it isn't necessary."* and then with another laugh, *"I wish I could get my own kids to help like this."* I won't even know about meetings with my father until after I become an adult, which was emotionally good, for my sake. There were never any legal documents handing guardianship to Judi and David, just a verbal agreement. As an adult, I would find out that my dad and stepmom would drop by now and then, when I wasn't around, to check up. Not so much out of concern for me. Judi would tell me, *"I always got the feeling your dad wanted to ask what you had told me about things at home, but he didn't ever really go that far."* I was also told that my father had warned Judi that I was "sneaky and shouldn't be trusted." That angered me, and I was glad Judi kept that from me while I lived there. Judi would tell me, *"I never saw that in you."*

*****

During the writing of this book, Holly would write telling me, *"I always knew there was something special about you. Your smile could light the room, but I also saw a painful darkness behind those beautiful eyes. Love ya, Holly."*

*****

The first thing I had to do was immediately transfer myself from Byron High School to Mayo High where Tim went. Mayo High didn't ask many questions, just a brief background on what was happening, where I'm living, and my transcripts from Byron. I get to Byron, and surprisingly boldly, a little sarcastically, I thank them *"for all their help"* and ask for my transcripts. I'm quite amazed that I'm able to do this all by myself without a parent or guardian of some sort. There are a couple phone calls between schools. I get my transcripts and leave. Mayo High has no issues with my transfer since I come with good grades and good school history, attendance, extra-curricular stuff, etc. I am elated, ecstatic! I feel like I'm free! Doing this on my own was a huge thing because I knew, somehow, I was going to finish school!

This transfer was a major jump up, like going from a low five A (AAAAA) school to a double A (AA). It is much larger and highly competitive. Since my extracurricular area was declamation/speech/theater, I was directed to the theater department and introduced to the speech team. Transferring this far into the year, their speech team is already full. However, to be fair, their drama instructor wants to see me perform from my dramatization of my adaptation of *A Day No Pigs Would Die*. I was petrified inside, being introduced to all these new people (new people scare me), but when asked to perform, I immediately get into character. By competition rules, I only have the three minutes to completely win the instructor (so I can compete) and the team (so I'm liked) over. As usual, I dig deep inside myself and feel the pain that moves me to tears, and in doing so, by the end of my allotted three minutes, half the team is sniffling and/or wiping their eyes, and I get a thunderous applause.

Even though the team is full, an exception is being made, and I will be allowed to compete at their next meet. I end up "placing" at my first competition in my new school, beating someone out in my category and securing myself a place on the team. I skyrocketed through district and regional, all the way to state competition with my heart-wrenching performances. I have the honor of competing against all the other top rivals from the top schools in the entire state. After a long day of competing, tearful applauds, and accolades, I make it through all the rounds to finals, but in the end, I don't quite place. I realize "that's okay." I am so overjoyed inside by being here. My accomplishment in getting here, being considered one of the best in the state, is my biggest satisfaction. Due to my accomplishment, I "Letter" at Mayo High School. It seems that at these bigger more competitive schools, you don't have to be a jock and in sports to show you excel in order to earn a "Letter." I'm on the road to being the Craig I should be.

I will experience a lot of new and interesting things living with Judi and her family. When my competition season is over, Tim teaches me the art of skipping school. He and I will cause some mischief that no one ever finds out about. We were being teenagers. I'm doing things I would never normally do. No real harm, just being a bit of a rebellious spirit and having fun doing it.

Tim is actually the kind of guy that, in my old school, I wouldn't have hung out with. He smoked and also "smoked." He drank beer occasionally. I didn't drink again after that party night. Tim and Steve would still tease me about not smoking pot, always telling me, *"One day, you will."* I was always adamant about *"one day, I won't!"* Tim liked working on car engines. By now, we know "I Don't!" But it was different with Tim, and I would watch and help a little. Of course, he always had a girl, I admired him for that. When he would have a date, I would stay home with everyone else. If I wasn't working and when he got home, he would tell me about it in the bedroom before we went to sleep. I was always a bit envious because I didn't understand those feelings but pretended like I did.

Tim and I would spend many nights talking before sleep. If it wasn't girls, it was about his dad David. David has very bad anger issues. He and Tim didn't see eye to eye a lot. David didn't get physical, but verbally, he would explode, sometimes scaring me. Tim would get so frustrated and angry inside and nothing to do with all that anger that he would storm out of the house, get in his car, and take off. He would need to be alone, and later, we would talk in private. Those kinds of talks I could understand. One time, David was having it out with Judi over Tim. Tim had already left, and David wouldn't stop. He was so verbally explosive and frightening that I actually got bold enough and intervened. I don't know what came over me, but I managed to get David out of the house to calm down. His way of calming down was, *"Get in the car, Craig."*

David drives a flashy black with gold trim Camaro Z-28 that Judi bought him. I had never ridden in this car before, and with him extremely angry, I'm a bit nervous. We take off and he's headed for downtown Rochester, angry and cussing but slowly calming down. Unlike my father, David's not mad at me, and he's not a physical person, so he doesn't scare me in that aspect, plus I know he has a lot of concern for me. Of all places to stop at, the one place that will bring him back to earth is a strip bar. We spend the afternoon there. Me... in a strip bar. I don't know when, if ever, I've felt so uncomfortable and out of place, watching ladies naked boobs flopping all over. I still don't get it. Judi wasn't very happy when she found out later, after asking me, but she "swept it under the rug" and just let it be. What a day that was. Certainly a first for me!

I would also learn about hunting and trapping. I didn't care for it too much, tromping through knee deep snow sometimes helping to carry traps. I don't like the cold to begin with, but I owe it to this wonderful family that has taken me in to at least go along and help. They didn't force me. This is what they did for extra income and, sometimes food, during the winter. They trapped mink, muskrat, and beaver for their pelts, hunted geese, pheasant, and duck for food. There was one day that bothered me. When they were checking traps generally if something was caught, it was dead. However, this time, a mink was still alive. The trap had not killed it, and they had to drown the poor thing before they could retrieve it. That was unsettling but that is part of the life of people that hunt and trap. I could not kill anything.

One time, we actually had beaver for dinner. There was no way I was eating that. I saw it trapped and skinned and cleaned. At the table, I would never had known it was beaver just by looking at it on the platter. But nooo… I won't have that on my plate. Disgusting. Gross. That is until David looked me in the face and called me a *"wimp!"* Judi laughed. Okay, bullying and name-calling I left behind me at that other school and with that other family. I was not going to be a "wimp" here. I put a slice of meat on my plate very hesitantly. Everyone was quiet and watching me. With a frown, because I know this will be disgusting. I put a bite in my mouth. Oh…my…gosh… it was so tender and juicy and sweet! It was better than roast beef. I know I had seconds and possibly thirds. David had a proud look on his face, the kind I never really got from my father, and gave me a slap on the back.

We would also do a lot of fishing during the warmer months, mostly Judi, Tim, Danny, Aaron, and me—catfish, crappie, and trout. I never got yelled at if my hooks got snagged just lovingly laughed at. We had lots of fun. Tim had become like a brother/friend, Danny and Aaron like little brothers. Judi was like a foster mom. There was a closeness like I had never felt before, and it was warming inside. If I ever did do something wrong, there was never really punishment in this family. You just knew you had let someone down. Judi liked to talk things out if there was ever an issue about anything. That was very seldom. Odd thing is that no matter how much I felt cared for, I could never get rid of my feelings of worthlessness. I could look in the mirror and still see that ugly, fat assed, big butt, good for nothing, worthless me.

*****

When Aaron starts school, he gets harassed, bullied, and called names on the school bus because of the color of his skin due to his Caucasian/Korean mix. They called him "Blackie." He would come home in tears. I tried to make sure I was home in the afternoons so I could meet him down at the bus stop to walk him home. I knew his pain. Bullying is bullying no matter what the reason, and it makes you feel less of yourself. Aaron is a beautiful little boy, and I would always try to make him laugh and smile on our walk home. Aaron also loved to sit with me in the recliner in the afternoons or evenings after dinner and have me read him stories. Danny liked to play games and watch TV.

*****

Judi is deathly afraid of spiders, and I had to come to her rescue a few times when she would see one in her bedroom. I believe she learned that you can't jump on a waterbed to escape a spider without hurting yourself. Myself, I'm deathly afraid of mice and rats. Having a forest at the edge of the yard means those disgusting little beady-eyed rodents are in the garage. This first winter I'm there, they actually get into the basement where our bedroom is. Just outside of the bedroom is the laundry room, and on the other side of the wall, from my bed, is the junk/miscellaneous room. One night, after I go to bed (Tim is either at work or on a date), I hear some sort of rustling noise in there. I get out of bed and very cautiously go into that room. Just so nothing runs over my feet, I climb up on a small table to survey the floor that we really need to clean up one day. I know I heard something, and if it's in there, I need to be very quiet because it has heard me. After a couple minutes of quiet, I hear the rustling again, more like something nibbling on paper. I haven't seen it yet, but I know it's there, so I quietly get off the table and rush upstairs to Judi's bedroom, David's at work. Loudly whispering through the door, I tell her there are mice in the basement. She tells me there can't be, they have never had mice down there. She tells me to come in before I wake Danny and Aaron, and I tell her what I heard. She reluctantly gets out of bed, goes to the closet by the back door, and gets a mousetrap (they are kept for the garage). And to appease me, she gets a little cheese, baits it, goes downstairs, and places it on the floor behind a small dresser drawers. The whole time, she's laughing at me telling me I'm crazy.

Judi goes back to bed. I crawl back under the covers but can't get comfortable at the thought of little mice possibly running around in the room. It really has me creeped out. Within ten minutes, I hear a "SNAP" then a "SQUEEK, SQUEEK, SQUEEK, SQUEEK!!!" oh… my… gosh…!! I jump out of bed and run back upstairs yelling for Judi, frantically knocking on her bedroom door. She's climbing out of bed again, saying, *"For goodness sakes, Craig, what now?"* She's wanting to sleep, and I won't let her.

"It snapped! It snapped! It snapped!"

"Oh, for crying out loud. Are you sure?" she asks as we go back down the stairs.

I won't go in the room by myself. I need Judi as my bodyguard. I get on the table and check it out, as long as she's there. I see the trap, and *"Yes, there it is,"* I tell her. I see the gross little mouse just laying there with a little blood around its nose. I get really brave and slowly reach down to retrieve the trap with the dead mouse. Just as I almost have my hands on it, the mouse starts to flip and flop and squeal. I fell back off the table right into Judi yelling out of complete disgust and fear. Judi just busts up laughing!

*****

To this day, for Christmas, Judi sends me a package loaded with mice or rats. Ceramic mouse musical Christmas tree, Christmas stocking with a big stuffed, cute as can be, mouse. Anything mouse related she will send. My curio cabinet is full of mice.

Same Ole, Same Ole

ℬ ℭ

All is not completely great inside of me. I still see my mom
and Emily occasionally, just day visits, no overnights anymore. I don't know why. I don't really know why I care. I
think despite all the abuse, I'm still looking for some sort of approval.
That I'm not that bad, ugly, worthless kid she's made me believe I
am. Granted, she has told me she's proud of me once. My mother
doesn't change.

When I drive over to spend the day, she will always manage to
get in her sarcastic, hurtful, little quips at me, putting me down in
some fashion. Even though she has seen me in a musical, she still likes
to make little insults if I'm singing to the radio in her car when we go
out. One day, I was in the back seat keeping beat to the music with
my hands drumming on the seat. Her comment was, *"See, you can't
even keep a beat."* I was keeping an "offbeat" in between the regular
beats that's called, *"Syncopation, Mother, it's called syn-co-pa-tion."* I
think I had just about had it with her, also because my reply came out
very bitter, slightly disrespectful. And I've never used the word *mother*
before in addressing her, especially in the tone that I did.

Sometimes after these visits, I would make another visit to the
apartment above the bookstore. In that apartment, I wasn't ugly or
anything. Never made fun of. They didn't see me how my mother
did. I was admired and wanted. Here I was considered good-looking
and sexy. At times, his young good-looking college buddies would
be down from the Twin Cities. Although deep down inside it was
demeaning, to a small extent, there was a certain excitement in
knowing that people wanted me and would pay for it. Even though
it helped me to block out my mother, I would still go home feeling
a little empty inside.

Other times, I would just go back home and lay on my bed for a while or just quietly sit in the recliner. Sometimes, almost as if sensing something wrong, Aaron would come over and ask to get in my lap and read him a story. Judi used to tell me that I would look confused and be really distant for a while. One time, she came downstairs just as I was coming up. She asked me to have a seat on the bottom step with her so we could talk. Even though she already knew, she would still ask, *"How was your visit with your mom?"* She was always so sweet when asking. Never wanting it to seem like she was prying but just wanting me to open up. I tell her that sometimes I have bad dreams of being chased by my mother but I can never remember the rest. At the end of our talk, she says, *"I want you to know that we truly love and care for you."* That was weird and uncomfortable, but it still made my eyes water. I grew up believing I was undeserving, unworthy.

As I fought back stupid tears and not knowing really how to reply, I just tell her, *"That's nice. Nobody has ever told me that before."*

Judi is also a Christian, although we never went to church. And many times, if I was staying up late (both of us waiting for Tim to come home), she would talk to me about the Bible, about God's love and the love Jesus has for us. The love that Jesus has for me. She loved to talk to me about Jesus when we were alone. She would tell me that, *"Jesus loves you no matter what, Craig."* Also making it a point to remind me that, *"I have come to know you better than you think I do, and you are not the person your parents made you think you are."* I never quite know how to take what she says. I have only ever seen myself in that one way.

I believe in God. I know the main stories of the Bible and of Jesus, so yeah… I believe in Jesus. But not "BELIEVE, believe." I had gotten to a point where I basically believed the Bible was just a bunch of really good stories. I do ask questions of things I don't understand. I debate issues of the Bible that I find hard to believe. Sometimes Judi would say, with a little sarcastic, knowing laugh, *"Craig, you can debate the Bible all you want and I will win because quite simply, the Bible is the truth and that's that."*

*****

It will still be another thirty years before I realize that within myself.

*****

One day, Judi has a friend over for the afternoon, very nice lady and pretty. She's part American Indian. Cherokee, I believe. She knew a secret about me that would soon stun and embarrass me. Later in the day, after Judi's friend had left, Judi would have a "sit-down" with me. Whenever Judi wanted to talk about something serious but sensitive, she would always ease into the conversation in a very relaxed, comfortable, casual, caring way. I would be sitting in "my" recliner (mine because that's where I read to Aaron), and Judi would be sitting in her recliner crocheting (she loves to crochet things for people). *"You know, Craig. My friend says she thinks she sees you sometimes near where she lives."*

I don't have a clue. Maybe around where my mom lives? And I don't realize she's "fishing," so I follow along. *"Oh, really. Where's that?"*

"You know, down Broadway near where you and Tim work, there's a bunch of apartments above those businesses down there?" My heart either skipped a beat or completely stopped for a split second. I froze. I could feel my face starting to turn red as my mind spins at whirlwind velocity speeds trying to think of something to say. I've been found out. My deep dark secret has been let out of the box. I guess Judi could see how uncomfortable I became because she lets me know that I don't have to say anything. She does, however, tell me, in her most caring way, *"I'm not going to tell you what to do because I'm not your parent, but you know that I love you and care about you as if I were and I don't want to see you get hurt. My friend lives in one of those apartments across from the one she says she sees you going into. Craig, she's dating one of the officers in the sheriff's department and says there are rumors of suspicious activity in that apartment. If you want to talk to me about...anything...you know you can. I just want you to be careful."* This is definitely a topic I cannot discuss with her. There were

no details as to what kind of "suspicious activity," but it definitely put me on guard a little.

Judi cares about me a lot. I know that. She will do her best to guide, as she does her own children, but she also cares enough to let you make your own mistakes. I don't rely on Judi for spending money. I usually get three nights a week at work, averaging forty-five dollars a week. I have car payments and insurance. I wasn't groomed growing up, as my sister, to be prepared for college. I was taught to survive day to day, and be lucky I did. I have no idea where my future is headed except that I am going to finish high school…and I'm in a safe place. I needed the apartment above the bookstore to help me keep my bank account in a comfortable position. I keep Judi's advice in the back of my mind, but I still go see the guys above the bookstore that make me feel special, attractive, and not ugly. I'm a little more cautious and keep an eye out to make sure I'm not being watched. Besides, as far as I know, I'm not doing anything wrong. However, one time, I go up there, and Paul is there, but the other guys have black eyes and bruises. It seems Paul has a couple older brothers that had been "tailing" him and found out where he was going. They put two and two together, and they beat up Harry and the two guys that come down from the Twin Cities. Paul is still brave enough to come over because, like me, he feels special and he gets paid for what we do. Harry is more careful about who he opens his door for.

A Bright New Year

శు   ళ

My first Thanksgiving and Christmas with Judi, David, Tim, Danny, and Aaron are the best and warmest I have ever had in my life—the feeling of a real family despite their own dysfunctions. There is real thankfulness at Thanksgiving and such warm heartedness at Christmas and not just because of the beautiful tree and glowing embers in the fireplace. A lot of presents are homemade from the heart, mostly the ones from Judi. Very special they were. It was slightly awkward inside because I'm not used to such real love. My mind and heart have a difficult time trying to figure out where that fits inside of me, like there's an extra piece to a puzzle and there was no place made for it. I push that awkwardness aside and enjoy the moment. Relish it. I will contemplate it all when I go to bed and shed a happy tear that I also don't understand before I fall asleep.

The New Year comes around, celebrated Minnesota style. It's too cold outside, and we are all toasty inside, with the fireplace burning, trying to stay up until midnight. David, who usually works nights, is lying on the couch, me and Aaron in "my" recliner, Judi crocheting, Tim and Danny playing a game on the floor while we all watch Dick Clarks New Year's on TV.

I hate Minnesota winters, but spring slowly rolls around. Tim and I have still been skipping school once in a while, creating our own little teenage mischief. I still have unfulfilling visits to my mom's that continues to lead me to the apartment above the bookstore, my bank account continuing to grow. Only nowadays, there are two new people hanging around, another slightly younger guy from my old high school and a guy in my grade from my new school. We all carry the same dark secrets. This is all very curious. We never knew each other existed.

174

Sometime around the beginning of April, I get word from the drama instructor about auditions for a summer repertory theater company, and he thinks I should audition. He shows me the audition/casting notice, it's for a theater company of seventeen at a college up north. I find out it's near the Canadian border. It's a paying job that also supplies living quarters in an on-campus apartment section that's empty for the summer. It says to have a prepared monologue for the audition. As a general rule of thumb, most monologues or soliloquies are taken from Broadway shows or Shakespeare plays. He tells me not to look up any theatrical monologues but that I should go with my already prepared *A Day No Pigs Would Die*. It's my own monologue that he says is the perfect length for an audition piece. He knows this is the perfect dramatic reading for me since I was considered one of the best in the state with this piece. If I rehearse with him a little to brush up, he thinks I would definitely have a shot with this theater company.

I'm excited that the drama instructor thinks this positively of me, so I agree. I fill out the forms and application so he can send them in immediately. Within a week, we're notified of my audition date. It will be on a Saturday in a couple of weeks. I am extremely excited! Soon, I will be driving up north for my first audition for an actual paying acting job. Wow! Judi has been proud of me through all this—my speech competitions and now this audition. I tell my mom about it, but she basically shrugs it off as no big deal, giving off that vibe of *"You'll never amount to anything."* Even though I should be used to that by now, it really hurts inside in a way I can't describe. I want to be proud of myself, but instead, I feel exactly how she makes me see myself. I don't know why I feel I need to prove myself to her.

The weekend of the audition is here. It's about a five-hour drive. Luckily, I have "my money" in the bank, and I can afford a hotel, so I leave late Friday afternoon around four o'clock. I drive about three hours somewhere north of Minneapolis/St. Paul and find a hotel. This is great. I'm seventeen, eighteen in about four weeks, money and checkbook in my pocket, and this is my first big solo road trip to audition for a big acting job. Well, big for me at this point in my life. I feel so grown up, Professional. Ready to take on the world. I feel like I'm really starting to live my dream. I find a hotel and get a room. They have an indoor pool, and when I go out to grab some fast food to bring back, I see a K-Mart. I go inside and see they're already putting summer stuff out, so I'm able to find a pair of shorts. I buy them, grab some food and back to the hotel. I eat and then go down to take a dip in the heated indoor pool. When I get there, some other people are already in the pool, a family with kids my age. My insecurities (my mother made insecurities) immediately surface—ugly, big butt, fat ass, in these shorts. I'm half naked in front of strangers, and I know they're seeing precisely what my mother says I am. I put my towel down and get in the hot tub instead of the pool. With all the bubbles, you can't see me from the neck down. My parentally twisted, magnifying mind had it all wrong, though. They weren't paying any attention to me. They were too busy having fun. That's okay because I felt safer in the hot tub anyway. They eventually left, and I returned to my room. I look in the full body mirror, as I changed, and am really disgusted with what I see, what my mother has made me to see. I see no reason to go over my audition piece since I know it so well, so I just go to bed. Auditions start at nine o'clock, so I need to be up early for the last two-hour drive.

Saturday morning, I get my wake-up call at five o'clock from the front desk. *"Oh, boy,"* I say to myself as I take a deep breath and look in the mirror. I'm a mixture of nervousness and excitement inside. I look at myself in the mirror saying, *"You can do this,"* trying to push all deep rooted insecurities aside. This is the day. A huge day for me. I shower, dress, pack up my car, and head out by six o'clock. I should make it there by eight. I'm too nervous and excited to eat, so I drive straight through up to the college.

I'm good at navigating with a map, so I have no problems getting there and finding the college. They have signs directing everyone, who is up for the auditions, to the parking lot near the auditorium. There are so many cars, and I'm having to fight my fears of all these new people I will be meeting. I park and head toward the auditorium following little directorial signs saying I need to go inside to sign in. I do so. In the hallway there's a line of people at a big long table with about ten other people sitting behind it sorting through piles of paper. I keep hearing, *"Name? (Sort, sort, sort) Here you are. Thank you for coming to the audition. You can have a seat inside the auditorium. Next."* Person after person, it's the same thing. I'm sure it wasn't hard to memorize those lines. I get up to the table.

"Name?"

"Craig Walter."

Sort, sort, sort. *"Here you are. Thank you for coming to the audition. You can have a seat inside the auditorium. Next."*

I go inside the auditorium and take a quick glance around. It is at least as large as the Civic Center back home. There are already a lot of people here, at least a hundred or so and more people outside waiting to come in. A lady gets on stage to talk to us, letting us know the audition process will start promptly at nine o'clock. There is no special order.

"Your names will be called as they appear at the top of the stack of audition forms. We a have a lot of interest in this year's summer repertory program and many people to audition for a company of seventeen. All auditions will be recorded. If theater is what you want, then this program is an excellent paid learning experience for those that will be chosen. When you are finished auditioning, you are welcome to stay and observe, or you may leave. Please be quiet when entering or leaving the auditorium. Notices of decisions will be sent out the first weekend in May. Work starts the beginning of June. Good luck. Break a leg and please be patient. It will be a long day."

I'm all excited inside. I wonder if this is how it is on Broadway, not that I have ever had any plans for New York; Hollywood is my destination.

Auditions are about to start, and the lady takes her speech out to the hallway. I've found a safe seat to myself, but it's not long before others are sitting around me casually chatting. I don't know how to casually chat. I can't instigate a conversation. I was raised locked up, beat up, and told to shut up, but eventually, the conversation is directed toward me. *"Hey, how you doin'? I'm so and so, drove all the way from such and such. This is, whomever. We just met. What's your name. Where did you drive from? How long did it take you? I was talking to so and so over there. She drove from North Dakota."* Idle talk like that. When I'm asked the questions, it's a little easier to talk, just don't ask me anything too difficult or personal.

The director of the repertory company gets up on stage to introduce himself, and shortly thereafter, one by one, they start calling names. There are so many people here, and I have found out that this isn't the only day of auditions. Boy, oh, boy, I don't stand a chance, my insecurities starting to rise. I believe I have a good audition piece, but one after one, after one, I listen to so many good people. Some funny, some serious, and with all the people to audition, who knows how many more on the other audition date, I don't stand a chance. I have such an inferiority complex that I always think everyone is better than me. I always do. Looks. Talent. I never think very highly of myself, but I keep telling myself to relax and relish this incredibly exciting, once in a lifetime moment. This is your dream. Then my name gets called. Immediate panic! As I walk down the stairs, in the auditorium to the stage, and all eyes on me, my mind is racing about everything other than my performance I'm about to give. Is my butt too big, fat ass in these slacks? My nose is too big and ugly. This is a big audition, actors are supposed to be good-looking. My hair, my ears, my clothes. My mother, *"You will never amount to anything!"*

I make it to the stage. With the stage lights up, I really can't see all the people out there, but I know they are there, judging me, quietly criticizing me on my looks and all my imperfections. I don't like other people my age. They are cruel and harsh with their condemnations. This is how my mind is thinking as my heart is racing. From beyond the lights, I'm asked, *"Name please."*

"Craig Walter."

Then the director's voice, *"Whenever you're ready."*

A quick deep breath and instantaneously, as if my life depended on it, I'm in character and start the introduction to my monologue from *A Day No Pigs Would Die* by Robert Newton Peck.

As I have done many times past, I relive Robert's childhood trauma when he has to assist his father in the butchering and bludgeoning of his pet and best friend, Pinky, his prize pig. When I'm done, I get a huge round of applause and some whistling of approval from my fellow auditioners. The director says, *"Thank you,"* and someone calls the next name at the top of the stack. As I go back and take a seat in the auditorium, to observe some more, I get a lot of whispered compliments, *"That was so good." "You made me cry." "You're going to be one of them." "My eyes are still all watery."* I really do enjoy the adulation, slightly embarrassed because I never think I'm really that good, but I do eat it up inside a little bit!

I stay and observe until about midafternoon. So many good people but I need to get on the road back home. The drive back to the same hotel was kind of euphoric and depressing. I felt on top of the world from the experience and the admiration I received, but now it's over and that "high" I was feeling has faded and diminishing very quickly, fast becoming a distant memory. I get dinner, do the hot tub again, there's no one there, go to bed, and head home Sunday morning. This has all been so surreal, dreamlike. This day has been so exhilarating that if my acting never goes anywhere, I think I could die happy with this experience. Once at home, I get to relive the whole experience with Judi, she's very happy for me, then again on Monday to the drama instructor.

By the end of the first full week in May, one week before my eighteenth birthday, I get home from school and check the mailbox at the end of the driveway. Walking back to the house, flipping through the mail, there is a letter addressed to me from the director of the drama department and repertory company at the college. *"Oh my gosh. Oh my gosh. Oh my gosh. Judi, Judi, Judi,"* I'm hollering out as I burst in the back door.

"What in the world is the matter?" Judi's in her chair crocheting as I come in waving the letter in the air. I have no idea what's in it. I'm so excited but scared, afraid of the disappointment that might be inside that envelope. My hand is actually shaking. *"Well, open it, for crying out loud,"* Judi says with a little excited laugh. She's also anxious.

I can't stop nervously saying, *"Oh my gosh, oh my gosh."*

I slowly open the envelope, unfold the paper inside, and start reading. *"Thank you for your sincere interest in our theater program."* I'm already thinking *denied. "Out of over two hundred applicants/audition-*

ees for this year's Summer Repertory Theater Company, you have been selected as one of the seventeen to complete our repertory cast."

"OH - MY - GOSH!!" That's about all I can say. I don't know what to say. I know my eyes are as big as can be, and I can hardly breathe. I'm in utter disbelief! How many people? I'm selected? I show it to Judi as if I don't believe what I'm reading and need another set of eyes as proof. She gets out of her chair to give me hugs and praises and *"Thank you, Lord's."* We're both excitedly talking at the same time as Tim comes in the house from school wondering what's going on. We show him the letter. Acting's no big thing to Tim, so it's no big thrill to him, but he is very happy for me. I call my mom to tell her. I get a *"Congratulations. That's nice."* No excitement from her. I was surprised to even get the "congrats," but that's okay because Judi more than makes up for it.

I have to be up at the college by the beginning of June to start my first paid acting job. What an early birthday present. Is there a cloud higher than "Cloud 9?" If so, I'm on it! At almost eighteen, I feel like I've hit the "Big Time"!! My dreams are on their way to coming true.

"They Say the Neon Lights Are Bright."

Well, I'm not actually going to Broadway, but I do love that song, and I feel like I'm going somewhere big!

Of course, I'm not graduating with my friends in Byron as I thought I would, coming home from Kansas. Now I won't be attending a graduation ceremony at Mayo High School either. I need to be up north starting my first acting job. Need to be up there Saturday, the last weekend of May, because we need to get our campus apartments and we start working Monday June 1. No graduation ceremony is no loss to me considering this incredible opportunity I have.

Friday afternoon, just like audition weekend, my car is packed. I'm going to travel the same route, same hotel, and arrive Saturday morning. We all say our goodbyes. Judi is full of her hugs and *"Drive safely. Call when you get to your hotel. We're going to miss you."* Of course, I have to call when I get to the college also. I give hugs to Danny and a big one for Aaron. Tim even gives a hug. I'm betting he's glad to be getting his room back to himself.

When I get to the college, Saturday morning, some of us have already arrived. We're all supposed to meet in the auditorium at ten o'clock for a meeting and receive our apartment assignments and roommate. This is going to be a real test for me—a group of seventeen strangers and sharing an apartment with one of them. Keep my secrets secret, and hope people don't start asking anything too personal. If conversations stick to acting and theater or the movies and our dreams, I'll be good. Ooh, boy, I feel like I'm sweating inside. We're going to be together for three months.

*****

A year ago, I spent the summer with my grandparents. That was the best summer of my life until now.

*****

It will be a whirlwind of a summer. A summer of hard work. A lot of fun…and more hard work. Our company of seventeen is made up of nine guys and eight girls. Obviously, we are all of some talent to have made it here. We get our apartments and roommates. Being an odd number of guys, one of us will get an apartment to himself. I'm not the lucky one. I'm not used to living with a total stranger, but I end up with a pretty cool roomy, Richard.

We have three shows we will be doing this summer: *See How They Run*, a hilarious British comedy; a very suspenseful thriller, *Night Watch* by Lucille Fletcher; and the Neil Simon comedy *Prisoner of Second Avenue*. Each of these shows will have a double cast, each cast with its own performance schedule. Even though our director has a good idea how he wants each show to be cast, we still read for the parts.

The first day of our first week, we are told how hectic the summer will be. We will earn enough to get by, and there will also be some free time. Then we jump right into reading, casting, and rehearsals. There will be no time to waste at the start.

In *Night Watch*, I will take on the very solicitous and furtive lead role of John for the second cast. For the production of *See How They Run*, I am delighted to be cast in the very comedic role of the Bishop of Lax for both casts. During the readings, I immediately become friends with Kevin because of his wit and love for horror movies. He will also be in both casts due to his hilarious portrayal as the reverend Humphrey. We will later become cohorts in a little devious Alfred Hitchcock style thriller of our own. In *Prisoner of Second Avenue*, I take on a very minor supporting background role in the second cast.

The first three weeks are a whirlwind of a marathon. We have five days for each show to block all scenes, learn the script, memorize lines, build our characters, become our characters, build the set, have dress rehearsal, and be ready for opening on Friday night for a full weekend of performances. We barely have time to eat and sleep. When any of us are not rehearsing, we are building sets. We will do twelve-hour days, 6:00 a.m. until 6:00 p.m. working strenuously and tirelessly in the theater. We take a dinner break and then back in the theater until 10:00. After that, if we're not too tired, some of us will get together in our apartments and continue running (rehearsing) lines. Our director even took us through hypnosis in order to memorize the scripts faster and then build our character. We all realize the seriousness of meeting the production deadline of opening night and fully comprehend that we are not in high school anymore. Up until now, this is the closest to professional theater any of us have ever been, and it's all extremely exhilarating. I go to bed every night completely exhausted. A wonderfully fulfilling type of exhaustion.

Week one, we rehearse, block, and build like crazy until all hours. It pays off because we open our first Friday to a sold out audience and standing ovations for *See How They Run*. Our whole weekend turns out to be a sellout.

Week two is the same thing: rehearse, block, and build until all hours. Opening weekend for the thriller *Night Watch* is sold out.

Week three with *Prisoner of Second Avenue* is a repeat of our first two weeks: exhausting schedule, sold out audiences all weekend, and all three shows get great reviews.

All rehearsals include both casts for each show, and both casts alternate during the weekend so everyone performs. Our intense efforts and work has paid off. Theater has never felt so rewarding.

When we don't have a scheduled performance night, those of us not performing will take on the backstage duties of tech work—props, wardrobe, makeup, set changes, etc.

Now that all the shows have opened, our schedule relaxes a little. We will still have rehearsals during the week, just not as strenuous. The big difference is that on the weekends, we perform more than one show. Show schedule for the summer has already been advertised for our audiences. We will perform, for instance, *Night Watch* Friday night. Change sets Saturday and rehearse *See How They Run* for that night. Change sets Sunday and rehearse for *Prisoner of Second Avenue* Sunday night. For the rest of our summer, it's mostly the weekends that are hectic. I wouldn't have missed this for the world.

We don't get to go out on the weekends, due to show schedule, but our weekday evenings are pretty free now for movies or pizza or whatever we want. One time, someone got a VCR, and we rented the movie *Fame*, which had come out in theaters the year before. Of course, being actors, we all loved the movie, so we spent an evening having a *Fame* party, singing and dancing to the movie as if we were in it.

*****

With a company of seventeen young adults, fresh out of high school, living and working together so closely day in and day out, we are not all going to become good friends. We each come from a different social and familial background. There will be little conflicts here and there. Things get a little stressful with our demanding schedule, but we all basically get along, some better than others and some even make a "connection" during the course of the summer. Things like that can't be helped. Some of the group are smokers. I, being the type that wants to fit in, decide to take up smoking under the pretense that it's relieving some of the serious stress due to our hectic schedule. Although "I never inhaled" in the beginning. By the end of the summer, I was smoking like a pro.

I was also one that made a "connection" over the summer. You see, my roommate Richard also has the lead role of "John" for the first cast of *Night Watch*, so we spend much late nighttime running lines for the other shows also and just talking. It turns out that Richard, who is very good looking, has the same curiosities that I do about men. Only thing is that mine aren't so much curiosities anymore and I subtly let him know that. Eventually, due to our late-night chats, one thing leads to another, and we have our own little secret trysts that no one ever finds out about. It was great—our own little private romance, someone else that shares that part of life with me and it's my own roommate. I'm attractive to someone else, and it doesn't involve money, and I don't feel demeaned or degraded. There is actually a pleasant emotion involved. I like this guy.

A problem does arise out of this, however, because a couple of our late-night talks about our "curiosities" would lead into talks about religion. Despite Richard's desires, he has a strong religious upbringing. I don't discuss my childhood, but we do talk about our beliefs. Richard tells me he likes me but can't finish the summer living with me and the temptation. He becomes so guilt ridden that he ends up moving out and moving in with the guy that got an apartment to himself. A part of me feels bad, but hey, I have an apartment to myself now.

It's slightly awkward working together, under the circumstance, nobody knowing the real reason we aren't roomies anymore, but we mask it pretty well, and we still get along. I don't remember the lie we made up as to our parting ways, but it seemed to be pretty believable. Richard will still find his way to my apartment a couple more times over the summer. What I don't get is we are raised being told it's wrong but, if it is so wrong, why does this attraction feel so normal.

*****

Now onto a little creative fun of my own with my cohort Kevin. We both love horror films—*Friday the Thirteenth, Halloween,* Hitchcock's *Psycho,* for example. I believe we were just talking about movies and simultaneously concocted a real life flick of our own that we were going to stage one night when everyone went out for pizza.

Two of the girls in our company have their apartment right behind mine. We're on the second floor, outside doors with steps leading up. One of the girls brought her cat, Fluffy, with her for the summer. The scene for our thriller takes place in the girl's apartment.

Everyone goes out for dinner at a local pizzeria, except for me and Kevin. We say we're going to head off to the movies. It's summer break so hardly anyone is on campus, and it's northern Minnesota, so we're all in the habit of leaving our doors unlocked. We all head off in our own directions. They are off for pizza; me and Kevin to the movies. After everyone else is out of site, Kevin and I circle back to the apartments to set the scene for our legendary thriller prank.

We let ourselves into the girl's apartment. We borrowed a trench coat from wardrobe, put it on a hanger, and hung it from the shower curtain rod outside of the bathtub so you can see it from the separate vanity area. Kevin had a pair of hiking boots we put on the floor under the trench coat. In the vanity area, we wrote "HELTER SKELTER" across the entire mirror in ketchup and in very large letters. Both the vanity area and bathroom had dimmer switches, so we dimmed the lights for effect, closed the bathroom door just enough so that in the dim light it looked like a person was in there, and we turned on the shower for an added sound effect. We already had some prerecorded scary type music that we were going to have playing just inside the front door. Before we left, we found a stuffed toy cat that we hung from the living room ceiling fixture and got a knife from the kitchen that we dipped in ketchup and left on the vanity counter. The last thing was to loosen all the light bulbs so only the vanity and bathroom lights worked. The scene was now set. All we had to do was keep watch. When we saw them returning, I ran in, turned the music on low, and shut the front door. Then we both hid in the nearby bushes. It was so difficult to stay quiet. This is going to be classic, like a scene straight out of a horror flick.

When everyone got back, they all said their good nights and headed off to their own apartments. The girls climbed the stairs and stopped at their front door. They heard the music. We couldn't hear the music, but we could hear them whisper with fear, *"Oh my gosh! Someone's in there! We need to go get the guys!"* They quickly and quietly backed down the stairs, and when they got to the bottom, they took off running to the other side of the building to the other guy's apartments. Kevin and I are about ready to bust out laughing but have to stifle. After a couple minutes, we see three of the guys coming, one of them carrying a baseball bat. They climb the stairs with the girls at the back of the little pack. The guy with the baseball bat cautiously opens the door and steps in first, slowly followed by the others. The girls enter last. After a short period of time, we hear a scream and knew our prank had worked, until the two girls come out on the front porch, one of them crying. She can't find Fluffy. That is really the last thing we did was to put Fluffy in my apartment. One of the girls crying, the guys coming out saying *"We need to call the police."* tells us that our little classic "scene right out of a horror flick" may have backfired.

Kevin and I are flooded with guilt when we see the crying, and we come out of the bushes to try to calm the situation. I run and bring Fluffy back. We explain that we were just doing an Alfred Hitchcock type scene and that, if it had been on candid camera, it would have been perfect. Everyone's reactions were flawless. Couldn't have been any better if it was scripted. Kevin and I clean the mirrors, screw in light bulbs, and put their apartment back in order. The girls are a bit upset, but Fluffy is back and no real harm done. The guys are probably angrier because we got the girls upset. But hey, it was just a harmless prank. We're all theater nuts. Before long, all is forgiven, and everyone sees the humor in it and can laugh about it. It was truly classic. Legendary.

*****

I recently found Kevin on Facebook. He now lives in the Los Angeles area and works behind the scenes of a well-known television sitcom. We had some good chats on line, reminiscing, and both agree that, after thirty-five years, we still harbor a little guilt about that prank. "Classic!" "Legendary!"

*****

My incredible summer of living my dream does eventually come to an end. I was able to eat, sleep, and breathe theater for three months, and it was phenomenal. We opened and closed shows left and right for the last two months of summer. Played to sold out audiences and great reviews every weekend. It has been an absolutely unbelievable experience. All the work we did. All the audiences we played to. All the applause and ovations. We strike the sets. Props and wardrobe back into the theater department storage for the upcoming school year. Apartments cleaned and cars packed. We say our good-byes and head off in our own directions back to our hometowns or cities never to see each other again, at least for me.

It feels so good to be back home at Judi's house. I missed them, just hangin' with Tim, playing games with Danny, really missed reading to Aaron, although everyone is really shocked to see me smoking. Tim, not so much. He thinks it's cool that I am, and I feel like I fit in more, smoking with Tim, Judi, and David.

I had kept in touch with Judi all summer, calling just about every week. My first evening back, she tells me she has a confession to make. She never brought it up during the summer because she didn't want to take a chance on spoiling this opportunity I had. Mayo High had been in touch with Judi, shortly after I left, and they didn't think they could graduate me, without attending summer school, due to poor attendance. Judi said that she told them where I was and what I was doing and there was no way I was going to be able to come back to resolve the situation. After a couple days, they called her back saying that due to my good record and grades coming into Mayo, part way into my senior year, I did keep my grades up and, with my accomplishments in such a short period of time, they decided I would be able to receive my diploma. It was mailed to me, and Judi couldn't wait to give it to me. Wow! I graduated high school. Not how I had imagined, but I did it.

I love living with Judi, Tim, and the boys. I have always felt safe here, but I'm an adult now. I can't live here forever. I wasn't raised with any focus toward a college education, nor was I encouraged to prepare for any kind of future. I was raised to survive the day, which, somehow, I managed to do fairly well all these years. I have my dreams, but that's about it.

I go back to my aimless, minimum wage job at the fast-food restaurant. After the events of this summer, my job is incredibly unfulfilling. I still go and visit my mom and Emily. Nothing has changed there. My mom shows no interest in my summer accomplishments. There's no way to really impress her. As far as I'm concerned, I'm still a worthless good for nothing in her eyes. I also continue to pay visits to the apartment above the bookstore. Emotionally, I know I'm cared for at Judi's, but I have this need to feel physically admired, and I get that above the bookstore. Plus, I get paid. I like to make sure there is a good amount of money in the bank just in case. I have learned that I need to be prepared for those "just in case" moments. I have this fear now of never having enough or not having anything. However, these days, I only do it when the guys from college come down. I don't quite get it, though what good-looking guys from college see in me, but I like it.

There is still another need inside me. A need to break free. To get away. I'm still too close, in proximity, to my family. On occasion, my mother still haunts my dreams, but Judi is there to talk to about it if I feel the need. There are no shows at the Civic Theater, since I've been back, with character profiles that I could play. I feel that there is a talent inside me that is becoming dormant. I feel stagnant. I desperately want to be acting again. This past summer was unbelievable. I craved the applause and attention on stage, and I want more.

Fall and winter arrive. We have a great Thanksgiving. It's always a warm feeling at Judi's house around the holidays even when David's temper tries to spoil the mood. Preparations for Christmas are always festive, just a glow and tenderness and caring and love that I never felt as a kid. For Judi, Christmas is more about Jesus and giving than anything else. That's cool. I like listening to her talk about the Bible, even if I'm not sure I agree. I've always liked the stories of baby Jesus. I would sometimes wonder where was God when I was little.

This winter seems to be one of the coldest I can recall, daytime highs in the negative single digits, lows in the negative double digits, And some windchills reaching close to -40 degrees. It is so cold that some power lines are snapping and the snow crunches under your feet when you walk across it. I have always hated the cold and the snow. I am going stir crazy. There is nothing for me here. I despise the weather. I never liked living here to begin with. All I have is my fast-food job and the apartment above the bookstore. Ken and other old friends have already gone off to college. I wasn't groomed or nurtured in that direction and have no real desire for college anyway. I can't keep staying with Judi and the family when I should be on my own.

California keeps beckoning me in my mind. I mention it to Judi, but that's a huge, scary move. It was one thing to run away at thirteen, but I'm old enough that I need to think this out. Judi mentions that David's parents live just outside of Los Angeles in Simi Valley, wherever that is, and I might be able to stay with them. She tells me, almost warns me, that they are *very* religious. I ponder over different thoughts and ideas. I have money in the bank from work and the other thing. I like my Camaro but wouldn't feel safe on a cross-country drive by myself, and I don't have it paid off. I end up dismissing any ideas that were floating around in my head because none of them seems very realistic. Ooh, I don't know what to do, but this is not where I belong or where I want to be.

It doesn't take too long for my mind to do an immediate about face. The year 1981 comes to a close, and the first week in January 1982 is so cold I can't deal with this anymore. This freezing cold, stagnant, going nowhere life here. I feel like that "good for nothing, wont amount to anything" person that my mother had made me to believe I am. My mind snaps like some of the power lines have been doing in this cold, and I make an impulse decision. I am leaving. I'm getting out of here. Let's start this train rolling and get "this show" on the road.

I start everything moving so fast. No real plan when I get to California but Judi talks to David's parents. I can stay with them, at least for now. I don't know them, never met them, but at least I got that out of the way. The majority of the country from here to California is in winter mode, so I'm not driving. I've never done this, but I managed to book a flight on my own to LAX. Well, Judi put it on her credit card, but I'm paying her back. I talk to the small car dealer, in Byron, who sold me my Camaro. He will take it, sell it for me, and pay off the bank, and if there's a profit (he said there would be), he can go ahead and keep it. I just want out of here.

Tim and two other friends come with me, following in Tim's car, the day I take my car back to the dealer. We have to stop by someone's home, a friend of one of our friends, for about half an hour. The temperature is so cold that in those thirty minutes, my tires froze to the pavement and one goes flat. It takes us over an hour, taking turns sitting in the heated car, to change that tire snapping three of the five lug bolts in the process. We drove another eight miles to the dealer on two lugs that were positioned fairly opposite each other. While we're in Byron, I go by the bank and close out my account. After I pay Judi back, I will still have nearly a thousand dollars. I feel rich.

I see my mom one last time just because I think I should, also to kind of throw it in her face that, *"Hey, I'm outta here."* But I don't really do that. Of course, I don't even talk to my father, but I know Judi will let him know, not that he's going to care. I want to completely disappear from them and sever all ties.

All I have fits into two suitcases, and by the end of the first week of January 1982, I'm on a flight to Los Angeles, California, where I've always wanted to be ever since I was a kid because that's where Hollywood is.

*****

Over a year ago, Judi had taken this wounded bird into her nest and nurtured it back to health, and now it's time for me to leave the nest and fly on my own. And, boy, do I intend to fly!

*****

During the writing of this book, I would be in touch with Judi, as I always have over the years, discussing memories. She wrote one time, saying,

"I remember the day you left for California, I cried after you left, I was hoping the weather would get so bad you would change your mind! Well, you left, and for weeks, all I did was worry. Finally, I just said to God, 'He is yours, Lord, all I can do is be faithful and pray for Craig.' And lo and behold, the Lord worked His miracle in your life, Craig. How awesome our Lord is. Love you, Craig, keep following Him, and I know He will take you to places you didn't know possible. Judi."

GOD'S NOT DONE WITH ME YET

CALIFORNIA,
HERE I COME

GOD'S NOT DONE WITH ME YET

Free at Last

℘ ❧

I am on my way to the land where dreams come true! Lights. Camera. Action. I tried in 1976 at thirteen and finally made it in 1982 at eighteen, with a lot of turmoil in between. I grew up being worthless, a nothing, and a nobody. Well, I am going to make it. I am going to make movies that people will remember. My name on the big screen. I am going to win an Oscar one day. I feel like I'm fulfilling my destiny. I'll show everyone, all my tormentors and intimidators growing up, especially my mom! I am going to be somebody! Wish I could tell my old friend Jim. I wonder what he's doing these days.

I had intentionally left my winter parka with Judi when the family saw me off because I knew I wouldn't need it where I was going. As we approach the airport, I can see those famous arches at the terminals that you always see in the movies, basically saying, "You have arrived in LA." Another movie moment is when I get off the plane and in the terminal. I don't know David's family, but there are three people holding a sign that says "Craig," just like you see in airport scenes in the movies. David's parents and one of his sister's have come to meet me.

I have never seen such a hustle and bustle in one place before. So many people rushing hurriedly back and forth trying to make it to their terminals as we scurry through to baggage claim to get my two suitcases and head outside. When we finally step through the doors into the California sunshine, I kind of think of Dorothy in *The Wizard of Oz* when she steps out of her front door into a new colorful world. But everyone's wearing jackets here. The captain at landing said the temperature was in the low sixties. Feels like summertime to me. I am definitely in a whole new world and a couple thousand miles away from everything I want to forget…and the cold. I am going to set the world on fire. Cut loose. Do everything I possibly can. Experience life to its fullest. I am going to do it all! I am going to live! Hollywood, here I come!

Well, first, I need to settle into my new temporary home at David's parents' house. The drive to Simi Valley takes almost an hour. We pass through Santa Monica and cross over the famous Sunset Boulevard through Bel Aire. Across the famous Mulholland Drive, through the San Fernando Valley and into Simi Valley. I don't see Hollywood, not yet. But I know from TV and movies and a map I have that Mulholland or Sunset will take me there. I'll figure it out.

I have never seen so much traffic or so many fancy cars on, what they call out here, the freeways. People are zipping in and out at all speeds. I see a lot of Porsches, a couple Ferraris, a lot of Corvettes, BMW's, Mercedes, and some of the huge fancy houses in the hills. Boy, do people have money out here. That's what I want—everything. A part of my mind is saying, *I'll show them*.

Simi Valley is kind of a quaint little city. It's own little valley tucked away from the more frenzied areas we passed through. A lot of really nice white adobe houses with terracotta roofs and exceptionally manicured yards. I'm told they shot a movie called *Poltergeist* here in Simi Valley. It's coming out this summer. I also find out that *Little House on the Prairie* is shot in the hills just outside of Simi Valley, along with *Father Murphy*. I absolutely love *Little House…* I have to get out there somehow. I'm fascinated and excited just at the thought of movie making and TV and being so close to it.

So I have a place to stay when I get here and a decent amount of "pocket change." A fairly good start. David's parents have a beautiful house outside. It is extremely neat and clean inside. I can tell they are religious by some of the novelties and curios around their house. Bibles, crosses, and artfully framed Bible verses. Judi told me once that they believed in "speaking in tongues" and "casting out of demons." I found that oddly curious and strange, maybe even a little scary, but they seem like really nice people, and they have told me I don't have to go to church with them if I don't want to.

I have a room and use of the spare car. Over the weekend, I'm introduced to family friends. Strangers are really difficult for me, but I force a sociable part of me to the surface. I'm starting a new life, a brand new beginning. I'm going to make it better than what I left behind. But I feel so transparent that everyone can see that bad boy, so I stay guarded and desperately keep my past hidden as I meet new people. I want people to like me for me before I let anyone into my private world, so I steer clear of any personal conversation. I never really "belonged" or "fit in" anywhere growing up, but this is a new life, a fresh start, so I'm going to make it good but stay guarded. I find out from one of the family friends that there are job openings working with handicapped children at a facility just over the hill. I know I need to get a job, at least for the time being, because I have no idea yet how to get work in the movies.

That Monday, I drive over the hill to the facility. I also found out that the hills I just drove through is where the movie ranch is that the Manson Family used to hang out at. It's kind of creepy that I drove along the same road as they did. I arrive at the facility, and I've never really seen or been around anyone handicapped before, so I'm given a tour of the facility, and my heart breaks. There are so many children, boys, and girls in wheelchairs or walking. Some are severely handicapped physically and mentally and some only mildly. Children with autism or cerebral palsy. Some from childhood accidents that left them disabled. All were there either because their families couldn't take care of them or they didn't want to take care of them. Some of their parents visit, and a lot of the parents never do.

I was flooded with emotions inside. Many times, I have told people that *Little House on the Prairie* can be so emotional that I could cry if Laura Ingalls was milking a cow, but seeing these children so many just left me wondering, *Why?*

I took a job there that started immediately. They were always in need of personal care technicians. Despite how I was raised, believing I was just this horrible person, I knew deep down that I had a lot of good, a lot of love inside of me. The love I have for Judi, Tim, Danny, and Aaron, reading to Aaron and being his somewhat protector, was one thing. That was more of a family love. Helping to care for these children who depended almost entirely on me, I was able to pour out all my love and compassion when tending to their nearly every need. Some were very high functioning mentally and emotionally; some not so much. Some have to be fed; some feed themselves. Some have diaper changes or have to be taken to the toilet; others can do that on their own. Some have to be bathed, yet still others are independent in that. What they all seem to share is the inability to be judgmental and they love unconditionally. All I have to do is take care of them. Care for them. And love them back unconditionally. It is such a type of emotional freedom I can't describe. There is a real joy to doing this kind of work to be giving to other children what I never got.

*****

I really didn't know what I was doing, but I started praying for the children. I don't pray, but I was asking God why they had to be like they were and praying for Him to heal them.

*****

I worked the evening shift, which usually consisted of dinner with the children, TV/entertainment time, and getting them ready for bed then into bed by nine o'clock because most of them go to special education school during the week. Even though I know I will never be a parent, there is something so special about bedtime with these much less fortunate children. Some like a little story read to them and that was just up my alley. Very precious times.

I make friends fairly easy, mostly with the girls, though. I guess because I don't feel as intimidated by them for some reason. With guys, I tend to keep my distance a bit longer. Since I'm attracted to guys (not all), I'm afraid they might sense that, and it scares me because guys have a tendency to want to hurt someone like me. I would be considered a threat, when I'm really not, and wouldn't be given a chance, so I don't give them much of a chance to begin with. I just want people to know the "good me" and be able to accept all of me. But that has never really been the case in life, so I always remain protective of my inner self and only let everyone see only one side of me.

It really becomes a challenge when I keep getting invited out after work since day one. I declined a couple times then felt I was being rude so I finally accepted an invite to just hang out at Jill's house, a co-worker. Just a bunch of us hanging out. This is also the first night I smoke pot. We are just hanging out around the pool with a couple friends from work along with Jill's brother and some of his friends. One of the guys just lit up a joint and started passing it around. When it got to me, I mentioned that I really only smoke cigarettes. Never have tried pot. I was kind of embarrassed feeling like I was the only person ever to have never smoked pot. It didn't take much coercing before I gave in, wanting to fit in and be cool. The first hit was harsh, not smooth like a cigarette. I started coughing so hard that my eyes watered. Everyone was laughing. The incessant hacking and coughing made everything rush to my brain, and I got so high so fast. It was an incredible feeling. I also had a few beers along with everyone else, they didn't have any hard liquor, but I spent the rest of the evening talking and laughing so freely. I'm feeling like I finally fit in. I am whole. I feel free at last of anything that bound me. I never thought I would smoke pot. Now I can't believe I never tried it earlier. Between alcohol and pot, I loved it. I can remember Tim and Steve telling me, *"One day, you will."* if they could see me now.

Even being high, though, I still have to keep myself in check and not let anything secret escape my now looser lips. I know I want more. I ask one of the guys there, and he sells me a small bag for ten bucks. It's called a "dime" bag. Wow, my first drug deal. I now have a "connection," a "go to person." I don't know how to "roll," so he gives me a small pipe from his collection and also shows me how I can make a temporary pipe out of aluminum foil then tells me I can do the same with an empty soda can or the empty cardboard tube from a toilet paper roll. He says that one day, he might take me to a "head shop" where all sorts of paraphernalia are sold. I didn't know what that was, but I do know that I need to be careful and keep this out of sight at David's parents' house.

*****

I don't know it, but this night would be only the beginning of my long, slow journey down the road of addiction and self-destruction.

*****

Lights, Camera, Action (My First Movie)

☜ ☞

Staying at David's parents is all right. I pretty much stay to myself. I'm sociable just enough to stay courteous and considerate. Once they asked me how I came to be living with David and Judi. I just told them Tim and I were friends at work and I needed to transfer to a bigger school where competition was tougher in the theatrical area but needed to live in the district and my family said it was okay. Other than that, I stay away from personal chitchat.

One evening, they told me they had guests coming over, husband and wife, for a prayer/healing meeting. As I was about to head to work, I heard them all in the living room so figured I should leave through the side door, but something caught my attention. It was a low, constant, continual…mumbling? I couldn't figure it out, so I quietly took a peek into the living room. I saw a man seated in a chair. David's parents and another woman had their hands on him and were quietly speaking something. I couldn't understand any of the words. It was a different language or something. This was kind of creepy to see. Then out of nowhere, someone would say, *"In the name of Jesus I cast thee out!"* Okay, this is a little way too bizarre for me. Feels like some cult thing going on. I quietly leave for work.

*****

I would witness similar "casting out" events a few more times while I stayed with them. I never ask about it. I'm afraid to, but I don't know why.

*****

At work that night, during the children's dinnertime, I overhear another technician, Allison, talking about a friend who is working as an extra on a movie being shot outside of Simi Valley. I asked about it, and she told me it had something to do with burning a village and they needed a bunch of people. I asked, *"How do you find out things like that?"* She said there had been a story in the paper a few days ago with a casting notice. She knew where they met because she had to drive her friend out there early this morning, had to be there by 5:00 a.m., so I asked her where that was, and she told me. I don't have to work tomorrow, so my mind starts devising a plan of action to get work in a movie.

As soon as I get home from work, I tell David's parents I will be up and out early in the morning, since that's out of the ordinary for me. I set my alarm for 3:30 a.m. and go to bed. I can hardly sleep because of my excitement inside. I really don't know what I'm doing, but I'm going to start by sneaking my way out to where I'm told everyone meets.

I finally get some sleep, but it seems like only minutes before I have to jump out of bed when the alarm rings. I shower, dress, jump in the car, and head out. I find the street I need that leads to the edge of Simi Valley and turns into a dirt road that heads off into the hills. It's so dark at four o'clock in the morning that I can't see the hills, only the dirt road in front of me. I want to make sure I'm early so I don't miss out on anything. Before I get on the dirt road, I smoke a tiny bit of pot to mellow me a little. I'm supposed to drive about two miles to a big gravel parking area. I see headlights in the distance behind me through my rearview mirror and lights in the distance in front of me that aren't moving. That must be it just ahead, the parking area. I pull in, park, and get out of my car as if I know what I'm doing. Inside I am so nervous and don't have a clue. I almost feel like

I'm committing a crime of trespassing. Someone asks, *"Are you part of the extra's cast for today?"*

My heart starts pounding, and there's a fear inside because I'm about to lie. *"Yeah,"* I said rather surprisingly calm and casual.

"The bus is supposed to be here in about thirty minutes," he tells me. There are some people smoking, so I light a cigarette and kind of hang out and mingle as more and more people start to show up. I get involved in idle chitchat, faking my belonging there pretty well. I like this pot. It makes me feel really relaxed. I don't feel as self-conscious or inhibited as I usually do. Some people, production crew and other extras, are talking about various movies or shows they have worked on. I'm a little envious but excited all the same to just be standing here around this movie small talk.

By four-thirty, there's already a large number of people here, and busses start to show up. Everyone starts boarding the busses as if they do this every day, so I just follow the crowd. I have this "pot giddiness" excitement going on in my mind because... I... HAVE... NO... IDEA... WHAT... I'M... DOING!! But it's all so exciting. I'm getting on a bus that's going to take me to "who knows where." I might get in trouble. Maybe even arrested, but *When in Rome...* and I want this so badly!!

The busses are taking us out to what is referred to as "location" where they're shooting today. A lady sitting next to me is an extra also. Since I really didn't know what to do and not wanting to sound stupid or suspicious, I casually ask her, *"Who is it we see to check in with today?"* It sounded like a smart question to me, and it worked.

She tells me, *"Roxanne might already be there or will be shortly."* So I know to keep my eyes and ears open for a Roxanne.

When we arrive on location, I'm in awe. Off in one direction, there's a road lined with poles that have fake decomposed bodies speared onto them leading to a bridge and a fortress wall and behind that a pyramid. In another direction, there's a small area that looks like a tiny burned out village with dead bodies speared to poles also. I heard they shot the burning of the village the day before. In another area way off in the distance is a small pyramid. There are trailers for dressing, makeup, and wardrobe. There are big movie camera booms that take the camera and operator way up in the air, lights, generators, and cables all over. There's a couple catering trucks. This is a lot like what you would see on TV if you were watching "the making of" something. I'm actually on a real movie set. This is all so cool. I feel like I'm in a dream.

A voice calls out for all extras. I follow the small crowd, maybe about fifty, over to where a lady is waiting. That is Roxanne. She's giving instructions, taking her roll call, and handing out pay vouchers, telling one group she has called out to go straight to wardrobe to see so and so and another group on standby for the director to look over. When she's done, I find a break in the moment, nervously go to her, introduce myself, and I tell her what I did to get here on location, waiting to get in all sorts of trouble. What I get is just a quiet verbal chastising, but she tells me that since she has a couple of "no shows," I can fill out one of her agency's pay vouchers to make sure I get paid for the day then I need to go with the group that the director is going to look over. Roxanne tells me that tomorrow, they are doing night scenes and she can put me on the extras call sheet for that but I need to come by her office to sign with her agency first, the "Model's Guild Agency," so I can get future work. She gives me her business card. I tell her I will be there first thing in the morning. I fill out my voucher, and now… I am officially working in my first movie. Well, as soon as I find out what I will be doing.

I learn that the movie is called *The Beastmaster* starring Marc Singer, John Amos, Tanya Roberts, and Rip Torn. I've heard the name Rip Torn before but not sure who he is. Tanya Roberts I'm familiar with because I watch *Charlie's Angels* and she's the newest Angel. John Amos I know from the sitcom *Good Times* but mostly from his incredible portrayal of Toby (adult Kunta Kinte) in the epic miniseries *Roots*. Marc Singer I remember from the miniseries *Roots: The Next Generation*. I can't believe this. I absolutely loved both of the miniseries. To think I was watching them on TV at home in Minnesota just a few years ago, and now I will actually be working in a movie they are both in. Oh… my… gosh!!

The director eventually comes over and takes a glance at us and starts pointing saying, *"You and you and you and you,"* until he chooses about ten of us, one is myself. *"You are my farmers with Marc on the hill when we're ready. Wardrobe will be calling 'farmers' when they're ready, so stay alert."*

I'M GOING TO DO SOMETHING!!! Oh…my…gosh!!! Well, I'm going to be a farmer in a movie…that's enough for right now. I am so thrilled inside, but I try to act like everyone else. Based on conversations I've heard, most everyone is used to doing extra work and being in movies. This is nothing new for them. Me…?? There is so much excitement inside me right now. I have to keep it suppressed, but I can't wait to get home tonight and call Judi!

The caterers have already put tables out loaded with pastries, donuts, and such, nothing fancy. There's coffee, juices, milk, and various fruits for everyone—cast, crew, and extras. There's a lot of us, and they keep the tables full. That's good because I've started to get the munchies.

Before too long, I hear a "farmers" call to the wardrobe trailer. This is all so cool. I go with our small group, and we get fitted with a type of a tunic and loincloths. I learn very quickly that you can't be shy in a dressing trailer. We all strip in front of the wardrobe lady for our loincloths. Some of the guys have very nice bodies, and my mind goes straight to my inferior thoughts of, *fat ass, big butt* (although I'm not). Thank goodness for this pot, it helps to diminish those thoughts a little.

When we're dressed, we're taken a little further out from the village into the hills. I also learn there is a lot of waiting around that goes on during the making of a movie. Cameras and lighting have to be set. Waiting for the main actors to get through with makeup and wardrobe. The director and everyone involved behind the cameras getting into positions. When Marc, whose character is Dar, arrives on location, my mental jaw drops. He's just in his loincloth without his tunic. Extremely sexy! He has the kind of body I want. My mother wouldn't be calling me "fat ass" or "big butt" if I looked like that. We all meet and shake hands. Marc is very pleasant and friendly. And this man is gorgeous!

The director calls us together and sets the scene.

We are farmers from the village working the fields when we see the Juns (bad guys) heading toward our village. We know that's bad news, so we race toward the village with Dar in the lead.

Even though there will be sound recording, there will also be live verbal directions given that get edited out.

Of course, we won't actually see the Juns, we pretend we do. We don't actually see our village either, especially since they shot the burning of it the day before. I have always heard that movies get shot out of sequence. This is very interesting.

We do a lot more waiting then get called to makeup ourselves. Seems we need to get dirtied up, a little more, since we are farmers. The makeup person has a large portable makeup station. She and her assistant take us one at a time and sponge some dirt-looking makeup on our faces, arms, and legs. After we get made up, it's about time to get things rolling. We're given very crudely made wooden pitchforks and hoes to farm with. We go to the top of the hill where cameras are set to start. We will be farming, following verbal directions while cameras are rolling.

Now…they really don't say "lights, camera, action" it's more something like *"Ok…places everyone…Quiet on the set…Scene ##, take# (clapboard), Sound speed…aaaand…action"*

"You're farming…you're farming…you hear dog start barking (even though we don't) rush to the top with Dar. You see the Juns coming…aaaand cut. Let's do it again. This time I want to see a lot more of…Make sure you let Dar get to the top first. Okay, back to starting places everyone…Quiet on the set…Scene ##, take # (clapboard), Sound speed…aaaand…action"

Of course, when we get to the top and see the Juns, all we really see are the cameras and all the people behind the cameras. We will do this over and over and then over and over from different camera angles. The fun scene is the long shot we do as we're running down the hill toward the village. We did a number of "takes" on that one also, one of them being my fault. As we're running down the hill, camera panning us left to right, I trip myself up and fall undoing my loincloth. Luckily, there's always someone from makeup and wardrobe around to do touch-ups in between shots. I wander over to wardrobe to get myself tucked back in and safety pinned up and back to the hill to finish the shot. We get quite a bit of exercise, and it takes a good part of the morning to shoot this one small segment of that scene in the movie.

Caterers have tables ready for lunch, nothing fancy. Meat trays, box lunches, veggies, and drinks. Then the rest of the day, I'm in different wardrobe being a dead body as they finish up the burned village scene. Again, there is a lot of waiting in between shots setting up camera angles, smoke machines, lighting, etc. We finally finish up (a wrap for the day) just as it's starting to get dark, somewhere between 5:00 and 6:00 p.m. It has been a very long and incredibly exciting day soaking in and absorbing absolutely everything I could, watching all the different intricacies, firsthand, of a movie being made. Me, right here in person and now I am actually in my first movie! What a dream this day has been!

Judi gets an earful when I call her after I get home and washed up. She is genuinely excited and happy for me, more than I could ever think my mom would be, but I call her also and end up only being able to leave a message.

I go to the Models Guild Agency the next day and register with them. Roxanne has a meeting with me about her agency and things I will need to do. First and foremost, I need pictures, 8 x 10 headshots. I find out that working in Hollywood is not all that cheap. You need headshots, and that costs a good deal of money. I can make that happen, though.

Roxanne continues to get me work on *The Beastmaster*. I will usually smoke a little pot each day I work before I get to our parking area. Sometimes, I actually keep my little pipe and a small bag in my pocket. If I feel the need, I will smoke a little in the porta-potties. It seems to help me escape the insecure, inferior me that I believe myself to be. I am more comfortable around people. It really helps because I'm not as apprehensive when I actually get to meet John Amos when I work in the crowd scene at the pyramid and when we pull the bridge off the tar moat and cover the tar with dirt. John was a very nice guy. I mentioned to him that I loved his show *Good Times* and how incredible the miniseries *Roots* was. He said that Toby was an amazing role for him to be able to portray. There really wasn't a lot of time for chit chat, but for as big of an actor as I perceived him to be, he was just very down to earth and genuine. I also work on the night shoots for the same scene when the moat gets lit up. It gets very cold at night in the desert hills outside of Los Angeles in the winter. Under our robes, we were able to wear our regular street clothes, which helped to keep us a little warmer. They also kept a lot of coffee and hot chocolate at the catering tables through the night.

The most memorable day was when I get to work with Marc again. I call it the sword fight scene. I'm selected to be one of the Juns that captures the tiger. It was a tiger spray-painted black. I get a little different wardrobe and more dirty make up. I'm holding the rope that's wrapped around the tiger's neck then wrapped around the pole. Dar (Marc) comes onto the scene to rescue the tiger. I grab my sword, and with another Jun on the ground, we head toward Dar to square off. However, I get killed. There were other Juns on horseback that Dar had to kill. One of them got it right in the back with Dar's boomerang style weapon, the cappa. This is where my close up comes in. By the end of that "shoot," Marc's main shots were done, so he was already gone when the director needed a close up shot of Dar's hand pulling the cappa out of the dead Juns back. Enter my hand. They put Dar's leather wristband on me and told me what they wanted. The cappa was just stuck in a piece of balsa wood covered in black cloth for a close up no one would ever know. They needed my hand to go down at a certain angle with fingers spread just right. It took about five or six "takes" to get that one little shot "just right." That was my close up.

I only briefly got to meet Tanya Roberts during the pyramid shoot. We had just been standing around, waiting, and she was nearby waiting to go up on the pyramid. I just had to tell her I always watched *Charlie's Angels* and hated that it wasn't going to be on anymore. She gave me a polite *"Thank you"* and said she loved working on the show.

It was interesting doing the crowd scenes at the big pyramid, where they would do all the long shots, and you can see the people at the top of the pyramid. Off in a separate area, they have a mock up of the very top of the pyramid, maybe about eight to ten feet tall, and we can watch them do all the close-ups at the top of the pyramid.

All in all, I get about two weeks worth of work on *The Beastmaster*, my first movie. What an amazing experience this was. It was like living a dream, even though I was an extra. Although, I learn that extras are an important part of movies. Just being a tiny part of this was an incredible experience. The hustle and bustle. Make up, wardrobe. *"Action." "Cut." "That's a wrap for today. Good work, everyone."* Every day was usually a good twelve-hour day with a lot of waiting around that you get paid for and food. Just seeing how movies are made and the tricks used. A camera on the ground pointing up with the tiger on one side and a shovel full of raw meat on the other side to coax him into jumping over the camera for a close up of him made to look like he's jumping on or over someone. I was told by the trainer that they would have to make sure he was hungry before they could do these types of close up tricks. The little trick with the cappa in balsa wood for my hand close-up. During my sword fight scene, one of the ferrets runs away with an arrow. They had to use fish line tied to the arrow and the ferret to make it look like the ferret had it in its mouth. After this, I probably won't look at movies the same way anymore, I'll be wanting to pick apart the scenes in my head from now on. Anyway, shooting for *The Beastmaster* is done in Simi Valley. Now I'll have to wait for it to open in theaters some time later this year.

*****

The Beastmaster is released in theaters in August of that year, 1982. I am one of the first in line at the nearest theater. In the farming scene, I don't know which farmer is me, same as in the pyramid and moat scenes. I'm just part of the crowd but love knowing I'm a part of it. However, in the sword fight scene, oh my gosh! Oh my gosh! There I am, plain as day. Yep, that's me all right! That's me holding the tiger! That's me getting killed! (They actually brought in a stuntman for the short sword fight, and they dubbed in someone's voice for the "death yells.")

There it is! There it is! That's my hand! For a split second, you see the close-up of my hand pulling out the cappa. I wanted to jump up in the theater and tell everyone, *"That was my hand! That was my hand!"* I wanted to tell everyone that was me in the sword fight also, but that whole scene, after all the time it took to shoot, lasted maybe thirty seconds on screen. But hey, that was thirty seconds of me *and* a hand close-up! Eat your hearts out all you punks back in Minnesota!

*****

Me (one among the crowd scenes)/ *The Beastmaster*
1982 (Tanya Roberts, VW)

Livin' the Dream

℘ ℨ

P alm trees, beaches, mountains, sunshine every day, and warm weather all the time. In the wintertime, you can be at the beach part of the day, and if you want, you can be up at Big Bear or Lake Arrowhead in an hour and a half to go skiing.

Movie studios, Beverly Hills, Hollywood—the first time I go into Hollywood, I am awestruck just by the fact that "I am here!" I walk down Hollywood Boulevard looking at all the celebrities stars in the sidewalk, the famous footprints in front of the Manns Chinese Theater. This is bad. I'm acting like such a tourist, and this is going to be my home. I'm almost embarrassed. At least I don't have a camera with me. Too funny.

As I continue walking down Hollywood Boulevard, I'm actually surprised at how dirty the street and sidewalks are. There's trash all over the street and sidewalks, even though there are trash cans near every corner and in between. This doesn't really matter to me because I am just ecstatic to be here. There are homeless people. I feel bad for them but think that if things got so bad that I were to be homeless what better place to be than sunny southern California. I watch, with a great deal of empathy, while a homeless lady has an argument with the Security Pacific bank building, at the corner of Hollywood and Highland, and wonder what could happen in someone's life to get them to this point. There are street vendors hocking their wares, mostly fake gold bracelets and necklaces. Others are selling maps to the star's homes. Double deck tour busses are driving up and down.

I've traveled far enough down the Boulevard now that I can see the Hollywood sign. Yep, I'm here! Just a little further down and I'm at the famous Hollywood and Vine intersection. Just about a block up is the iconic Capitol Records building, and a little further down, the famous Pantages Theater. This is all just so amazing. I can't begin to really describe how exciting it is that I'm wandering around where I've dreamed of being my whole life.

I'm actually on a bigger mission today. A little further down is Gower Street. When I get there, I turn right, walk quite a few more blocks past Sunset and down to Santa Monica Boulevard. There are the walls that surround Paramount Studios. I walk around trying to figure out, *"How I am going to get inside?"*

The main entrance to the studio is actually further down around the corner on Melrose. When I see the main gates, I realize I'm not going to be able to just walk in that way. Back around where I came from are doors leading into the office areas. I go to one, open it, and walk in. That was easy, except that I can go no further without seeing the lady at the window. I take a quick look at the directory and tell the lady that, *"I'm here to see..."*

She asks if I have an appointment. Of course, I don't and she says I need one to enter. I say thank you and leave. I walk down along the low walls lined with trees and think, *The walls are taller than me but not by too much.* I look around, mostly to see if there are any security cameras. I don't really see any, so I hoist myself up onto a tree branch, climb a little higher to just above the wall, stretch my leg out real far, and take one giant step onto the top of the wall. I carefully lower myself on the other side and drop to the ground. I have just scaled the walls of Paramount Studios. I'm in and my heart is pounding. I know I shouldn't be doing this, but this is rather exciting. Quite the adventure.

Once I'm in, I glance around to make sure I'm not being rushed by anyone. The coast is clear, so I just start to casually walk around. I am fascinated with the back lot, the make-believe houses and streets that could be "Anywhere U.S.A." All the huge sound stages that look like airplane hangars. I actually walk into an open sound stage for the movie *Airplane II: The Sequel.* They have a set for an airport terminal built in part of the sound stage and a mock up of a cockpit in another area. I love just walking around feeling like I'm a part of it, wishing I was working here. Maybe I'll be "discovered" while I'm here. Ha, ha.

I walk around the lot some more and see the sound stages for the sitcoms *Happy Days* and *Laverne and Shirley.* "Oh, wow!" I love these shows. So does my mom. I walk across the lot. All the doors are shut, but I'm going to take a chance anyway. I try one of the doorknobs, and it turns. I cautiously open the door, being very watchful but nonchalant and remaining very composed, as if I do this every day. I go inside, and I'm behind the sets of *Happy Days* where all the dressing rooms are with their names: Tom Bosley, Marion Ross, Henry Winkler, Ron Howard, Erin Moran, and Scott Baio—Scott, of course, being my favorite. Who doesn't like Scott Baio? There is no one here, so I walk around the sets of the Cunningham's living room, Fonzie's apartment, Al's Drive-In, breathing it in and fantasizing about being on the show. I come out of my little daydream because I need to keep moving on. There is so much to see. I appropriate a couple of *Happy Days* items as collectible souvenirs, tuck them inside my shirt and pants pocket, and head next door to the *Laverne and Shirley* sound stage. I don't get far in here. I have to walk past dressing rooms to get to the sets, but one of the doors is open, and a radio is playing. There is no way I can sneak past this, so with my heart pounding, I casually walk to the dressing room, and inside is David L. Lander, who portrays "Squiggy" on the show. I need to stay relaxed and spontaneous, so I politely say hello, and I can't help but to tell him that I love the show and my mother especially loves him and, keeping my nerves in check… *"Could I get your autograph for her please?"* He's really nice, gives me an autograph signed to my mom, but tells me that I really shouldn't be here. I tell him, *"I know but I really just had to see. Thank you for the autograph."* I turned around and left the sound stage and started walking across the lot again. It wasn't long before two security officers came up to me and asked to see a studio ID. Of course, I didn't have one, and they knew I wouldn't, so they escorted me to the main gates and off the lot. No trouble, just a polite escort out. This has been an amazingly exhilarating day.

*****

Eventually, I will become friends with Lucy Casado, the owner of the restaurant, Lucy's El Adobe, which is directly across from the main entrance to Paramount Studios. I help care for Lucy's son

Darryl at the facility I work at. Lucy is acquainted with just about every celebrity you can imagine and many political figures dating as far back as JFK. Her restaurant has a wall plastered with their signed pictures. Through Lucy, I will meet the likes of Emmy award-winning actress, Betty Thomas, from the Emmy award-winning TV drama *Hill Street Blues*, award-winning pop/country artist Nicolette Larson, Grammy winner Linda Ronstadt, Golden Globe and Emmy winner Danny DeVito and his wife Emmy winner Rhea Perlman.

*****

I will also have the privilege of meeting the very good-looking, incredibly athletic, Olympic decathlon gold medal winner, Bruce Jenner, at a celebrity golf tournament raising money for the handicapped and disabled children. One of the kids I took with me to the tournament, John, is a big fan of Bruce's. Bruce was a great guy and said, *"Since you have a camera, why don't you take a picture of the two of us."* I was glad he offered because I was a bit starstruck, a bit enamored, and a bit intimidated by him that I was afraid to ask.

*****

Bruce Jenner and John. Another one of our
kids (another John) in the back.

*****

I find out where the sets are for *Little House on the Prairie* in another area of the hills just outside of Simi Valley. It's quite a hike through private property to get there, but I am determined to see Walnut Grove. It's at least a mile hike before I come upon the Ingalls house. Of course, it's a façade, but I have to look inside anyway. It's just used for storage. Once a week, since the show started, Michael Landon and Melissa Gilbert take us back to the 1800s, and the opening credits always start right here on the Ingalls farm. Further down the road is the Garvey's house and even further is the actual town of Walnut Grove. It's like a fantasy walking around the outdoor set of a TV show I love so much. Favorite episodes come flooding into my mind. I would love to be able to find work on this show.

What I'm not aware of is that there is a security trailer near the "town" with round the clock security. Each building facade I enter sets off an alarm the second I open a door. They finally catch up to me when I'm in Walnut Grove, and they tell me they've been looking for me ever since I first opened the Ingalls house. I don't get in trouble, they just drive me back to where I first came onto the property.

I do, at one time, meet Kevin Hagen, who plays Doc Baker. I was auditioning for the musical *The Sound of Music* at a dinner theater in Woodland Hills on Ventura Boulevard, and he was there to audition also. I got a little star struck because I've watched him for so many years. I got to read a scene opposite him as Rolf and he as Captain Von Trapp. I was excited when we met, but he brought me down to earth when he told me he was, *"Just another actor trying to stay working."*

*****

From then on, I would keep my outward enthusiasm down when I met anyone big or famous.

*****

For the next six years, I get a lot of work as an extra on many movies, commercials, or music videos. Roxanne is good at making sure my headshots get submitted for various roles for any project to get me work. Sometimes, I find my own casting calls through film industry trade magazines.

One time, I manage to get an audition for a yet untitled Francis Ford Coppola film. For me, it was a fiasco. I was slightly stoned, and I don't think the script we read from was even for that film. I couldn't get my head together for the cold reading. Even having smoked some weed, I still felt very insecure next to the extremely good-looking guys I was reading with. Even though I don't know what the casting people are looking for, I just assume the better-looking guys are going to get it and that counts me out. On top of the fact that this is a Coppola project and my anxieties were running high. The weed wasn't working with me too well that day.

Another time I find there is going to be an open casting call for the TV series *Fame*. The movie was incredible, and I would love to have a shot at the series. Open casting calls are sometimes referred to as "cattle calls," and that's exactly what this one was. Hundreds of us lined around the block near the studios, literally hundreds. Everyone wanted to be in *Fame*. *Fame* was so huge that there were local network news stations outside interviewing people. I didn't get interviewed, but I made darn sure I got in front of one of the cameras, mostly because I knew I didn't stand a chance in hell to win a role for this show.

It was a very long day as they slowly filed us in groups into holding areas inside where we would hand in our resume and 8 x 10 headshots then wait to be called to audition. Once inside, it's a rather quick process because there are so many people. Read…sing…and/ or dance, depending on which talent(s) you wanted to showcase. I did all three. Of course, I'm not a professional dancer, but for a show, I can mimic and learn pretty quickly. It also gave me the opportunity to meet, well, introduce myself and audition for the incredibly multitalented Debbie Allen, the star of the movie and the series.

That open casting (cattle) call was quite an experience. Of course, I did smoke some weed that morning just before I got there. I'm still very intimidated by others, and it mellows me. Needless to say that out of the hundreds, I didn't get a callback. However, the day had not been a complete washout because I did end up with a cameo appearance on the news that night.

*****

I'm never happy with my own pictures/headshots because I always see the person I grew up believing I was, but if there's a camera around filming, I will do what I can to position myself and make sure I'm somewhere within that cameras frame.

*****

One memorable project Roxanne got me work on was a two-day shoot for a music video working with Ashford and Simpson for their song "Count Your Blessings." I am mostly familiar with who they are due to their hit song "Solid" (Solid as a Rock). I love that song! I had heard stories of theirs being one of Hollywood's long-standing, solid as a rock marriages. They were an absolutely amazing couple to work with. Watching them work together, you could see how much in love they were with each other. It was beautiful. The funny thing is that most people don't realize that music videos are lip-synced to the already recorded song. The two of them would keep forgetting the words to their song. A good portion of the time was "cut… rewind… retake." They would get a little frustrated but had a good time with it.

The song didn't hit big on the charts. I thought it was a great song, but then I might be a little biased since I worked on the video for two days. The only time I saw the video was one day, months after the shoot, when I was walking through Macy's. They had TV's in the corners up near the ceiling always playing VH1 or MTV when I heard a very familiar song. I looked up and there it was, the video for "Count Your Blessings." I watch it, and…yep, there I am! It's always interesting how much of a two-day shoot gets edited down to a three-minute video, but nonetheless, there I was.

*****

Back then, VH1 and MTV strictly played music videos back to back all day long.

While writing this book, all I have to do these days is YouTube the video and the memories flood back. Both days of shooting, I was a little stoned. Aaah… but I wasn't the only one.

*****

Other little projects were a Public Service Announcement for a major beer distributor. A Spanish Mcdonald's commercial. A commercial for Redken Beauty Products that we shot at the mansion, in Beverly Hills, of co-founder Paula Kent Meehan.

Redken had come out with a new hair mousse. For the commercial, we were at a fancy, intimate, dinner party when the butler brings out the highly anticipated dessert on a silver tray under a dome. When he lifts the dome, there it is…ahh…chocolate mousse (the bottle of the new hair mousse). It is another fun two day-shoot. Commercials always seem to take two days. It was the first time I had ever been in a mansion. We were such a small group that Paula told us to feel free to look around. The fireplaces in the house were so big you could stand in them. Koi ponds, pool, and tennis courts are outside. What a way to live. I never did see that commercial, though.

I was honored to meet the legendary George Burns when I get a week's worth of work on his movie *Oh, God! You Devil*, part three of the *Oh, God!* franchise.

The comedy *Surf II* did not do well at the box office in any respect. There was never a *Surf I*, but I did get to work with the very hilarious Ruth Buzzi. I know her best from her years, during the late sixties and early seventies, on the comedy variety show *Laugh In*. I would later run into her again at a party at a friend's house in Woodland Hills.

*****

I briefly get to meet the beautiful Valerie Bertinelli while working on the film *Another High Roller*, which was later changed to *The Seduction of Gina*. I used to watch her all the time in the sitcom *One Day at a Time*, and she is married to the incredible guitarist/rocker, Eddie Van Halen.

One of the most grueling days working on that was when we were shooting a full day inside a bar in Culver City. We're wearing winter attire, under hot lights, smoke machines going, drinking "near beer" and eating stale popcorn, while outside the temperature in surrounding LA is in the nineties. For the movie, it's supposed to be wintertime somewhere in the north.

Sometimes, as an extra, you can be treated "less than" by some celebrities, which is fine because I'm still getting paid, but Valerie Bertinelli treated everyone with such respect, almost like you were a friend of hers.

*****

I met Treat Williams while working on the film *Dempsey*, the story of Jack Dempsey. I'm just part of the crowd in one of the boxing matches. I was not familiar with him before this film.

What was ironic about this movie is that when I saw it on TV, I recognized another actress in it. I'm certain I know that face. I do some research and find out it's a lady I had worked with on stage in *A Midsummer's Night Dream*, in Minnesota. Lana Schwab (she changed her name), I called her family back home to track her down out here, and she has been doing quite well herself. She got her start in *Twilight Zone: The Movie*.

*****

I didn't get to meet Gary Busey but was in some scenes with him in the movie *The Bear*, the story of coach Bear Bryant. I was one of the male cheerleaders of an opposing team during a big game sequence. Even if I don't get to meet one of the stars of the movie I'm working on, it's still amazing just being able to work on a film, being in front of the cameras and around all the action.

*****

The film I believe I had the most fun on was *Back to School* with Rodney Dangerfield and Robert Downey Jr. I only know about this movie because a female friend of mine has an uncle who is an art director on the film. I hear the band Oingo Boingo is going to be in it also.

Rodney Dangerfield is a renowned comedian, and Robert Downey Jr. I've only seen in *Weird Science*. *Back to School* also stars Billy Zabka from *The Karate Kid*, and Keith Gordon whom I was familiar with from the Stephen King movie *Christine*. But Oingo Boingo is really the reason I want to try to get work on the film. I think their music is hot. They also did the music for *Weird Science*. Would love to be able to meet them. I talk to Roxanne, and she's able to get me some work on the film.

There are two most memorable scenes for me working on this film, one being "registration day." We're actually shooting in some public building in Burbank whose interior resembles that of a college. All day long we're up and down the stairs, back and forth across the lobby. *"Action"*... *"Cut"*... *"Action"*... *"Cut"*... up and down the stairs and a lot of waiting in between. However, I do get a nice close up as I'm walking behind Rodney Dangerfield and Burt Young while they're talking at the bottom of the stairs. Then just a lot of orderly disorder for the rest of that scene.

The other *most* memorable scene for me is the party scene. It wasn't too bad spending a couple days on the sound stage at MGM with Oingo Boingo, dancing while listening to "It's a Dead Man's Party" over and over. The dorm set for the party was so cool. During one of our many breaks to reset lights and cameras, I wandered to the restroom off of the soundstage. While I was in there, one of the stars of the movie came in. It was just me and him, and straight out, he asks me, *"Hey, man, you got any blow?"* First time we meet and he just casually asks, *"Hey, man, you got any blow?"*

I was taken aback, caught off guard, surprised, but without even thinking, I said, *"No, but I've got some weed. Never go anywhere without it."*

He said, *"Could really use some blow, but that'll work."*

I loaded my pipe, and we lit up right there in the bathroom. It wasn't my first trip to that bathroom. We chatted just a little about the movie and the scene we were shooting. How cool it is that Oingo Boingo is here, but dancing at a club when stoned, or wired on blow, is more fun. He wasn't a big star or anything, so it was kind of like catching a buzz with a friend. The next day, he came on set with the party favors he preferred, and I got to "hang out" with him a bit again.

*****

Years down the road, I become a fan of his. I see him and his run-ins in the tabloids and hear about him on the news. I follow his rise to stardom ultimately leading to an Academy Award. I never did get to actually meet Oingo Boingo, those days at the studio, but it was cool and a lot of fun to be on the same set with them. And we got to listen to "It's a Dead Man's Party" over and over and over.

*****

Craig Walter

Height: 5'10" / Weight: 150 lbs.

Now, I never did anything big myself, but I would have to say that the absolute highlight of my years working in the industry would culminate with the open call for a big national commercial that I went on. A long line of people with pictures and resumes similar to the open call for *Fame* but not quite the "cattle call" as *Fame* was, possibly because no one knew what the commercial was or who the commercial was for. Even though the casting call was hyped up a bit, any specific details about the commercial were being kept secret. Roxanne informed me about this one.

It's a fairly long line of hopefuls stretching out the back door of an office and down a back alley, but it moves fairly quickly. You NEVER know what they're looking for at a casting call. I'm always checking out the other guys in lines at casting calls thinking *"Yeah… he's really good looking. He'll make it. I wish I was that good looking."* or *"Those guys have really nice bodies. The way they look in their clothes… I don't stand a chance"* My mind always gets mired up in comparing myself to others. I always lose. I'm sure glad I smoked a little weed before I got in line.

When I do get into the back door, I can see up ahead at a table they're just taking our pictures and resumes. Most are being told, *"Thank you, we'll be in touch."* Some, not many, are being told to go see "so and so" down the hall. I've heard the *"we'll be in touch"* line many times before. I'm always guessing they're looking for "good-looking," so I always cancel myself out but go through the motions anyway. You never know. When I get to the table, I'm ready to say *"Thank you"* in return, but they look at my picture, look at me, and say, *"Go see 'so and so' down the hall."*

Okay, my heart is pounding! There have been a lot of people told "Thank you," and I get told to go down the hall. I'm directed into a room and given some papers to fill out. Some others are doing the same thing. Then we're told we are in the commercial and to just make ourselves comfortable for a while until they have finished looking at everyone. Someone asks what the commercial is for, but we're told we will all be told when they have everyone they need.

We're only in there for about an hour, but in that hour, there's a lot of excited chatter and speculation about what it could be that's so big and so secretive and we are going to be a part of. A person from casting finally comes in to give us instructions and a map. *"It will be a two-day shoot."* Commercials always seem to be two days. *"Call is at five o'clock tomorrow morning downtown at the Shrine Auditorium."* Wow! Cool! The Shrine is where they host some of the big awards shows—Oscars, Emmy's, the Grammy's. I will actually be inside where all of everybody who is anybody gathers for these shows. *"Wardrobe is your own. Where what you would wear if you were going to a rock concert. This is a national Pepsi commercial featuring Michael Jackson and his brothers. This is the first time the Jackson Five have been reunited, and this commercial is to promote their 'Victory Tour'."*

Okay…Okay…Okay….What did she just say…??? Michael Jackson…!!! The Jackson Five…!!! I'm going to be working on a commercial with…OH MY GOSH…!!! This is the biggest "OH MY GOSH" ever for me!!! There is an excited buzz all around the room. I cannot wait to call Judi tonight!

"Show up on time and be ready to work and have fun." That's it. Casting is complete, and we're sent on our way. OH MY GOSH!!! This is totally radical.

There's about thirty, maybe forty of us? We are all on time. I generally don't bring a camera when I'm working on something; *The Beastmaster* was the only time because it was my first movie. I don't think I should have a camera, but I am not going to miss out on an opportunity like this. Michael's about the biggest thing around and him with his brothers all together. I took a Kodak 110 camera with me because it was slim, and I could slide it down inside my pants so no one would notice. And I'm feeling pretty good, as usual.

The day is like any other shoot. A lot of waiting, but when we get started, we're moving. The stage is set as if the Jackson's were giving a concert. We're doing all the close-up shots. We are part of the "fake" audience, and we have to sing "You're the Pepsi generation" to the beat of Michael's "Billie Jean." We even have cue cards to sing from. At the ever so familiar words *"…rolling aaaand action,"* The Jackson's come running out on stage with everyone, cheering, going crazy, and singing to the prerecorded music. With all the commotion going on, I reach down my pants, pull my camera out and up to my eye, zero in and snap two quick shots and then… PANIC! Michael looked right at me when the flash went off. Everyone kept performing until we heard, *"Cuuut!!"* Then I thought I was a dead man! Any buzz I might still have is gone. This is a definite "buzz kill." For whatever it would be worth, I hid my camera in an inconspicuous place near the stage. I thought for sure I would be confronted and, at worst, possibly kicked off the shoot. But nothing ever happened. Either way, I didn't dare risk any more pictures for the rest of the day.

However, at the first real break, I would find a quiet place to light up a bowl and regain that lost buzz. And of course, I'm not the only one who knows how to find these "quiet places."

We spent most of the morning shooting and reshooting and singing and singing to the Jackson's coming on stage from every angle. After we break for lunch, we do all the backstage shooting. A handful of us are selected to act as hair and makeup people in the dressing room shots while a small group of us, myself included, are to be backstage groupies for the shots when they go running onto the stage.

They're setting up the backstage shots, marking our places so it looks like a crowd but leaving enough room for the Jacksons to come through. Places have to be marked since we do a number of takes. I'm backing up so my place can be marked, I bump into someone, turn around instinctively, kind of laughingly, saying, *"Oops, I'm sorry."*

A very soft voice replies, *"It's all right."* He holds out his hand and says, *"Hi, I'm Michael."*

OH MY GOSH!!! Okay... this is an even bigger "'Oh my gosh'" now than my last biggest "Oh My Gosh" when I got on this commercial! Michael didn't even have his glove on yet. It was a very soft, gentle handshake. Not like I would expect, but... I just shook Michael Jackson's bare hand. Okay, I am like so totally star struck now. Outwardly, I maintain, inside I am so "WOW!! OH MY GOSH!!" and thinking about the pictures I took earlier. *"It's incredible to be able to work with you! I love your music!"* Boy, did I just sound stupid or what!

Michael replies with a simple but humble, *"Thank you."*

Wow! Then a voice yells out, *"Places everybody!"* And that was it. That was the extent of my meeting Michael Jackson, and there was not a word mentioned of my picture taking earlier.

The rest of our long day was shooting backstage and dressing rooms. Friday's shoot would be a late call, 3:00 p.m. The Shrine will be filled up for tomorrow night's shoot. It seems radio stations have been giving away free tickets all day to fill the Shrine to make it look like a real concert. I know people will do anything to see Michael, but it will be interesting to see how a crowded auditorium reacts to "take after take after take." I have retrieved my camera by the end of the day, and of course, I am going to call Judi the second I get home. It has been an amazing day!

Friday's shoot starts out exciting. We know it's not a real concert, but the auditorium will be packed and filled with the frenzied enthusiasm of a few thousand Jackson fans. By the time we, the paid actors, get there, people have already been lining up out front. We, of course, get to use the more prestigious rear entrance. Before the general audience is allowed in, the director, Bob Geraldi, goes over instructions. Most of us will remain in the front. A few of us will be dispersed throughout the audience and given auto flashes to give the appearance of flash photography. I am one of those people. I was hoping to remain up front but think this might be better since I actually have my camera with me. Up front might be too risky after my close call yesterday. I get placed about ten rows back, which is not bad at all. I would have to pay good money for a seat like this if it were a real concert. Instead, I'm being paid for this.

The general public is slowly ushered in. After everyone is seated, the director explains to everyone how the evening will proceed. The probability of retakes, time to reset the stage, doing the same thing over and over, this is prerecorded music, please be patient and with each new "take," show the same amount of enthusiasm and excitement every time. This is "The Jacksons!" The audience is definitely excited. I'm excited, even though I went through this yesterday. With the Shrine filled to capacity, there is so much "Jackson" energy in the air.

When we get rolling, everything is going great. It's incredible, all the lights and the explosions going off on stage! I am in awe so much that I couldn't take my eyes off all the action and just kept waving the auto flash around in the air while I kept pushing the flash button. I didn't want to miss a thing on stage. We were told earlier that it was going to be pretty spectacular. This was totally radical! The audience is perfect. The Shrine filled with screams of excitement when the Jacksons come running out. Calm and patient in between takes while everything gets reset. The pyrotechnics take the longest to reset. Then they are full of massive amounts of energy when the cameras are rolling again.

I am so awestruck and caught up in the excitement of acting as if this is a real concert that I keep forgetting that my camera is in my pocket. Finally, around the sixth tape, I pull my camera out. I know how the scene runs, so I wait for the lights to open at the top of the staircase, on stage, to the silhouette of Michael's pose while the explosions of the pyrotechnics start going off all around him. Since I've already seen it a few times, I just put my eye to the lens and *click, click, click*, and all of a sudden, there's a huge commotion on stage. I pull my camera down to see some people on stage have rushed Michael, and it looks like they've taken him down. Wild screams of panic have suddenly filled the air throughout. Pandemonium erupts all over the auditorium. It's almost as if a President had just been assassinated. No one knows what has happened. Confusion, panic, and fear are so prevalent all through the Shrine Auditorium. Girls are screaming and crying in hysterics.

The commotion on stage is subsiding a little, and the crowd surrounding Michael moves off stage, with Michael in the middle of them, and someone comes out on stage with a microphone to calm everyone down. There is now an eerie silence throughout the auditorium as we all wait to hear what has just happened. We are not being told anything, "Everyone, please remain calm, everything is going to be all right." I move a few rows back to the front with the rest of my people, and security starts to systematically, row by row, clear out the Shrine Auditorium except for those of us who are working. I think we have only been shooting for a couple hours or so. I'm told that some of the rest of the Jackson family were seated not too far behind us. Would have been cool to meet them.

After the Shrine is cleared, we are kept back for another hour and are told that Michael's hair had caught fire from one of the explosions and had been taken to the hospital.

We finally get to leave around ten o'clock. As I race home to call Judi, I also search frantically for a One-Hour Photo shop that is still open. I manage to find one just before they close. I won't get them in one hour, but I tell the man how important they are and what they are of. I will be back first thing in the morning to pick them up. When I get home, I call Judi and, just about anyone else I know, spreading the story before it hits the airwaves as if I was some Hollywood gossip columnist.

When I get up in the morning, I see the *LA Times*. The story is big. There is a picture of Michael coming down the staircase with a glow behind his head. I rush to pick up my pictures that has Thursday and Friday's shoot on them. Thursday's two pictures came out okay. There's Michael and one of his brothers looking right at me. The second picture shows another brother looking at me. Fridays pictures... Oh my gosh...perfect sequence of Michael coming down the stairs. The last picture looks strangely very similar to the one in the *LA Times*.

*****

The Pepsi commercial, January 26 and 27, 1984, is not the last thing I work on, but it was by far the biggest thing I ever worked on. Meeting Michael, working with the Jacksons was incredible on top of being a part of something that made the news worldwide.

I will end up going to the "Victory Tour" concert three times.

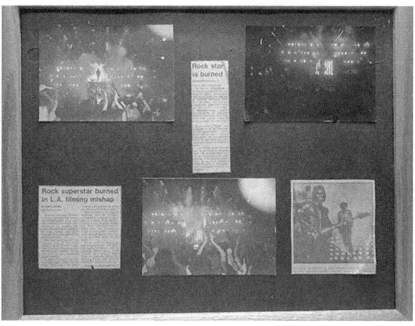

Living a Lie
(My Two Life's)

୫୦ ୦ଌ

I certainly was living the dream or so I liked to think. When I would call home, I played up all the extra work making it sound more glamorous than it truly was. It was exciting to me, but I made it out to be way more exciting to everyone else, mostly to make myself feel important. I was important. Movies need extras. However...I was never as important as I liked to think I was or as I wanted to make others believe.

*****

I don't stay in Simi Valley for very long, only a couple months. I started to feel suffocated by religion. Their house was a godly house, but I wanted to live life. I wanted to experience and see all sorts of things. Everything.

While working on *The Beastmaster*, I make some on set acquaintances, and through idle chitchat, I start to find out about nightclubs in West Hollywood. Rage, Mother Lode, Studio One, the kind of nightclubs that are intriguing to me due to the patronage I hear they attract and I decide I'm going to take some evening trips into West Hollywood to check them out.

It was those late nights that prompted a "talking to" by David's parents. Their home is a Christian home, and my late nights out are not cohesive with their Christian faith. I understand that. They have taken me in. They are my hosts. I need to be sensitive and respectful to their beliefs. I'm embarrassed that I may not have been. And I'm embarrassed about where I've been, that they don't know about, that would definitely conflict with their beliefs. I thank them for their generosity and let them know I will be moving out. Besides, I really don't want to feel like I'm being smothered by religion, especially this kind that talks in a funky weird language, they call "speaking in tongues," and casting out of demons you can't see… so how do you know they're out or if they were ever really there.

I have made a handful of friends while working with the children, and for a period of time, I am afforded a couch at someone's home, here and there.

My first couch will be at Jill's house, she still lives at home. Her parents are cool with that. They say they're used to their kids bringing home friends to crash from time to time. It also helps keep me in a little tighter with Jill's brother who can supply me with weed whenever I want, as long as I have the cash, that is. We're tight but not that tight. He is also the person that introduces me to a "head shop" that sells all sorts of (drug) paraphernalia, as long as you call it by its proper name. For instance, a "bong" is called a "water pipe." If not, then you're asked to leave the store. Slang terms indicate that the merchandise will be used for illegal purposes. I learn quite a bit from him.

I decide I'm close to wearing out my welcome, not really, but that's what I say when I realize through people at work that Jill has a crush on me and I need an excuse to "exit" the premises. Besides, it's Jill's very cute pot dealing brother that I have a small crush on, and that part of my life is still a deep secret. This makes it very easy to leave with no hard feelings and everyone still friends. Their parents tell me that the couch is always there if I'm ever in a bind.

Ironically, I'm also the love interest of someone else at work. My supervisors thirteen-year-old daughter, Rene, has a crazy crush on me. She makes me cards and even went as far as to make me a cake for my birthday. She's really sweet, and I'm flattered, but if she ever found out about my secret life, I think she would be so crushed. Although when she asked, I did promise to go to her senior prom with her. It would make her day and her life, if her mother offered me a couch.

There will be about three other couches I crash on, through friends at work, for about a month at a time. During this time, dreams of my mother chasing me have started to come back on occasion. I always wake up in a panic and sweaty. It's very unnerving and difficult to go back to sleep, but when I wake up in the morning, I can never remember anything beyond being chased. It will usually bother me through part of the morning, and I struggle trying to remember more of the dream to make some sense, but I always end up, somehow, just pushing it out of my mind. Interesting that I never had these dreams when I was at David's parents' house.

Despite my couch hopping for a while, I'm still working with the kids, getting work as an extra as often as I can and learning to use the LA Rapid Transit District (RTD), the city bus service that crisscrosses throughout the entire city, and San Fernando Valley, to get you literally within a couple blocks from where your destination is. It just takes a little more time, so I have to schedule carefully. The bus is inexpensive, so I'm able to start saving a decent amount of money.

Before long, with all the movie work and the kids, I'm able to buy myself a used "narc" car. It even has the holes next to the sideview mirrors where the police spotlights used to be mounted. Shortly thereafter, I get my first apartment. It is not cheap, even for The Valley in Canoga Park. Twelve hundred dollars a month for a two bedroom one bath, but it's nice. I'm feeling rather proud.

I make two very good friends, through working with the kids, Andrea and her husband Don. My first very cherished friendship in LA. Aside from his job, Don plays drums in a country band. They have two small children of their own, Jacob and Conner, that I would babysit on occasion. I will become Uncle Craig to the boys. Jacob and Conner look up to me, love when I babysit, and that always made me feel very good inside. I spoil them like crazy with lots of hugs all the time. Our friendship is so close that they know about my childhood, but I would be destroyed and devastated if Andrea and Don found out about my deep personal secret.

There would be times when they would find another babysitter on a Friday or Saturday night and Andrea would gather some of our friends from work and we would head to whatever country bar Don was playing at that weekend. Of course, being uneasy in a crowded social situation, I would always make my way to the bar rather quickly.

*****

Things are going good. I love working with the kids. The feeling that I'm being of some nurturing benefit to these children and giving them the love and attention they desperately need is so fulfilling. I love making each one of them feel that they are special. They satisfy a deep emotional need inside me that was never touched while growing up in an abusive home. A need to be able to give and share love from within me at the same time allowing myself to receive the love coming from these children. A love that does not have conditions attached to them. I grew up not feeling loved and, as such, not being able to express love. This is a very safe way of experiencing both the need to receive and the need to give.

On the days that I get movie work, I'm continually enthralled by just being around all the action, even though as extras, we spend a lot of time sitting around in between takes. The atmosphere of just being on a set and around the stars is intoxicating in its own way, and a little pot always enhances that feeling.

I also have such incredible self-image issues any time I'm on a set, on location, or a casting call. Even though the weed I smoke calms my mind about it, I still have to look in the mirror when I'm not under the influence and I see a "fat ass, big butt, good for nothing." I'm five foot ten inches and weigh one hundred fifty pounds. I know I'm not a "fat ass, big butt," but through my mind's eyes, I see what I have been told I am. Remembering Marc Singer, on the set of *The Beastmaster*, and how I want to look, I decide that since I'm finally settled and on some solid ground, I'm going to join a gym.

I am determined that I will not allow myself to look anything like what my mother has always said of me, so I join a well-known franchised gym and begin a solid regimen of cardio and weights. Slow at first, of course, because I'm a little soft. Not fat, just not muscular. I'm very shy about my body, especially in the locker room, but

I watch other people, guys that have what I want, and I put together my own solid routine. I am going to sweat! I am going to work! I refuse to be what my mother has always said of me! I work out five to seven days a week at the gym and sometimes at home in my apartment. At home, I just do supplementary push-ups and sit-ups.

The company my best friend Ken works for has transferred him to LA for a short time. One time that Ken was over to my place, watching me do my at home workout and holding my ankles to assist my sit-ups, commented, *"You have muscles in your abs I didn't even know we had."* I liked hearing that, but no matter how hard I worked, I could see it in the mirror, but my mind would still tell me otherwise. I will continue to push myself. I drop to one hundred forty pounds of very lean muscle and maintain a twenty-nine-inch waist. One time while talking with a trainer at the gym, he took some measurements and my weight and said I was at a six percent body fat. I liked the sound of that. I'm sure my cigarette and pot smoking helps me to stay at this size. I always smoke a bowl before I get to the gym. It not only helps my shyness but it also helps me to just zone out and focus. I will usually indulge in a Hershey almond bar for energy before my workout.

I quickly find out that the gym is a very cruisy place and I'm being subtly checked out quite a bit by various guys every time I'm there. Good-looking, muscular guys. I'm not sure what they're seeing because I'm never really quite happy with what I see, but I do like the subdued attention, and I always give a subtle smile and a nod back. My membership allows me access to the gym on the other side of The Valley in North Hollywood and the one in Hollywood. They are all cruisy.

*****

My introduction to the dance clubs came when I was still living in Simi Valley, which then prompted my moving out of David's parents' house due to my late nights. I had found my way into West Hollywood to check out the clubs I had heard about and ever since then West Hollywood has become my playground.

Studio One was the first—my first club. I was very nervous at the time because I was still not comfortable with myself, my body or my sexuality and from what I heard, these are gay clubs. I know I'm not straight because I've never been attracted to girls "that way," only guys. These dance clubs are supposed to be frequented by mostly men, which sounds so cool, but how can I be gay? I can't be. I'm not supposed to be. But I'm so intrigued and curious that I just have to check them out.

Traffic along Santa Monica Boulevard is extremely heavy on weekend nights. Finding parking where you don't have to pay and where you won't get a ticket is nearly impossible without having to walk a few blocks back to where all the action is. I take the walk, but before I leave my car, I smoke a heavily packed bowl of weed. I know I'm going to need this going into completely foreign and unfamiliar territory, but I'm excited at the same time.

I'm feeling really good, and when I get about a block away, I can already hear the music coming from inside the club, and there's a long line to get in. I'm uncomfortable waiting in line by myself because there are so many good-looking people, and I'm certain they are giving me the "look over" ending up with bad reviews. Once I get inside, though, my whole world is transformed. It's so loud…and people everywhere. Lights are flashing, strobing, spinning, a machine shooting jets of mist onto everyone on the dance floor creating an almost hypnotic, illusionary fog effect. A pounding, pulsing beat of high energy dance music that seems to resonate and reverberate through every fiber of my being. This whole scene is intoxicating. It's crazy, being high and feeling all this is wild. I feel like I'm part of the world now. I feel like I belong.

It's a mixed crowd, men and women, but mostly men. Good-looking men. The women are beautiful also, but my interest, of course, is in the guys. Immediately, I'm being "checked out," given the "once over" as I squeeze my way through the crowd. It's packed. I see one of the bars and make my way toward it. I'm starting to feel self-conscious around all these great-looking guys, and I know that a drink on top of my weed buzz will help me to loosen up a little bit more. The bartender sets down a drink for the guy next to me. "Long

Island Ice Tea. That'll be…" I don't know drinks, and that one looks good, so when the bartender asks me, I just tell him, "A Long Island Ice Tea," as if I order them all the time. I was hooked with my first sip. It's fairly potent, so I try to drink it slowly as I start to mingle.

I'm stunned that there are so many men and some women in one place that are gay, and there doesn't seem to be anything wrong with that. Maybe I'm worrying about myself too much. I also see that straight people come to these clubs and don't have any issues. That's interesting and somewhat confusing but also very cool.

Guys start coming up to me, very good-looking guys, wanting to dance, wanting to buy me drinks, wanting to talk. Of course, the music is deafening, so you have to go out to the patio where it's not so noisy and you don't have to yell. I'm a little embarrassed by this atten-tion, but these "Ice Teas" are definitely getting rid of my inhibitions and insecurities. I actually feel kind of normal. I even get on the dance floor. It was great. I have never danced outside of the theater, and this makes me feel alive, like I have never felt before. People want to dance with me. I didn't even know I could dance. I seem to be attractive to many. By the time it's last call at the bar and then the club closing for the night, I'm fairly inebriated and feeling on top of the world. I have never felt so normal and popular. Out of many, I finally accept an extremely handsome guy's invite to his home in Beverly Hills.

I don't get home until after four o'clock in the morning. I had a great time and somehow managed to get home in one piece and into bed. Something was looking out for me. When I wake up later that morning, no longer under the influence and mostly clearheaded, I look in the mirror and staring back at me is that worthless, good for nothing, won't amount to anything, fat ass, big butt. But I was admired and well-liked by many last night. I felt like I had finally fit in somewhere. I belonged. On the other hand, I'm also feeling guilty. I'm confused. But the attention I got I loved!

*****

By day, I was living a very straight life. I only smoked pot when I worked on a movie or when I went out to the clubs. Drinking was strictly a weekend thing at the clubs. Nobody, my friends nor my coworkers, knew I had a secret life. Ken is the only person I have confided in. It was scary because he's been my very best friend for years, but he mentioned that he had always figured as much. Although I have a very difficult time accepting it myself, Ken remained a steadfast friend.

The Dark Side

ℰ℧ ℭ℞

Santa Monica Boulevard, heading west toward Beverly Hills, is lined with bars and clubs—Studio One, Rage, Motherlode, Gold Coast, Revolver, and Micky's. West Hollywood has become my main stomping ground. I work with the kids or movies during the week, the gym every evening. I know I'm cut, but I don't "know" that I'm cut, so I'm always checking my backside, making sure I don't have what my mother says I have, but I think I'm pumped and ready for the weekend.

I start going out to the clubs every weekend. I'm always a little quiet and uncomfortable at first until I get a little (sometimes a lot) of weed, "Ice Tea's," tequila shots with beer chasers, or vodka 7's into my body, then I can loosen up, and I start to feel normal. Not the ugly worthless thing imbedded in the back of my mind so long ago. I can let people come up to me, and before I know it, I'm talking and carrying on.

It doesn't take too long until the pulsing beat of the music, the excitement, the energy of the crowd. My slight intoxication has me on the dance floor. Before long, I'm sweaty from all the dancing that I even take my shirt off like so many other guys. Generally, I would be too shy about this, but under the influence, I feel much more confident about my body, and it seems I fit right in.

Throughout the night, mingling about without my shirt, I am continually getting hit on, and admiring guys are complimenting, wanting to touch my abs and chest. This is all so unreal, being desired in this way, to have the kind of body that so many seem to want.

Weekend clubbing becomes a ritual, I thrive on the attention. I realize that with all the invites from so many good-looking guys, I could go home with just about anyone I want. I don't really understand it, but I go with it and learn to be a player. I make a lot of acquaintances at the clubs. They all want something from me, I get all the drinks, and I play the room and take my time choosing the perfect one for after the club.

*****

Clubbing is also how I'm introduced to cocaine. Already stoned and partially intoxicated, I am willing to try almost anything else. Who hasn't seen Al Pacino in *Scarface?* Cocaine is a rich man's drug. Very seductive and very enticing. I'm easily coerced into the bathroom at the club to do my first line. The adrenaline rush, when I snort that first line, is phenomenal. Hits me faster than alcohol or weed. I am wired ready to take on the night. I am dancing with energy I've never had before. Before long, we're in the bathroom doing another "toot," a "bump," a line. I learn to snort it, smoke it with my weed, freeze it on my gums. I am totally amped and feeling so much a part of the world. It seems the higher I am the better I feel about myself.

Sometimes, if I know I'm going to have cocaine or blow or if I know it will be involved, I'll end up at club Probe, an all-night club, when it's underwear night and you check your clothes at the door. I need to be high and have already done a line before I get there to repress my inhibitions to feel comfortable walking around in my bikini briefs showing off my body. The only time I am comfortable with my body is when I'm high and even more so when I'm wired.

I know I work out hard for this body. And I know others want a piece of it, and I love that feeling. So I know how to tease, entice, and tantalize to get what or whom I want. I am able to go home with someone different, of my choosing, just about every night from the clubs.

*****

From the clubs, I'm introduced to the bathhouses. I have actually made a couple friends through the clubs, Khashi and Sal.

Khashi's family fled Iran when he was little, and Sal is of Spanish descent. I like them because they are both gym rats like me and very attractive. Khashi with his striking Middle Eastern features, and Sal with his exotic Spanish traits. I don't allow myself to make close friends, but if I'm going to make friends with guys, I want them to be masculine and good-looking. Besides, they're both players like me, so we have fun picking and choosing and playing the game. Sal and I very briefly dated, but I don't like attachments of any kind. I learn from the clubs that I'm desirable, so sex is all I'm after. Sex is what affirms myself worth. Sex is a declaration that I am worthy of others company and not that fat ass big butt. I can't get that affirmation if I'm with someone. I need that confirmation from many.

Sal is not a drinker and doesn't do drugs. He likes to experience everything with a clear head. Khashi is more like me. If you can drink it, smoke it, or snort it, I would generally try it and so would Khashi.

One Friday we were doing the clubs, Sal had already left with someone well before closing. Khashi and I are having a wild time, already stoned, some drinks and a little coked up, when one of the many guys we had been flirting with all night had mentioned about a time he had gone to The Hollywood Spa. I'm thinking, *A spa...ooh, how Cosmo.* Then I'm told it's a bathhouse (Khashi had been there before). *"Okay...??"* Then I'm told what a bathhouse is. *"Okay!!!"* It's a sex club, like there are swingers clubs for straight people, there are bathhouses for gay people. I have never heard of such a thing, and I'm *extremely* intrigued. We leave the club before last call and head toward The Hollywood Spa. There's no bar inside, and I have plenty of weed and a little blow, but we stop at a liquor store so I can smuggle in a bottle of my own to make sure I keep my night going.

When we get there, the man at the desk informs me I have the choice of just a locker, a room, or a room with a TV showing nonstop X-rated movies. He explains the cost differences. I pay the price for just a room and leave my wallet, except for some bills in my pocket, and my car keys in a private lock box at the desk. I have a pint bottle tucked in the waist of my pants and other party favors in my pocket. The man hands me a towel then a buzzer sounds allowing me entrance inside. Khashi is behind me, he got his own room.

When I get inside I have this sense that I'm walking into a lair of unseemliness. It's dim, dark. An aura of something almost unsavory, sordid, and forbidding hangs in the air. But being high makes it stimulatingly, intriguing. There's club music playing but not as loud as in the dance clubs. There are two floors. On the bottom is the large TV room playing regular movies. A number of vending machines. There's a fully equipped workout area. The second floor is where all the rooms are—sauna, steam room, and hot tub. This place is as large, if not larger, than any of the dance clubs.

There are men on both floors roaming around (cruising), either nude or with only a towel around their waist. We find our rooms located on different halls. I change into just a towel around my waist and shortly, Khashi is knocking on my door. He is dressed the same, just a towel. We do the last of the coke, smoke a bowl, and take a swig from the bottle. Khashi is hot, but before we head out on the prowl, I take a last look in one of the many mirrors, check to make sure my "ass isn't fat," pat my flat-ripped abs, check my biceps, bounce my chest muscles, wipe the powder from my nose, take a hard sniff, look at Khashi, and "let the game begin." We both have our own agenda, but since we're both under the influence, we make a pact to check on each other throughout the night.

Many people have their doors open as an invite, kind of like door to door shopping. You can meet and hook up anywhere throughout the building and have a room to go back to. There's a lot of good-looking guys, and we have eight hours paid for. I'm very choosy, so I'm in no hurry. I talk with many who all try to get me to come to their rooms. I watch their eyes while we chat. I see them roam all over my body. I devour their compliments and enjoy playing the game. One guy notices my jaws grinding, a side effect of the coke, and says he has some party favors I might like in his room. I tell him that would be cool but only if my friend can come. Khashi and I do drugs together when we're out. I point out Khashi and the guy says sure. I wave Khashi over, introduce the two, and we head to his room.

When we get there and shut the door, the guy pulls out a bag, but it's not coke. It's something called "crystal," which I have never tried. Khashi has, before we ever became friends, and told me it's like doing blow but stronger. I'm all for that because I'm coming down from the coke. He lays out three lines. I take mine like it's nothing, but, boy… it hits hard real quick! It is many times more potent than cocaine. There is an immediate rush of like electrical energy raging through every fiber of my body! I am so amped and wired! I stay only long enough to be polite. I have so much energy I need to leave and get around. Being on this crystal makes my need to be desired even more compelling. At some point, I end up back in my room to smoke a little bowl to mellow me just a little. I spend the night staying high and on the hunt for that one out of many possible, that seem so unobtainable, that if I can get him, my mission of seeking my worthiness will again have been accomplished. And it does.

When I come down from the drugs and alcohol, I am again in that state of looking in the mirror and seeing that worthless good for nothing. I don't see what other people see when they are complimenting my body.

I become a frequent guest of the bathhouses like I do the dance clubs. The majority of the time I go by myself, but sometimes, I also go with Sal. Each of us with our own itinerary. Unlike me and Khashi, Sal doesn't do drugs, but I love the way they make me feel about myself. While I'm being standoffish, getting high, playing the game, and enjoying the chase, Sal keeps me informed of guys that have seen us come in together that are asking him about me, wanting to meet me. Sal says they're intimidated by my body and shy about approaching me. I think that's hilarious, but me intimidating…?? I love the thought, I crave the attention, but intimidating…really?

I'm very, very selective and particular about what I do and who I do it with. I have many wild experiences in the bathhouses, and I always leave having gotten what I went there for. Complete satisfaction. Validation. Feeling of self-worth.

*****

I accompany Sal to some private house parties that he gets invited to. These, for the most part, are regular parties. Lots of hot guys, alcohol, weed, other stuff, pool, and hot tub, but there are separate parts of the house set aside for other semiprivate activities. I don't care for all that. I am more the "keep it low key, anonymous hookup" type person, at private house parties.

*****

I find out that the adult bookstores have a lot of activity. There's a bookstore just a couple blocks from my apartment, one in North Hollywood and one in West Hollywood. The alleys and parking lots behind these stores are very cruisy. I manage to meet many people in these areas for anonymous hookups. I often bring people from the bookstore near me back to my apartment. The short drive makes it much safer since I'm already stoned and the police tend to patrol these spots a little more frequently. On weeknights, I become a continual visitor to these back alleys always seeking that one anonymous encounter that will let me go to bed that night knowing I am desired.

There are also parks in the city that are very popular for meeting other guys—North Hollywood park and Griffith Park. Griffith Park is huge. The major part of the park encompasses The Valley side of the mountain with one very long and winding road that traverses onto the Hollywood side. A couple or more miles of just carefree cruising. You could do all the driving and check out who was parked alongside the road or be like me. I would pitch my lounge chair, strip to my speedo, grab my pipe, catch some rays, and let the people come to me. Absolutely any time of the day, on any given day, I can meet someone in Griffith Park or North Hollywood Park if I want. If I don't find someone to my choosing, then there's always the bookstores the clubs or the bathhouses.

In Confusion

& &

This is how my life has been evolving. I love children, and working with the handicapped kids is an incredibly fulfilling job. Deep in my heart, I know I'm needed by these little hearts. I love getting extra work in the movies. Being on set or on location is part of realizing my lifelong dream. I have Andrea and Don, friendships that I cherish, and there boys whom I adore and spoil. In this part of my world, I only let people see the one side of me—the very caring, compassionate, loving, straight guy. I have other, not as close, friends at work, but I don't dare let anyone see my secret side. I'm scared of losing these friendships, but I really struggle with my secrets.

I still have those dreams of my mother, more frequently now. Between the dreams and looking in the mirror, I'm constantly reminded of that "bad ugly boy" inside of me. I can't help that I'm attracted to guys. I've never been attracted to women that way, and that really confuses me because I'm very masculine and nobody would ever guess that I have those inclinations. I wish I *was* like other guys.

Smoking pot helps with my feelings, and my introduction into West Hollywood nightlife makes me feel like I'm not alone anymore. And the drinking and drugs I start using make me feel whole, like I really belong. My heaviest use starts out only on the weekends, but "coming down" in the mornings, after my nights out, I am filled with guilt. I look in the mirror and see in myself what my mother had always said, "Worthless, good for nothing, fat ass, big butt, won't amount to anything."

In my confusions and guilt, I decide I'm going to go the religious route that I had always steered clear of to make myself really normal like regular guys. I had heard about a church, the Assembly of God church. I believe that's the church that David's parents went to. They do the laying on of hands and casting out of demons. I found out where one of these churches was and told myself, *"This has got to be the way."*

I was feeling desperate inside and chose this coming Sunday. I stayed home that Saturday night. I didn't do the clubs. I did smoke pot and drink a little and visited the bookstore near my apartment to get my daily needed affirmation then went to bed.

The next morning, I made my way to church. I was apprehensive when I got there, but I made myself go in and take a seat in the very large and crowded sanctuary. I wasn't sure how I was going to get someone to lay their hands on me but was sure that somehow I would get some sort of a sign. Well… I got that sign!! It wasn't what I expected! About halfway through the pastor's sermon, a man on one side of the sanctuary to my left jumps up out of his seat with his hands in the air and started yelling out something in some strange language (tongues), and the split second he finishes, a lady on the other side of the sanctuary to my far right jumps out of her seat hands raised spewing out the translation in English. Clear as day, I could hear them as if they were coming through the speakers. There was an eerie hush in the sanctuary when the two finished and the pastor quietly said, through his microphone on the pulpit that, *"The Holy Spirit is here with us."* I don't know about the Holy Spirit, it seemed like *demon language* to me, and it scared the crap out of me! I didn't want to be rude and leave with everyone watching, so I stayed for the rest of the service, not being able to stop thinking about the freaky show that just took place. Was it for real? I left as soon as the service was over. I had my pipe and a bag under the seat in my car, ducked below my dashboard, and lit up right there in the parking lot of the church. I felt better now on the drive home. That was totally bizarre! Really freaky! I am never going to go to church again!

Out of Control

ℰᴏ ᴄᴙ

I resumed my regular life. I'm always clear headed when working with the kids I love so much, but I do smoke weed on movie sets especially on locations. My usage of everything else, alcohol and other drugs including my beloved weed, will slowly evolve and increase.

Before I'm twenty-one, I am arrested and spend time in jail for drunk driving. Jail…not fun! Scary! I plead no contest in court and spend a small fortune in fines, court costs, alcohol education class, and do a crap load of community service cleaning horse stalls. I also have to attend AA (Alcoholics Anonymous) meetings.

All of that doesn't hinder my increasing use and activities.

I discover a drug street lined with low income apartments on either side. Whenever I'm low on weed and can't reach my supplier, I can drive down this street any time of the day or night, be waved into any driveway, and score a dime bag, a small bag with ten dollars worth of pot.

One evening, I get waved to the back of a driveway and end up with a gun pointed at my temple and a guy demanding my money. In a flash, I envision my brains splattered all over the passenger side window, and I give him the ten dollars in my hand. I get nothing in return for my extreme, almost peeing my pants, inconvenience except a warning to keep my mouth shut. Like I'm going to run to the police and explain my being there? I exit the driveway shaken up, hands trembling, drive down the street, pull another ten out of my wallet, turn around, and find another driveway to score a dime bag. When I'm out of weed and desperate for that high, a gun isn't going to scare me off.

A few times, I have been stopped by the police, questioning my reasons for being in this particular neighborhood. I always have a story. Bottom line is, when I'm high, I feel good about myself and the world around me. When I'm not, I don't. I will take the extra risks sometimes when needed.

*****

At one of the parties, I go to with my friend, Sal. I'm getting stoned with another guy out in the backyard, and he explains that if I want an even more intense feeling with my high to try self-asphyxiation/strangulation. He explains it to me and then demonstrates on himself with his belt he has taken off. It's a trip watching as he falls to the ground briefly passing out then coming to. He says, *"It's like what it must feel like to die, but you can't die because your body goes limp before you reach that point."* I'm curious, intrigued about almost anything that can put me in an altered state of mind.

I wait until I'm in my apartment alone to experiment. I'm getting high and use my belt as he did. As I slowly start to fade away, I'm taken back to when I was a kid and my mother would stand on me. I'm feeling that beautiful sensation of just floating away into nothingness, peacefulness, and then total blackness.

I don't think I'm out long, but I come to on my hands and knees shaking and convulsing and seeing flashes of light, like fireworks in the sky, inside my head. At the moment, I'm not in control of my body. What a rush. This is so out of control. But I love that floating away feeling, that sensation of….just nothing.

I continue to make a habit out of this, being very careful that furniture is out of the way so I don't hurt myself. I just want that feeling of being "taken away." After a few months of doing this, on and off on occasion, I get careless and people start to wonder what these marks are on my neck. I feel I've taken this too far and need to quit. It's not entirely easy, but I redirect my focus and spend more time at the gym.

I'm meeting more guys at the gym. I work out at the two in The Valley and the one in Hollywood. I'm finding the gyms to be not much different than the clubs. I'm tuned into my workout, but my peripheral vision catches whomever is checking me out. I have an ab routine that requires six hundred reps, in sets, using the incline bench and the hanging upside down inverted sit up apparatus. This is what usually catches the interest of other guys. I can meet someone new at any of the gyms just about any day. This is how I meet the Chippendale dancer. For a while, we have regular get-togethers. I see in the mirror I have a really good body. But my mind refuses to believe it. I rotate around looking at everything, especially my back side my mother loved so much, and still wonder what someone like a hot Chippendale dancer sees in me.

This need to be desired, to feel desirable, is like a drug in itself. No matter how I see myself I need someone…a different someone… on a daily basis letting me know that I am attractive, that I am worth something. I need validation. I thrive on knowing I'm attractive… Hot From the gym. From the clubs. From the cruisy alleys behind the adult bookstores. From the cruisy parks. From the bathhouses. I want my body to be liked by the type of people I had always wished I looked like, so I partake in random, rampant sex from all these places, on pretty much a daily basis, to get that validation that seems such a critical need to me.

It's as if I have to make up for every single day growing up that I was made to feel like I was an ugly worthless nothing.

Eventually, I'm stopped and questioned, near one of the bookstores, on suspicion of soliciting sex, but I end up getting arrested for giving false information. Fortunately, they didn't look in my car for anything, or they would have found an open bottle and my pipe along with some weed.

On another occasion, I get arrested for having sex in my car with someone I picked up at the bookstore on the other side of The Valley. I spend a weekend in LA County Jail before I'm bailed out by Andrea and Don. They don't know the specifics, so I let them believe I was with a female. Due to the arrest, I'm fired from working with the children. Scared that everyone will find out the truth about me, being scorned, ridiculed, and end up hating me, before they have the chance to dump me, I dump my friendships with Andrea and Don and all other friendships or acquaintances at work.

I have allowed my acting endeavors to slow down, due to my otherwise active life, and my financial situation is becoming critical, so I take on a night job in a medical lab as a lab tech on the job training. This will also leave my days open, if I can pull myself from my other exploits, to look for acting work. It doesn't quite work out that way so well. I become friends with my supervisor. He's a Vietnam vet and a major pothead. On lunch breaks, around 1:00 a.m., my supervisor, an IT guy, and I always go out and get stoned. When we get off at 6:00 a.m., my supervisor usually invites us to his house where we smoke some more. Then I head off to the gym, get pumped up for a couple hours, and head up to Griffith Park to catch some sun...and whatever else comes my way.

This will become my new routine. Work, stoned, gym, park... whatever until around 3:00 p.m. Go home, sleep, be at work by 10:00 p.m. and do it all over. I might slip some movie extra work in there, but these other activities become more important. Work, stoned, pumped up, meet someone. Every day. The lab job is Monday through Friday so I still hit the clubs and wherever else, Saturday and Sunday nights. I become so entrenched in this sordid, disreputable, routine in life I have, that I can't see how everything else about me is slowly spinning out of control.

I'm constantly lying to my supervisor and friends at work about my regular daily life when asked, *"So what did you do last night?"* or, *"What did you do over the weekend?"* Nobody knows anything about my private life, but I'm always quizzed about it, enquiring minds always wanting to know. Even when I'm at my supervisor's house getting high, I don't divulge anything personal, always being evasive, fabricating believable stories. It gets tough keeping this up over the years.

*****

By the time I'm twenty-five, I'm going through an ounce of weed (one hundred dollars) a week, at least. Aside from weekends at the clubs and my other favorite venues, my alcohol consumption has slowly progressed to be an everyday occurrence. I'm going through a half pint of Peppermint Schnapps, or some other flavored liqueur every day, usually at the park with my pot. This also puts my cigarette smoking at about a pack a day.

I am still going to the clubs every weekend and still hitting all the cruisy spots. If I work it right and play the game, sometimes, I can get my other party favors for free; otherwise, I'm spending so much money on coke and crystal on weekends that I can't afford my apartment anymore. Being desperate, I resort to renting a room, the converted garage, in a rat-infested boarding house on the west side of The Valley for a couple months. There's enough room that I can bring what little furniture I have, but…me and rats do not get along, and these are big black Palm rats. I know I can't live like this for long.

At one of the parties I go to with Sal, I meet a guy who knows a guy that has some property for rent. It's one half of a tiny duplex in North Hollywood that he has available, which is cool because it places me closer to the gym on that end of The Valley, North Hollywood Park, and the North Hollywood bookstore and the bathhouse.

It's a tiny two-bedroom, one-bath, tiny kitchen and living room. There's a sizable rose garden in the backyard, about twenty lush bushes, and I can have the place for only three hundred a month if I keep the roses watered and pruned. Dirk, the owner, shows me how to properly prune, so I agree.

With the lower rent and my job at the lab I buy a new Nissan Pulsar with a sun roof. But it also means that I spend more on going out. Drinking. More money up my nose. In my pipe. Always needing to obtain, and then maintain, mostly through anonymous hookups, that feeling of belonging, that affirmation that I am worth something.

I still have those dreams. I can't seem to stop doing all that I'm doing and I can't keep up with the fallout. What bills I have keep getting behind. Phone disconnected. I keep interchanging my full name to get a new phone turned on. I'm okay with myself and the world when I'm drinking or high and out being wild, grabbing ahold of the attention from any and every direction I can get it. Half the time wondering how I drove home through West Hollywood, Hollywood and over Laurel Canyon into the Valley without incident. But always the guilt afterwards and looking at that "worthless, good for nothing" in the mirror. My life feels like it's in a spiral.

Eventually, I leave my job at the medical lab with enough in the bank to barely hang on for a very little while. But my fear of running out of money makes me desperate enough that one day, while looking at casting calls, I decide to go in a different direction for quicker money. I answer a casting call for an adult film. A porno.

It's a "straight" film. Two thousand dollars for a weekend shoot. How difficult could that possibly be? A lot of things take place at a casting call for an adult film, a *lot* of things. Already having a small weed buzz when I get there, I keep telling myself, *"Two thousand dollars, two thousand dollars."* I let them take nude pictures of me. They like what they see, and we go on to the next phase. "Two thousand dollars, two thousand dollars." With cameras rolling I could not conduct myself, could not function, could not execute, could not achieve, could not *do* what they wanted of me. No matter how they tried to coax me, I couldn't. Something in the back of my mind? I don't know. Considering how I live my life…I still could not do this. Even for two thousand dollars.

A week later, I try another "adult" casting call thinking it will be different this time because it's a gay film. I can do it. I should know how to block things out of my mind. I smoke a little more weed, and this time, I do some coke also. The result is the same even for a gay film. I get as far as nude pictures, but I can't go any further, and then I'm just feeling lower than life when I get home, look in the mirror, and ask myself, *"What the f___ are you doing?"*

I have not an ounce of self-esteem or any real semblance of… anything in my life, if I'm resorting to X-rated movie calls. That's how low I have gotten.

Memories of childhood keep coming back. I keep thinking about the dreams. A part of me wants to start up the self-asphyxiation thing just to have that "floating away" feeling again. To feel that escape, but I can't. My life is in such disarray. There's something wrong with me. If things had just been different growing up, I know I would be different. I want this to stop.

*****

I'm full of anger and confusion. My mind is just a murky, mud-dled mess. I actually try a little counseling through the free clinic, but I don't talk about my childhood. I can't. It's none of his business. So we just end up talking about my drug use and my drinking. How it seems that once I get a drink in me, I don't want to stop. I don't talk about all the sex either. He does ask but, again, none of his business. All I ever really tell him is how screwed up I feel my life is. His rec-ommendation, since I give him so little to go on, is AA. I did it a few years ago when I got my DUI and didn't think much of it, but I'll go again. After just a few meetings, I decide it's not for me. If I'm not telling my counselor personal stuff, I'm definitely not telling a room full of strangers my personal crap. I'm going to go my own route.

I haven't talked to my family in years. I severed all ties when I left Minnesota, except for my mom. I did send her souvenirs and was dutiful in sending birthday and Christmas cards. Why…? I don't know. Otherwise, that was it! I've kept in constant touch with Judi, of course.

Whether it's good or bad… for a while it's been mostly bad, I call Judi. She's always there to listen and to always tell me, *"I'm pray-ing for you."* Okay… yeah… fine. But *my* family… no contact!

I decide I need to do something. I need to know some "whys" and "whats." *Why* was there so much abuse? *Why* did you not love me? *Why* was my brother really taken away? I have always had my suspicions. This is one question that has bothered me for years. *What* happened that our family was the way it was? I have never felt any real love for my family. I wasn't shown it and wasn't shown how to. The only way I can think of to find any answers is to confront everyone I have dismissed from my life. And the only way I can think of to start would be to make a cassette recording, copy it, and send one to each member of my family. This is the only way I can think of to figure out why I feel so screwed up. I buy myself a tape recorder, some cassettes, and get started.

I wake up every morning about five o'clock, pack the bowl of my pipe with weed, and start to smoke. This is the only way I can pull up all those buried, painful memories and talk about them, even just to a tape recorder. But that tape recorder symbolizes every single person in my family. My mother, my father (will he let my stepmom listen?), my sister, and both my brothers. I've been in this 5:00-a.m. routine for two weeks now. This is how I unleash all my early years of pain, anger, frustration, confusion, and hurt. This is my way of confronting and dealing with my childhood and what happened in our family. I don't know if I'm going to get any questions answered, but I need to get this out of my head and hopefully stop the dreams. Maybe, I think, just maybe, my messed up life will start getting better.

This has not been easy, but I finish the tape, have copies made, and mail them off. Once in the mail, I can't take this back. They will either listen, or they won't. I will give them all time and then arrange a trip back home for an individual face-to-face.

The Reunion

ఴ ☙

After about a month, I start planning a trip home. I find someone through the personal ads in the *LA Times* that is heading to Minnesota and looking for another person to do a ride share. One long drive straight through, split the gas, and I take a Greyhound bus back to LA when I'm ready. The first call I make is to my father to make sure he had received his cassette and listened to it. He had and agrees to meet for dinner one night when I get there. My sister I talk to on the phone. She, being the eldest, had been witness to some of my abuse that took place in our home. My mother, I can't reach. My brothers, I will call when I get there. This will be a very short visit primarily intended to take care of family matters.

When I get back to Minnesota, I stay with Judi. It is so good to be back in her warm home and to see everyone. She makes sure I know, as always, that she's there if I need her. I call my father and make arrangements for a dinner meeting the next night. I also call my brothers. They had been told I was coming to town, and we made plans to get together for drinks the night after I meet with my dad.

Of course, I brought a bag of weed with me on the trip. I don't smoke it at Judi's, but I borrow a car and smoke a nice big bowl on the way to meet my father. I haven't seen my father since the day of the big fight some years ago. I'm a little scared and nervous, and this bowl has become about the only way I know to cope with all this.

My father's already at the restaurant when I get there, and the initial greet, handshake and small hug, is awkward, especially the hug. Immediately, I feel like the bad, bad kid from so long ago that should be punished for shutting everyone out of my life. But the buzz I have going helps me to shove those thoughts aside.

It's a very cordial get-together. While looking at the menu, I break the ice and "come out of the closet" and tell my father I'm gay. Aside from my best friend Ken, my father's the first person I come out to. He tells me he had always figured as much, probably in part because he saw the adult magazines when he threw all my belongings onto the driveway way back when. We share a little idle chitchat, but for the most part, I remain fairly emotionless through our meal and our talk. He says he listened to the tape I had sent and indicates he had no idea my mother was doing all the things she had done. At one point, I straight out ask him why my brother had been taken away. I share what I witnessed that morning, when I was so little, and offered up my speculations. He confirms my suspicions by telling me that there had been concerns of abuse. He never explains why for his own brutalness nor does he offer any type of apology.

The next night, I meet with both my brothers at a comfortable hotel lounge for drinks. I had to smoke a little for this meeting also. When I see them, a part of me feels bad. I was never close to either of them, through no fault of theirs. A wedge had been placed between each of us since day one. My mother especially saw to that. My younger brother was taken away and my little brother she spoiled while I got tortured. I had so much animosity toward him my entire childhood. But it wasn't his fault. This particular meeting was for me to clear the air. Explain my disappearance. Not only do I come out of the closet, but I'm going to bring the family secret out into the open with me, not to hurt anyone but to bring everyone onto *my* page.

My younger brother, the one taken, was not surprised at the revelations of my tape. When I bring up the incident when our mother burned his hands, I ask him why he keeps a relationship with her. Just like me, he did not know. The term "Stockholm syndrome" comes to mind. My little brother seemed to have been taken totally by surprise, shock, and disbelief at the mother I described, who seemed so different from the mother that raised him. I did not exclude the irrational beatings I endured from our father. When I would describe some situations, my little brother would start to get emotional. I felt bad but I wanted them both to know my reasons. That I was justified, for not wanting anything to do with our family.

Our get-together actually went well. I will never know the kind of bond that brothers usually share, but this did turn out to be a warm and friendly visit.

This has actually been a little draining on me, and I really don't know if I got anything resolved other than getting it all off my chest. I will spend one last day in Rochester with Judi and the family, savoring the closeness, then the following day hop a Greyhound bus for the trek back to where I belong.

*****

My younger brother, the one taken, is Charles. This was the last time I would ever see him. He passed away in his sleep at the age of thirty.

*****

Charles's gravesite.

Coming Unhinged

᪥   ᪥

I will never travel two thousand miles on a bus again. That was excruciating.

I've been gone for a week, and aside from my two family meetings, I have hardly smoked any weed and haven't drank and no companionship. I have some catching up to do.

North Hollywood Park is where I meet one of the stars of the very popular daytime drama *One Life to Live*. When Mark and I meet, he is just a very *GQ* looking man in a very hot convertible. I have no idea who he is. If I watched any soap, it was *General Hospital* during the Luke and Laura saga.

I never do the approaching, so aside from my constant companion, my weed, I always have a book with me to read so if I'm standoffish, stuck up, showing no interest, that is why. A book was a good thing to always have. It is all part of the game. However, I was very interested in this man when he came up to me. He introduced himself by name only—Mark. We chatted for a minute, but he was on his way to give an acting class. Okay… he's an actor. Cool. We exchanged phone numbers, and he says he will definitely call me in about three hours, a long time for me to wait considering how I like to operate. My time frame not theirs, but he will be worth the wait.

I make sure I'm home in time for his call. We make plans to meet somewhere. He chooses a bar in North Hollywood, a straight bar. I don't get it, but he says he will explain.

It's strange for me to preplan meeting someone in a bar, acting like we're just buds going for a beer, when we had met earlier in a pickup park. I'm the "quickie" person. I don't have any use for taking the time to get to know someone. I never let intimate strangers into my life. But this guy was different. Mark tells me who he is, his character is some big bad guy drug dealer on *One Life to Live*. Sounds pretty cool but I don't watch the show. It doesn't really mean anything to me other than this really, really, good-looking cover of a *GQ* magazine type guy wants to know me. He emphatically tells me that nobody knows this part of his life so he has to be extremely low key. He's on hiatus from the show right now, hence his being in LA, and he gives acting classes while he's here.

Well, we hit it off right away. Mark is the first guy I actually allow to get close to me. I quickly become emotionally attached and infatuated with him. I didn't know I could feel this way about a guy, and I don't understand it. I also don't understand how someone with his looks and status would want anything to do with the likes of me. Worthless me that can't keep his life together. I curtail all my promiscuous activities. I still smoke weed and drink a little every day, mostly under the radar, but otherwise, I try to put up a good front to impress him because I just don't feel I'm good enough.

Mark loves to go camping. We go shopping, and I buy us a little tent and some camping supplies, and on weekends, we would head off somewhere into the Angeles National Forest. We always stopped at the grocery store for food before leaving. I would always hang a little behind because as we approach checkouts, the female cashiers would get all goo-goo eyed, trying to hold back their excitement and be like, *"It's you.....It's you...You're so and so on One Life to Live. I watch you all the time! Can I get your autograph!"* Even though it's really cool to be with someone that's kind of famous, I always wonder, every time we go through this, *What does he possibly see in me!*

Everything with us has to stay extremely hush, hush, so we just go camping or to a straight bar for drinks or just hang out at my place when he's free. Sometimes, I make dinner. I always have alcohol, and Mark does like to smoke a little weed. I have to be very careful with my drinking. Once I get alcohol in me and that buzz starts to take effect, I usually don't stop, and I don't want Mark to see that side of me. I only want him to see the real side of me, the nice side of me, so I rely more on the weed to make me feel the way I need to be.

One of my ways of trying to impress, win approval, and show I've got it all together is by putting anything we do on my one and only credit card. I figure that this way, he won't know that I really *don't* have it all together. I'm going deeper in debt by loving the fact that someone thinks I'm worth enough to spend time with. I'm hooked.

On days that Mark's not around, I'm desperately searching the classifieds for a job. I do find something else rather quickly. It's another laboratory job at a small privately owned environmental lab. I will be working with a great group of international people. I'll be dealing with all sorts of chemicals doing scientific testing. Pretty cool for someone like me who doesn't have an education outside of high school and can't really do anything. The best part is it's all on-the-job training. I still feel I have to keep my personal life a secret, for the time being, in order to be accepted. I actually make up lies about having a girlfriend.

In a sense, I have come out. My family knows and my friend Ken knows. I identify with being gay because that's the only attraction I've ever had or known. I just have a difficult time accepting it inside. It's a lot easier when I'm on something. I'm not into the 'gay scene' or 'parades'. I'm not the type that needs to let the world know. People I meet, in general, see 'masculine', 'straight', no one would ever know unless I tell them. In the past, I have jokingly told Ken, *"I think I'm a gay man in a straight man's body."* However...all I've ever known it to be about is just sex, until Mark. I didn't know I could have feelings like this for someone, especially a guy. So I cling to this and always make sure I'm available.

Mark and I are together every weekend and some week nights. It's really great. I'm glad this is a quiet 'thing' with us because I'm not into the social 'thing'. That's a whole different me that needs drugs to function in that world. Mark tells me how he got into acting, what it's like working on a soap opera, and I love hearing the stories of the celebrities he has worked with. I feel so small in comparison. My stories could never measure up. They're almost laughable in contrast. I've really done nothing but become a screw up, if he only knew. I really don't feel deserving of his attention. He presses me with questions about my life sometimes and wonders why I'm so vague and don't like to talk about myself. I tell him very little and work very hard to keep the majority of my life secret. I've always been ashamed of my life, and I don't think he would like me if he knew. In fact, I don't think many people would if they knew my childhood and what I had to do in high school, the things I do now, and how messed up my life is. I just need everyone, especially Mark, to see the nice me. The good me, that's the real me.

I have gotten so used to Mark's company every weekend and one or two nights a week. I'm emotionally dependent actually, knowing that this incredible person wants to spend real time with me. I felt really wanted, needed. But I too quickly will learn that, as they say, "All good things must come to an end." After just three short months, Mark has to return to New York. I'll miss the weekend camping. I'll miss the quiet companionship that never required much of me. My weekends and some weeknights had been very quiet and pleasant with Mark. There is definitely a type of emptiness that I've never felt or had to deal with before now that he's gone. I never thought it possible that I could feel this way about another guy. I just don't understand it.

*****

Work is going well at the lab. I've learned gas chromatography-mass spectrometry, liquid chromatography, all sorts of cool scientific stuff. Makes me feel a little smart. Some people at work that I have become friends with have noticed an unusually quiet demeanor about me that I have no explanation for when asked. I've kept up lies about a girlfriend for quite some time now, out of fear of not being accepted and being rejected, that I don't dare tell them about Mark and that his leaving has quieted me a little. Keeping up this facade is killing me inside, pretending to be someone I'm not. Kelly, my younger supervisor, and Maureen (Mo) are two people I have found it the most difficult to keep up this lie around. I have grown very fond of them as work friends and have so much admiration and respect for them. I just can't jump that hurdle and let them into my personal life out of fear.

With Mark no longer in the picture, I dive right back into my old routines of the clubs, bathhouses, and the cruisy areas. Guys from the gym. My constantly needed validations. I have Crystal and coke when I can get it. I have picked up my old pace very quickly: work, gym, cruising, clubs, bathhouses, drugs, validation, like I never lost stride. This was the best way to get past Mark and keep getting what I needed. But the pace keeps getting faster.

I'm smoking pot every day, morning, noon, and night. That's the only way I've been able to start my day for quite a while now. The best way to get rid of any guilt and be able to look at myself in the mirror…kind of…it makes it easier anyway. I always have a bowl and a bag in the car. I'm glad liquor stores open early because I'm now in the habit of tossing back a couple miniatures on the way to work, tequila or green apple Smirnoff, along with hitting the pipe. This is definitely good for smoothing out a morning if it's been a wild night on crystal or coke, especially on many Mondays. I still try to keep that to the weekends but, these days, not unheard of on a weeknight now and then. Another friend at work, Mike, has noticed some of my mornings. It turns out he likes to do a little crystal or coke and always has a small vial with him for an occasional "bump" of his own. He has offered me a pick me up, at times, to help me get over the morning hump. The only problem with that is that I want more. I will have to go to my car during break and retrieve a miniature from under my seat or smoke a little to mellow me. My life is really starting to spiral out of control.

*****

Around this time, I meet a very gorgeous guy in Griffith Park, much in the same fashion that I met Mark. I'm lying in my chair, only in my shorts, advertising my body (I had just come from the gym). I have already smoked a bowl and am innocently reading a book. I see that he's interested, I am too but don't make it obvious. I just give a glance and go back to reading. We keep this up for a little while. I like to play the game. You're interested, you need to approach me; otherwise, it's your loss. That's my attitude. I know what I see in the mirror at the gym. Even if my mind doesn't see it, I know I have the body you want. That's why I work so hard at the gym. For you and all those like you that I wish I was. Oh, there are many others around out here today, Griffith Park is big, but no one as striking as this one.

He eventually pulls his car, a beautiful new Miata convertible, up next to me and introduces himself. His name is Lucca. He has a beautiful tan, piercing blue eyes, dirty blonde hair, and a sexy accent. I ask about the accent. He says he's from Brazil. His father is Brazilian, his mother is Czechoslovakian. He's an advertising executive, speaks Portuguese, and obviously hits the gym regularly. All that wound up into this one incredible package that has been pursuing me. Once again, I feel that I'm not good enough even though inside I never really feel attractive. I love that others do, especially someone like Lucca, whom I wish I was more like.

I only live a couple miles away, and....well...I wanted to head in that direction, but we ended up talking for quite a while. Not my style, but this guy is taking a big interest, reminiscent of Mark. Lucca wanted to exchange numbers, so I did. It's the last week of the year. We are both with busy schedules and have plans for New Year's Eve. Well...I say I do. I can't let this successful guy know I'm a nothing. He will be at a party but says he wants to spend the beginning of the new year with me and wants to leave the party and come over right after midnight. I tell him I will make sure I'm home. We talk during the week, and I find out he's also "from money." He reveals to me that the worst thing that ever happened to him was when his father passed away, they had to release the housekeeper and he had to learn how to do his own laundry. He then asks if I can be home by one o'clock, after all the revelry, so he can spend the start of the New Year with me. Absolutely, I will.

The feeling, the idea, that someone cares, like with Mark, and wants to spend the start of the New Year with me, I grasp at the notion and latch onto the idea. Thus I start the task of losing myself in another person. I will go out of my way and bend over backward to prove myself worthy of this person who, in my eyes, lives such a high statured life.

Lucca is only the second guy I will ever really go out with for any extended period of time. With his striking good looks and exotic Portuguese accent, I'm instantly infatuated. As with Mark…why someone gorgeous, wealthy, and with a great career in advertising would want anything to do with me, I could not figure out. I'm just an uneducated lab tech, a "used to be wanna be" actor. There's no way I could possibly live up to any of his expectations, but again, I curtail most of my extracurricular activities to focus on him, making sure that every time he called, I would clear my busy schedule, that I never really had, to accommodate for plans with him.

We would go out to crowded restaurants, just the two of us. He's very social, I am not. I don't do good in crowds in a social setting where I have to be "normal". I would always require a couple drinks to calm myself while waiting for a table and play it out, force myself to act normal. We would have dinners out with his friends who are also successful. I could never fit in. There wasn't anything I could really contribute to conversations that intelligent successful people have, so I would sit there feeling stupid and insignificant wishing we could leave. As sociable as Lucca was, I would also get very jealous inside, silently accusing him of wanting everyone else and everyone else wanting him. The only consolation is that I was his eye candy and he did like to grab my behind, in front of others, and compliment on its sexiness. Yes…that "behind" that my mother always berated. Although I did enjoy that somewhat since I could never really believe it myself. However, it would also embarrass me and leave me feeling uncomfortable. The one thing I do feel good about mostly is that I refuse to let him pay for dinners. I need to show that I can hold my own, so I put our dinners out on my credit card, even though I really can't afford it.

These social outings were becoming too much that I started to have panic attacks. Many times, I would literally almost pass out in public. Lucca would get irritated with me when this happens and practically accuse me of faking. One time, I excused myself to the restrooms and only made it to the main lobby before literally passing out on the floor. It was very brief, and a couple gentlemen helped me up. I had to go sit in a restroom stall for a few minutes to compose myself before going back into the dining area. I would never tell Lucca for fear of scaring him off.

These attacks got worse to the point of my seeing a doctor. He asks general family history and such, but when he asks about drugs or alcohol, I downplay it, of course. I don't tell him I drink and smoke pot every day. I just have these really panicky feelings inside under certain situations, he doesn't need to know all that other stuff. He tells me I suffer from anxiety attacks and gives me a prescription for Xanax, not to be taken with alcohol. At least I have a diagnosis and can tell Lucca so he doesn't think I'm faking. Maybe we will do less social outings.

We talk almost every day. Since we are doing less social outings, I need to maintain his interest, so I'm the one calling him every day from work. So much so that Kelly tells me it's become obvious that I'm spending too much time on the phone while I'm on the clock. I let Lucca know we can go places since I'm on medication now, but he has other plans, a lot more these days. I find out, through my grapevine of Sal and Khashi, that Lucca is out at the bars and going to the underwear parties at the all-night club, Probe. I know what that means. I'm not stupid.

I become almost obsessed with needing his company to validate me. I start to pop Xanax and head into West Hollywood checking out the bars. I like the mellow feeling it gives me, but I also smoke weed on top of it. Not feeling the way I really want to feel yet, I grab a drink or two in each bar I go into. I start to make this a habit and wake up the next day at home not remembering the night before. One time, I actually see Lucca in a bar and wake up the next day in his house not remembering, as he tells me, that I was knocking on his door in the middle of the night. I'm feeling like I'm losing my mind.

We still get together at times, dinner at his house, and spending the night, just not as often as I would like. I do, however, make sure I keep a toothbrush there to make me feel more secure in this relationship. Unfortunately, I notice that there are more than two toothbrushes and quietly to myself make my own conclusion.

I'm becoming consumed with the need for Lucca's acknowledgement and admirations. I work out hard at the gym so I know he wants my body, but I need more than that these days. I need him to want me completely. My drinking at night increases while I'm tormenting myself about him and what he's out doing the nights I'm not there. I always have my weed and drink in the mornings before work, to ease my mind, then more weed at break and lunch. Sometimes, I need to rush off to the liquor store at lunch to grab a couple more miniatures. All this seems to be complicating my mind more, resulting in additional anxieties over the issue, so I increase my Xanax.

I know what the problem is. I'm not a successful person, and I need to be in order to keep Lucca's attentions. I think about it a lot and decide I need to enroll in college. I consider many different types of careers that I feel would impress him and finally trim my list down to court reporting or paralegal. They both sound like exciting careers with prestige, and there's a school in Van Nuys that specializes in both. I opt for the paralegal. Running around a law firm, law library, in and out of courtrooms, working on big cases sounds much more important and intriguing than just sitting in a courtroom as a court reporter. This would have to be impressive to Lucca. He would see how important and successful I can be.

I enroll in the paralegal course with a student loan and pay for all my "smart-looking" law books out of pocket, which I can't afford. Now I'm juggling work, school, the gym, still paying on my car, my weed, alcohol, and regular bills. My finances are spinning out of control trying to impress Lucca. I can't keep up with the three hundred a month rent on my North Hollywood duplex. I start searching the classifieds and find a two-hundred dollar a month room to rent in the lower Hollywood hills just above Hollywood Boulevard in between Highland and Cahuenga. It's just a room I'm renting in the manager's apartment of an apartment complex. It's another step down in living for me, but the balcony overlooks all of Hollywood to downtown LA, so I take it. I skip out on the rent in my North Hollywood duplex and move into my new "room" in Hollywood.

Even though I'm in school doing something important, impressing Lucca, I've become more ashamed of my quality of living. I used to have a very nice apartment once, and now I'm down to renting a room. One day, Lucca asks if I'll house sit for him when he goes to Australia on vacation. Lucca has a beautiful cottage type house in West Hollywood and a dog, Buster, that he doesn't want to board. Immediately, I think I'm more special than the owners of the other toothbrushes in his bathroom because I get to watch the house while he's on vacation, so without hesitation, I say yes.

Lucca keeps a fully stocked liquor cabinet, and he also likes to do a little coke. We had never done any together, but I had seen a vial he keeps in a bathroom drawer that I never asked about. He's not offering any money to house sit, it's a farther drive to work, and he's going to be gone for two weeks, so I know I will take full advantage of these amenities.

I'm feeling rather proud of having this distinguished trust placed upon me while he's gone. I enjoy being in his nice home pretending I'm the other half living here. I get along with his dog, Buster. He would sleep on the floor in the bedroom, sometimes, when I would spend the night. One thing I hadn't anticipated, however, was all the phone calls Lucca would be getting while he's in Australia. I let his answering machine take the calls, but the volume is turned up. All sorts of guys are leaving messages wanting to know when they will see him again or thanking him for a nice evening the other day or week, letting him know they are still available. This is all making me incredibly jealous and hurt. I'm not so special after all. I really wanted to be this one person's special person. It's a fancy machine, and I don't know how to turn the volume down, so I'm stuck listening to each message every time some guy calls.

I'm about to go crazy by the end of the first week at Lucca's house with all his phone traffic. I drink to ease the seething, jealous pain inside. I can't focus at work. I'm drinking on the way to class after work and can't focus on studies. All this I'm doing for Lucca, and yet I'm hurting so bad inside. Everything in my life feels like it's spinning completely out of control. It has been this way for quite some time now, and I don't know what to do. I'm basically out of money. I'm drowning in debt with my credit card, my car, school, bills, and Lucca. I'm being sucked under by some riptide of life. I can't stop drinking and smoking weed. I'm doing some of Lucca's coke to bring me up. Maybe it will get me in the mood to go out to a club or bathhouse and seek my own revenge on Lucca, but the coke only makes me more certifiably insane. These phone calls seem to not want to stop. My world feels like it's in total chaos, and I want it to stop. I want to get off. This needs to end. I need peace.

I don't know where the thoughts all come from between hurt, jealousy, anger, fear, abandonment, retribution, self-pity… feelings from so deep inside me that every fiber of my being seems to be fracturing to pieces. I just want him, that one person's attentions. I want to know that I'm good enough for someone like him. My whole life, I guess that's all I really wanted, was to know that I was just good enough for someone. I had to do something…something. My mind seemed to completely split from reality. When I went to work the next day, I had a plan in mind. I go through the day as if my life was in perfect harmony. I tell Kelly and Maureen how much I liked working with them. I pretty much tell everyone the same. I tell Mike thank you for the times he gave me the little crystal boosts to help me through some tough days. At the end of the day, I take a bottle of ether out from one of the cabinets, sneak it out to my car, and head off to class. I have a little to drink on the way and don't really pay attention to anything the instructor is saying because my mind is focused on events to take place later.

After class, I drink in the car all the way back to Lucca's house. Going through my mind are my mother's words "worthless good for nothing." I have become just that. I realize I have been that for quite some time. I'm not good enough, never have been good enough.

When I get to Lucca's, I go inside and feed Buster. Another phone call comes. This guy has called a few times looking for Lucca. He's not going to give up. Must have been good. After Buster is fed, I get into the liquor cabinet and proceed to drink quite a bit more. I have grown fond of tequila straight and Jack Daniels. They're both a little rough, but it does the job. Another call comes in. *"Hey, Lucca. When can I see you again? I had such a great time when we went out."* My mind is kind of numb right now, not really caring anymore. I go into the bathroom and do a little coke from Lucca's vial. I go back to the living room for more liquor and take out my bottle of Xanax. I still have about fifty pills. I proceed to swallow them, a few at a time, with my tequila and Jack, until the pills are gone. Still another phone call comes in. Do these guys not give up. I yell at the answering machine, *"Lucca's not here, you assholes!"* I want to take the answering machine and smash it against the wall. Instead, I get the bottle of ether I stole from work, go into Lucca's bedroom, and place it on the nightstand. I feel the Xanax beginning to take effect. I use the phone in the bedroom and call my best friend Ken. He lives in some place called Huntsville, Alabama. I just want to hear his voice and say goodbye. He was always the one person that I truly ever trusted. We talk for a little while. I hang up the phone. I unscrew the top on the bottle of ether. I cup my hands over the opening of the bottle and place my nose and mouth into my cupped hands and inhale as deeply…as… I… possibly…can…….

I don't know how, but I'm lying in a hospital bed with a very good-looking man standing over me. He introduces himself as my doctor. He asks if I know my name, my birth date, what year it is, and if I know who the current president is. In a raspy voice, I answer all the questions correctly and find out I'm in Cedar Sinai Hospital in Beverly Hills. I'm not dead.

*****

Over the course of a decade, living in the Los Angeles/Hollywood area, I will have had an estimated two thousand sexual partners in my constant, desperate need for validation and self-worth. Over this same period of time, I will also have spent, in the neighborhood of, $150,000 on drugs and alcohol in my attempt to cover up pain, anguish, shame, and guilt. At this point, I would never believe that in twenty years, God and Jesus will become the major players in my life.

GOD'S NOT DONE WITH ME YET

ALABAMA,
HERE I COME

GOD'S NOT DONE WITH ME YET

On the Road Again

ಬಿ ೞ

My car is packed to the hilt with only my belongings I have deemed important. My Michael Jackson Pepsi commercial pictures being the most important then my clothes. I sold most everything else I felt had any monetary value—a used computer I had bought for school work. It was mostly just for show anyway in case Lucca came over. I sold my king-sized Italian black lacquer water bed with under lights and massager on both sides. I sold a David Lee Roth autograph for two hundred dollars. I had met him at the department of motor vehicles one day when I was getting my registration renewed. It only took me a week after getting out of the hospital to take care of matters and get on the road.

About two hours outside of Los Angeles, I connect with Interstate Forty, which will take me most of the way across the country toward Alabama. No alcohol but I do have a bag of weed so the drive through the desert is not too monotonous. Although I spend a good part of my drive recalling the events of the last couple weeks.

Waking up in the hospital had definitely been a surprise. I was confused and relieved in a way. They kept me in the psyche ward, at Cedar Sinai, for a week with daily visits from a psychologist. During my stay there, my friend Ken calls to check on me and explains how he had called the phone company to do a trace but they couldn't. Then he called the LA sheriff, but they couldn't do anything without an address. He called my phone in my room I rented, and one of the other renters picked up and went through my "black book" to get Lucca's address. He calls the sheriff back, and an ambulance is dispatched to Lucca's address. My doctor told me I had already lapsed into a brief comatose state and they had to pump my stomach. By the end of the week and a few daily visits from a psychologist, it was deemed that I was no longer a threat to myself and it was safe for me to be released. Interestingly, the week laid up did not curb my appetite for cigarettes. That's the first thing I get when I leave. I've been smoking a pack a day for quite some time.

During that week, Ken and I talked quite a bit, and I came to the conclusion that I needed to get out of LA. But I only had two places to consider: Minnesota, with Judi, or some place called Huntsville, Alabama. I love Judi, but Minnesota is too close to my family and is too cold for about eight months out of the year. Alabama is a lot further south, and it can't be that cold in the winter. It's a lot closer to the equator, my mind tells me. Plus, I know one person there. This decision was not too difficult. With the sunroof off and the desert air blowing in, I feel like I've taken a huge breath of fresh air and am ready to start over. It is good to be alive.

*****

With prior notice, I make a pit stop for a week in Albuquerque, New Mexico, to visit my favorite uncle. My mother had two brothers. One is a minister I was never comfortable around growing up because I was the bad boy and just knew my minister uncle could see all that "evil" inside me. But my mother's youngest brother, about fifteen years older than me, was the cool uncle to me. I was always comfortable around him. I unbury some of the dark family secret of abuse and fill my uncle in on a lot of my life and what I did that led me to leave LA. Even though it was troubling for him to hear, he made me feel very much at ease discussing this. He even asked me once if I had ever felt as if I had been born into the wrong family. It made me recall the times I had wished I had been adopted because that could explain why I always seemed to be the outcast, the black sheep of the family.

After a much-needed and very rejuvenating visit with my uncle, I take a detour north to Colorado then across into Kansas to go see my favorite grandma in Rozel. I had also called her in advance to set up this visit, and since Grandpa passed away years earlier, she is really looking forward to my staying with her for a week. It will be good to see Grandma; however, I will not discuss the underlying reasons for my leaving LA. She will just know that I'm moving to Alabama where my best friend lives.

Rozel has a population of around one hundred. No liquor store, no bar. It's been three weeks since I've had a drink, one week in the hospital, one week packing, and a week at my uncle's. Even though I've had weed to keep me company, my mind is really wanting a taste of alcohol. I stop in a larger town about thirty miles out from Rozel and hit a liquor store. I figure a few swigs, now and then, from a fifth of rum will get me through the week without Grandma knowing, enough to just keep my mind at ease.

The week with Grandma is relaxing and comfortable, just soaking in the essence of Grandma and the old house. Grandma's a big hugger and hand holder, so there is always a warm feeling here. We spend time doing the sightseeing things she always loved to do when I was younger spending the summer with her and grandpa. We went to Fort Larned, Pawnee Rock, Dodge City, and the Santa Fe Trail, where there are still wagon wheel ruts embedded, seemingly petrified now, in the ground by all the wagon trains from over one hundred fifty years ago. It's been a wonderful week, and I'm very glad I made this detour, but I must be on my way.

I've kept Ken informed of my whereabouts during my cross-country journey so he will know when to expect me. I head back south toward Oklahoma City to reconnect with Interstate Forty going east. However, with the taste of alcohol I've had and the weed I've got, I feel a little bit in a party mood. I have with me a "men's" travel guide that shows me where, in every city around the country, I will find bars, clubs, or hotels suited toward my way of life so when I get to Oklahoma City, I am ready to sample a little bit of the lower Midwest, kind of country nightlife. It's been a month, and I need some excitement.

I arrive in Oklahoma City early in the evening and check myself into a very busy hotel, belonging to a well-known hotel chain that was listed in my guide due to its proximity to the types of bars and clubs I like to frequent. I casually peruse the lobby, look around, and see some guys seated in the lounge at the bar. I'm checking everyone out. I go to my room to shower and freshen up from the long drive before heading out to get some dinner and hit the clubs. As soon as I'm done showering, I hear the phone ringing. It's someone from another room that saw me checking in, saw that I was by myself, and wanted to know if I have plans for the evening. I found this call to be totally bizarre yet intriguing. The message light on my phone is also blinking. Is everyone staying here watching the new guy check in? I check myself in the mirror, especially my mother's favorite backside, and see that even with a few weeks absent from the gym, my body still looks good. My eyes see that, but my brain still never registers it, so I down a quick, stiff drink I've made with the rum I still have, smoke a small bowl, and head toward my car. I nonchalantly glance around to see who might be watching out their window, and feigning disinterest, I get into my car, put the bottle and weed under my seat, and leave.

After a quick bite, I head toward the clubs. Considering I'm in Oklahoma City, Oklahoma, I thought I would run into a lot of country boot scootin' boogie line dancing but was pleasantly surprised to find the clubs here are as mainstream as the ones I frequented in West Hollywood. Once I walk in, I lose myself to the feel of the pulsing beat, the flashing strobes and lasers, and the deafening sound of the music. Straight to the bar, I head, for my favorite Long Island Ice Tea and a shot of Tequila and lime. It doesn't take long before I'm ready to hit the floor to mingle and see who I can find. What does Oklahoma City have to offer? I feel like I'm me again.

I don't talk like they do here. Having an accent makes me a little more obvious, so when I'm asked where I'm from, I tell them Hollywood, California. It seems that being from Hollywood is really impressive to anyone I meet. I quickly become popular and engage in my usual game. I play coy and let others hit on me, act interested, and hit the dance floor often, the whole time waiting for that perfect guy who will totally captivate me.

It doesn't take me too long to hook up with an incredible-looking guy who becomes so infatuated with me that I stay in Oklahoma City, at his place, for almost another week partying with him and enjoying the attention. It's nice to know that even after my intentional near demise, I've still got it.

Since I'm in a moving transition, don't have any real ties anywhere, and it's not imperative that I go to Huntsville, he tries to convince me to stay permanently. That's a scary thought. At this point in time, the last thing I need is an emotional tie to someone. In fact, I really don't want anyone in my life like that again. I politely decline explaining that I kind of owe it to my friend in Huntsville to finish my trip. I pack my bags and get back on the road again. When I finally get there, I realize it has taken me nearly five weeks to drive from LA to Huntsville, Alabama. It was a trip well worth the time taken.

My New Home Alabama

℘   ℭ

I grew up in Chicago, Minnesota, and spent more years in California than I did in either of the other two. I'm going to miss the beach and the year round weather, but Huntsville is definitely slower paced than LA, which is good for me, but otherwise doesn't look much different than any other city I have driven through. They do talk different here: "Ya'll, fixin to, right quick" with a "twang" in their speech. I guess I am in the south. I find my way to Ken's apartment in the lower part of Monte Sano mountain. He has graciously invited me to stay with him. It's a one-bedroom apartment, so I will have the couch. It's been quite a few years since Ken's company had him in LA, so we spend a lot of time catching up. I also waste no time finding out that there are two clubs in town that are to my liking, so my drinking and nightlife pick up where it left off before I left LA, except for the drugs, I don't have those connections anymore. However, I will still dabble in weed a bit. That's always easy to come by. I also start to make many new acquaintances at the clubs.

I'm still behind on car payments, so I hit the streets and the want ads in search of a job. I quickly find one working at an animal clinic as a veterinary assistant, which translates to a glorified kennel cleaner and dog and cat bather. I do assist the doctor, in a small way, during routine checkups and vaccinations. It doesn't pay a lot, wages are somewhat lower down here than in LA, but I'm glad to have a job. Plus…I love animals.

When I say my drinking picked up where it left off, I really mean it got worse. We have two hour lunches, from 12:30 to 2:30 at the clinic, so the doctor can go on large animal calls or do surgeries. Across the street is a liquor store and a fast-food place. Every day at lunch, I drive across the street to get a pint of vodka, grab a small burger, fries, and drink, and head to the park just down the road. For ninety minutes every day, I will drink the whole pint and hope the burger and fries absorb enough alcohol so I don't get noticeably messed up. My body just needs that little bit of a buzz. Besides, there's only about two and a half hours of work left when we get back.

One day, the veterinary technician was out, and the doctor had a surgery scheduled during lunch and asked me to stay and assist. All I had to do was hold back flaps of skin on this dog with forceps so the doctor could dig around somewhere inside and do his thing. I don't know if it was my body revolting because of its craving for the midday drink it was missing or I just couldn't handle the sight of glistening, slimy, bloody, sinewy muscle tissue and organs. But I started sweating profusely, felt my body get cold and clammy, and nearly passed out. I'm generally not the squeamish type, so I blamed myself thinking it was my need for alcohol. Of course, I kept that a secret but was very embarrassed that I had to leave the doctor to finish up on his own. I actually thought I was so transparent and he could see my problem, but he never said anything, so I figured I was okay. That experience did very little to change my midday routine.

I also make sure I keep a bottle at Ken's for after work. Ken has a heart of gold. I've never seen him angry, always very passive and willing to do just about anything for you. Despite my best friend having saved my life and his immense generosity by inviting me to stay with him while I start my life over, I do not show the gratitude or respect in return that is greatly deserved. I am grateful inside, but instead of showing it, I end up, through my extensive drinking, taking advantage of Ken's kindness and hospitality. I abuse this friendship. I didn't set out to do so. I didn't just say one day, *"I'm going to abuse this friendship."* It's something that quickly evolved. My drinking got heavier, I would bring "guests" back to the apartment from the club once in awhile, to the point that Ken started spending more nights at his crazy girlfriend's house. I believe he would rather be there than have to deal with me.

One night, coming home from the club drunk with someone following, I jumped a curb in my car on an access road getting onto the parkway, the main artery running through the city, and stranded my car in the ditch. My new acquaintance behind me took me the rest of the way to Ken's and stayed for a while. The next day when Ken comes home from his girlfriend's, he takes me to where my car was left and pays to have it towed to a garage. They tell me my main frame is bent. Ken also pays to have that fixed, as best they could, so I will have a car for work.

Nevertheless, in spite of all Ken's giving, I continue to drink. I have not caught up on my car payments, nor do I even attempt to. I live so far away now, what are they going to do. Within a couple weeks of getting my car fixed, the repo people have found me. We are in Ken's living room watching TV and hear a bunch of clanging around down in the parking lot. We look out the window to see my car being hoisted onto a tow truck. I rush down, knowing I can't do anything, and they hand me paperwork. My attitude was *they can have it back, bent frame and all.* Once again, my best friend to the rescue. In all his giving, he loans me his twelve-speed bicycle to get to work, but that only lasts a few days. Because of the distance I have to ride, my doctor boss loans me an old van he has at his home.

I still completely abuse this friendship with Ken through my daily drinking. I lie, I steal, I nearly drain his bank account with my deceitfulness, and I manipulate to the point that he has to confront me in his most kindest way because that is just how good of a person he is. I realize I have completely and absolutely worn out my welcome. Ken doesn't ask me or tell me to leave, but I know it's time to go. One evening, I load up what few belongings I have into the back of the van and head to the parking lot behind the animal clinic where I will spend the night in the van. Just me, my belongings, and a bottle…until the police show up and want to arrest me for trespassing.

The doctor I work for owns the property, so I didn't have any worries about sleeping there in the van. I also have keys to the clinic. We, the staff, take turns feeding and cleaning the kennels on Sundays when it's closed. I will be able to let myself in early in the morning to wash up before anyone shows up for work. However, the building the clinic is in actually has two businesses, one side, the clinic; the other side, the doctor leases to a pet-grooming business.

According to the police, the owners of the pet-grooming business happened to be across the street at the fast-food restaurant when they called to report a suspicious vehicle and person on the property. Even though I had already been drinking a little bit, I tried explaining to the police that I worked at the clinic. I asked them to call the doctor to verify, even showed them I had keys to the building, but they wouldn't listen. They were intent on arresting me, so I made a break for the front door, quickly unlocked it, got inside, and locked it up just as the first officer got to the door. I turned off the alarm and called the doctor's house, explained the situation, and he was on his way. Through the closed door, I told the officers, there were three of them, *"I told you I worked here."* and said the doctor was on his way.

When my boss arrives, he spends a little time talking with the officers then comes inside and convinces me to go outside. They are still going to arrest me only not for trespassing but for resisting arrest because I fled from the officers. It didn't make sense. My boss bailed me out and went to court with me the next morning. I pled innocent and acted as my own attorney. As the proverb goes, *"A man who is his own lawyer has a fool for his client."* How true that is. That's one thing I remember from law school despite my drinking, but I still thought I was smarter.

Three officers, one spoke for them all. I asked, in court, *"Did I not tell you that I worked at the clinic?"* Officer replied, no. I was dumbfounded. Then I asked, *"Did I not show you that I have keys to the building?"* Officer replied, no. I cannot believe what I'm hearing. Then I asked, *"Did I not ask you to call my boss, the doctor?"* Again, the officer replied, no. That was it. I had no more questions. I was found guilty of resisting arrest and fined. I was stunned, in total disbelief. This officer flat out lied. Nothing I could do but move on. The bail money came out of my paychecks to pay the doctor back and my fine I eventually paid off. And life went on.

Needless to say, there wasn't a very good relationship with the pet groomers after that. I did eventually get an apology.

Trouble, That Familiar Road

ℰ   ℛ

My mother had a saying for me when I was growing up: *"Wherever there's Craig, there's trouble."* That seems to be true, in my mind, along with just about everything else she predicted about me: *"Worthless. Good for nothing. Won't amount to anything."* But I just keep drinking those thoughts out of my mind.

At the top of my priority list is finding a place to live and running a very, very close second is making as many acquaintances as I can at the club. I still need that physical validation that gives me the feeling of self-worth so you can generally find me at one of the two clubs on just about any given evening, especially when things are looking down. Even though I've been here a few months, I'm still considered the new kid in town, so I'm fairly popular. Coming from Hollywood, with all my stories, is a huge plus on top of the fact that I still have my gym body.

I'm trying to start saving money, never mind that I still smoke a pack a day, but staying in the van and washing up in the clinic is a big help. Drugs have been out of the picture since I left LA, except for a little weed now and then, but my drinking is at a level that I'm having to buy the cheap vodka, in order to save, so I will have a buzz before I even get to the club. Once inside, there's usually someone wanting to buy me a drink. During very busy hours, you don't want to leave your drink unattended at a table if I'm around. While you're out on the dance floor, I will suck it down without anyone noticing. My body needs to maintain its level of inebriation, without having to spend too much, in order to function.

One night, my functioning goes a little overboard. I wake up, or "come to" shall we say, in a cell at the city jail half naked. I don't recall a thing of the previous night. Although according to the arresting officers and I would later find out from other club goers, that my behavior was getting a bit too risque at one of the clubs and I refused to leave when asked so the police had to be called. I was arrested for public intoxication, and I was also banned from the club for a year. At some point, I pleaded my case with the owner, and he allowed me back after a month figuring things are just a lot different down here than in LA and I just had not acclimated yet. Yeah…sure…I'll go with that. This is also good because New Year's Eve is just around the corner, and I don't plan on *not* being able to go to my favorite club on New Year's Eve.

When New Year's does come around, I find myself in a little bit of a pickle again. The club is packed. I've been drinking all evening, smoking pot out on the patio with anyone that has some, and dancing with just about everyone. I'm feeling no pain and having a great time. After midnight, I decide I'm going to hang out with a couple guys I've met from out of town at their hotel. One of the guys is in a wheelchair. We get to the hotel and party some more, a few more drinks and a little more weed. I was already feeling really good when we left the club, but now I'm really wasted. After about an hour, the party starts to take a bad turn when I see the one guy get up out of the wheelchair just as the other guy tries to hold me down so they can get my wallet from my pocket. It's amazing how fast a body can sober up and come to its senses. Actually, it's just the adrenaline kicking in, but I was able to kick the wheelchair guy across the room when he tried to get on top of me, breaking a lamp in the process, which startled the guy trying to hold me down, so I was able to throw him into the dressing table, breaking the mirror, allowing me to make a dash for the door and get out of there. It was almost reminiscent of that last fight I had with my father.

I've been here ten months, arrested and in jail twice, and almost robbed once; but I have made a good many acquaintances in the meantime. One in particular, Kelvin, has taken an incredible liking to me. So much to the point that he wants to see me every day. He has my work number and always calls when the clinic closes. He doesn't know that I'm living in a van and bathing early in the mornings at the clinic before work, but I continually tell him I'll meet him at the club for happy hour. I feel a little awkward at the club with him because I don't want to give the appearance to others that I'm with someone. That will ruin my "one night stand" reputation. I need my validation from others and can't risk giving the impression that I'm out of circulation. I have absolutely no desire for a relationship, but he seems to want one. That's scary because I'm not going down that road again. However, I need a place to live, and this might be my opportunity.

Kelvin and I get along just fine in every way, but I can't be tied down, and he's getting a little too serious. One evening, I tell him my story, but nowhere near the complete truth, *"I like you but bad ex in LA. I'm not looking for anything serious, don't want to ruin this friendship, I really need a place to stay, etc., etc., etc."* Before I know it, I have a place to stay.

I get the couch in his comfortable one bedroom apartment, which will mean we remain just friends. Cable TV, a kitchen for meals, and I will get to take warm showers in the morning again. However, this will all be relatively short-lived. One evening, Kelvin brings a few friends over before going to the club. We all hang out for a little while, I'm invited to go along, but I decline. Very rare for me to turn down a club invite, but I'm already a little stoned and have had a couple drinks, but one of the guys is very good-looking, and I'm hoping he will stay behind. His name is Curtis, and he decides he's going to the club. I stay behind, disappointed.

The next evening, Curtis drops by. I'm not at all about getting close to anyone these days or letting someone get too close to me. I only want one thing. However, Curtis and I spend the night drinking and talking, well into the early morning hours.

*****

This is not how it was supposed to be, but Curtis and I will spend the next sixteen years together. The whole time not knowing that God is still patiently waiting for me.

*****

The Long One-Night Stand

෨ ෬

I only believe in one-night stands. Nothing too close. Nothing too personal. Might know your name. Probably won't remember it. Definitely "no strings attached." That's my attitude. However, Curtis is different. He is very intelligent and funny. Very good-looking. His family history is fascinating. His grandfather was one of the German scientists smuggled into our country during WWII to help start our rocket program under Wernher Von Braun. Very intriguing. I love listening to his stories. Plus…he drinks nearly as much as I do. That means I don't feel too guilty about how much I drink.

In two months, I will have been here, in Huntsville, for a year. In three months, I turn thirty. I remember telling my friend Ken, one time in high school after I was thrown out of the house, that I didn't think I was going to live to be thirty. I recall mentioning that to him again when he lived in LA for that short period of time. If I had gotten my way, I wouldn't have made it to thirty. Curtis and I really hit it off. I'm in love, and it looks like I will be celebrating my thirtieth birthday with him.

I end up meeting the family: his sister Michelle and her husband Ed, their three boys—James, fours years old; Wyatt, three years old; and Cody, one year old. I also meet his mom and dad, lovingly referred to as Granny and Grandpa since that's what the boys call them. I very quickly adopt the title of "Uncle Craig," and before long, Mommy Michelle is sending Cody my way, saying, *"Go ask Uncle Craig if he will change your diaper."* and then yelling out, as if I hadn't already heard, *"Uncle Craig, Cody wants you."* in a sort of sing-songy voice with a little laugh. I actually enjoyed diaper changing. I get to tickle and blow on his belly making him laugh and squeal.

Sprinkle him in baby powder making him smell really good. Play "This Little Piggy" with his toes. Diaper changing was like bonding time. He became my Code-man.

Now Ed was a little wary for a time. Curtis had someone else in his life, at one time, that Ed wasn't fond of. But by the time my thirty-first birthday rolled around, Ed gave me a card from the family that read on the front: *"Congratulations on overcoming your biggest hurdle."* open card: *"Becoming a member of the family."* Wow! That really meant something to me, being part of a family…and the family actually wanting me as a part of it.

We go on family vacations together, during the summer, down to the Gulf of Mexico. Curtis's parents would always rent a beach house for us all. Curtis and I even bought a van specifically for these vacations so the boys could ride with us. We'd play with the boys on the beach. Curtis and I would go deep sea fishing, and in the evening, Granny cooks up all the red snapper we had caught. I tried to keep it low-key so granny and grandpa wouldn't notice, but I would always sneak a drink or two…or…more…throughout the day to keep a slight buzz going. At night, after boys are in bed, the rest of us would stay up late drinking and playing cards. There was always plenty of alcohol. Summer family vacations were always great.

Back at home, the boys start spending about one weekend a month with us, always Friday and Saturday night and go home Sunday afternoon. Curtis and I have a large two-bedroom split apartment. A bedroom and bath on each end with the living room, dining room, and kitchen in the middle. The second bedroom is the study, which doubles as the nephew's bedroom. We have a patio that opens up into a mini forest out back where we love to build forts with the boys. On the other side of the woods, there's a Chuck E Cheese pizza within walking distance where we take them for fun nights out and go home exhausted after being endlessly taken through all the sky tunnel tubes. We always have a great time.

We take them out to movies. We rent their favorite movies. I dance and sing with them and swing them around the living room to the music when we watch *The Lion King* or their other favorite *Aladdin*, and we all, Curtis also, sing along to the soundtracks in the car wherever we go with them. The nephews love coming to our place on weekends, and we love having them.

Curtis and I also spend about one weekend a month, on average, at Michelle and Ed's. The boys always look forward to these visits from us also. After a daytime of playing, an evening of Ed grilling, the four of us adults spend the night, into the early morning, drinking and playing cards. The boys would get to stay up late. It was always a treat for them. I'm always the first one the boys wake up to change a diaper and get them breakfast so Mommy and Daddy can sleep. Of course, I can't start these mornings off without a cup of coffee with vodka, not to ease a hangover but to catch the morning buzz. This is a habit that slowly developed at home.

Whenever it comes to family get-togethers, such as holidays, I'm always seated at the children's table so the boys can fight over who gets to sit next to Uncle Craig. After getting all their plates and it's time for me to eat, someone is usually ready for seconds or is finished and wants me to go outside to play hide-and-seek. I love being an uncle. I adore the boys—building forts, playing hide-and-seek, going through the tunnels with them at Chuck E Cheese, changing diapers, presents at birthdays and Christmas, and just spoiling them. *"Come on, Uncle Craig. Come on, Uncle Craig. Let's do this. Let's do that. Can we do it again? Do it again. Pick me up. Pick me up. Again. Again."* I love that the boys adore me. I think it's because I'm truly a kid at heart vicariously enjoying a childhood I didn't have through them.

Michelle and Ed have a strong desire for a baby girl one day down the road. I wonder how that would be. I don't know anything about girls. I don't think you can rough house with them like you can with boys. My sister has two beautiful boys, and my brother has a beautiful daughter I have never met. They have sent pictures. I feel slightly saddened that there was such a wedge placed between us growing up that I was never close to my sister and brother and sometimes wonder if I would have been a good uncle to their children. Well, eventually, Michelle and Ed will be blessed with two more boys Jonathan, whom I nickname "Munchkin man," and Billy (William Alexander). More diaper changing for Uncle Craig. There are now five boys total for me to spoil, like I never was.

The boys pretty much have to be potty trained before they can spend weekends with us. The youngest, Billy, would be the only exception when it came around to him. Cody, the third born, is so excited when he spends his first weekend. About the only real rule we have at our house is…no running around the house. Cody has a difficult time with that at first. Even his older brothers, James and Wyatt, try to impress this upon him. I end up getting firm with him, one day and swat his behind, which is well padded with a pull-up and jeans. It's just a light swat, but my little Code-man just adores me and that little swat from Uncle Craig is like the end of the world to him. He just quietly looks up at me, and those huge brown eyes just flood with tears. With a whimper, he quietly says he's sorry and buries his head in my lap, and he wraps his little arms around my waist. I feel like I have just committed the most abominable act. I think about all the things my parents had done. I look at Cody's tear-filled brown eyes, and I give him a big hug while fighting back tears of my own. I didn't hurt him physically but knowing that I had injured him emotionally killed me inside. I will never do anything like that again…to any of the boys.

One of the biggest honors bestowed upon me is when Michelle and Ed ask me if I would be Cody and Jonathan's godfather. A few years down the road, I will become Billy's honorary godfather when Michelle can't remember who his godfather is. This is actually a sometimes really crazy dysfunctional family, but I hold them all dear to my heart.

A Midsummer's Nightmare

℘ ℭ

It's 1997, Curtis and I have been together for four great years. After an apartment then a rental house, we finally buy a house: a three-bedroom, two-bath-brick rancher. The clincher on this house was the Space Shuttle wall mural in the third bedroom. Because their great-grandfather's work played a part in the start of the space program, I told Curtis, *"This is the boys' room."* Now the boys will have a bedroom that's completely their own.

My alcohol consumption has also increased over the last four years. I've been drinking at least a fifth of vodka a day. I left the animal clinic and was working in manufacturing, better money, until I got laid off due to a company buyout. Now I'm drinking closer to half a gallon a day.

All of our big furniture has been moved to the new house: bed, couches, essentials, etc. So while Curtis is working, I do the rest of the packing from the rental house, but I can't finish because something is wrong with me. I don't know what is happening. I stay at our new home because I've started vomiting violently. I'm not able to keep anything down: juice, milk, water, crackers, nothing stays down. I think alcohol will calm my body, but it doesn't. Within minutes of taking anything, I'm in the bathroom bent over the toilet in painful bouts of vomiting.

I'm also starting to see things. At first, I'm seeing the comforter on the bed moving as if there are little rats crawling around underneath. When Curtis, comes home he's not sure what to make of any of this, so he goes about his normal routine of dinner, bed, and work, but I keep getting worse. I'm seeing ghosts. There's a lady that paces up and down the hall, I don't actually see her, but I can hear her chiffon dress rustling as she paces up and down the hallway as if she's guarding it or waiting for me to enter but I'm afraid to go in the hallway when I hear her there. I'm up all night in the living room desperately trying to sleep, but I can't. There's a demon cat with a cartoonish, caricature head, ten times the size of its body, on top of the television. The room is filled with hundreds of flies flying all around. The demon cat can stretch its head out to the middle of the room, opens its mouth to display rows of razor sharp teeth, the type you would find in the mouth of a great white shark yet grotesquely exaggerated, and snatch mouthfuls of flies. I just lay on the couch, terrified, watching this cat snatch flies until it eventually disappears, as morning rolls around, and I can safely get up and go to bed. However, I'm also hearing voices. I have a sleep mate that usually plays ocean waves and other soothing sounds to help with sleep, but now when I lay down and turn it on, it softly sings a very eerie, frighteningly sinister, whispered version of *"Hush little baby don't say a word momma's gonna—"*

I feel like I'm going insane. I'm vomiting and can't keep anything down. I'm afraid to go in the hall if the ghost lady is there. I'm afraid to be in the living room if the demon cat is around. I can't sleep. The first day wasn't so bad, but this has been going on for three days and getting worse. I'm seeing miniature wild animals in the house. A tiger only about two inches long is pacing in the cave on our table fountain. A koala bear is clinging to a stem in one of the peace lily plants while a gorilla roams around at the bottom of another plant.

Day four. I have spent the night in the living room watching demon cat with ghost lady in the hall. I can hardly walk now, so I just lay quietly in fear on the couch partly knowing that none of this can be real. When the sun starts to come up, the demon cat vanishes, but ghost lady is still in the hall. I feel like I'm completely coming apart, and I need to get up and get past ghost lady to talk to Curtis who is still sleeping. I keep telling myself, *"She's not there. She's not there. She's not there..."* Somehow, I make it down the hall past ghost lady, whom I can hear but don't see, and into the bedroom, but I stop suddenly when I see a black ghost lady kneeled at my side of the bed, her elbows on the bed with her hands folded in prayer. My body gets very cold, I go to Curtis's side of the bed and, in a panic, frantically wake him up to tell him about the lady across the bed. Curtis decides it's finally time to take me to a doctor.

At the doctor's office, they have to put me in a wheelchair because I'm so weak. I don't know what the doctor sees, but he tells Curtis to get me to the ER at UAB Hospital in Birmingham as quickly as possible. I don't want to go. I just want to eat something and get some sleep. I just…need to…sleep. Please. The doctor orders a sedative for me. It takes two people to help get me out of the wheelchair for the injection in my butt.

The entire ninety-minute drive to Birmingham is scary. I see ghosts standing in the middle of the highway that vanish as soon as the car gets close. There are kittens crawling out from under the dashboard climbing up my pant legs. I'm almost frantic. I can feel their sharp kitten claws through my jeans. Curtis keeps telling me there is nothing there, telling me to touch them. When I do, my hand passes right through them, but I can still see them and feel them and they won't go away.

We arrive in Birmingham, and Curtis makes a stop at a fast-food place for directions to the ER at UAB and also to see if he can get me to eat something. I try to walk in, but Curtis has to half carry me. I see police officers inside that can give us directions, Curtis says they are not there, but I know they are. I can see them. He orders a little food, but I can't eat. He half carries me back to the car.

*****

I find out a few weeks later that I collapsed in Curtis's arms on the way back to the car. A stranger helped him put me in the passenger seat. I was barely breathing. We were only five blocks from the ER, and Curtis ran every red light to get me there. Medical personnel rushed out to help. I had already lapsed into a coma. I was dying.

*****

I don't know where I am, but I'm in the most frighteningly, terrifying place. It's dark but yet it's not. There are horrible disfigured beasts, demons…things. Demon things that are beyond any physical description, all around grabbing at me as if they all want to tear me apart. They're trying to drag me down this dark, moist stone or brick, tunnel, or pit. I don't know which it is, but I desperately don't want to go. If they get me there, I'm certain I will never make it back. I claw at the stones with all my might to keep from being dragged down, but I'm getting nowhere. The harder I fight to get out, the further down they seem to be pulling me. I am frantic, filled with an overwhelming fear. They are all over. They're making loud guttural noises as if they are all cheering each other on. It's almost deafening. These gruesome putrid demon creatures. I can smell a stench. I am absolutely terrified because I can't escape them. There is no escape. There is no end to this. It goes on and on and on. I am completely exhausted trying to fight my way out of this pit, but I don't dare to give up. I have never felt so paralyzed with fear…ever. But I fight and I fight and I struggle. I see a female figure sitting on a throne. She's a dark figure with no discernible facial features, but I can feel her watching. She has the body of a serpent snake that trails off into the distance. Colored bands encircle her serpent body like those of the venomous coral snake. She wears a dark crown on her head and has the most skin crawling evil emanating from her. There is never a sound from her, but she seems to be in charge of all these horrifying creatures. I can feel the pure evil she exudes as she relishes in my despair, at the excruciatingly, tormenting punishment she has handed down upon me. I am filled with absolute terror. This has been going on for what seems like an eternity, and there is absolutely no escape.

Then I start to see a bright light. I hear beeping noises and human voices that seem far off and muffled. Everything is fuzzy and out of focus, but I can make out body forms. I'm in a room, someone has their hands all over my face. As things start to come into focus, I see that it's a doctor shining a bright light in my eyes. I try to look around the room I'm in and see a nurse opposite the doctor. The beeping noises are coming from monitors and machines I'm hooked

HE'S ONLY JUST BEGUN

up to. I have tubes coming out of my arm, wires coming from my chest, a mask over my nose and mouth, and my wrists are strapped to the bed rails. I'm scared and confused. The doctor is talking to someone, and I can't understand any of what he is saying. Still trying to focus, I look around some more, and I see Curtis, finally a familiar face.

The doctor leaves after speaking with Curtis, and the nurse comes over to change my IV. I don't know why I say this because I can barely speak, but when she takes down my empty IV bag, I tell her, *"You can get more of those at Olson's Mercantile in Walnut Grove,"* in reference to *Little House on the Prairie.*

As my head slowly becomes "unfogged," I learn that I have been in a coma for two weeks. That nightmare, or whatever it was, seemed so real. I'm told I had been strapped to the bed because I would thrash about at times. Among other medications, I'm also being given doses of Haldol to help curb the alcohol withdrawal related hallucinations. At times, I see rats climbing over things around the room. I'm petrified by rats. When the door to my room is opened, I can see the Ponderosa living room from "Bonanza" out where the nurse's station is. The massive stone fireplace, the leather high-back chair that Pa sits in along with the leather couch and the other high-back chair for Adam, Hoss, and Little Joe. At times, when I look over my right shoulder, I see a formal dining room with full table settings and a crystal chandelier. It's all so real to me, but Curtis insists it's not.

I've been on a catheter and diaper for two weeks. The catheter is painfully removed, and it seems Curtis has been doing diaper duty because the nurses are rarely around. That's funny because he has never changed any of the boy's diapers. He gets very frustrated with me because I don't have the strength in my legs to "raise myself up" to assist him. I feel very ashamed and humiliated with this diaper thing. I also find out Curtis has taken time off work and has been driving ninety minutes to Huntsville, to take care of our two cats, and back to Birmingham every day to be by my side. He said his parents finished moving us into our new house. I don't remember that I had left things unfinished.

Curtis also tells me that the doctor believes I tried to commit suicide. My diagnosis coming in was "salicylate poisoning." Typically, that's an overdosing of aspirin. I argue this point with Curtis. *"I think I would be the first to know if I tried to commit suicide…We just bought a new house. We have little nephews that I adore, and they adore me…We don't ever have aspirin in the house."* He tells me that since I was in a coma and they really couldn't ask me, he was compelled to tell the doctor my history: Teenage suicide attempt…LA suicide attempt…My drinking. He didn't know what to believe except that I was dying.

Being out of work and uninsured, the hospital needs me to recover as quickly as possible, but the doctor won't release me until he feels that I can take care of myself at home while Curtis is at work. It will be another two weeks in the hospital regaining strength in my legs. I try real hard because I don't want to be in here any longer either. I do remember one of the first things I wanted, coming out of the coma, was a cigarette, even though they had me on a patch. We make frequent trips down to the smoking court. What they don't know is that my brain is telling me…*I also really want a drink.* My doctor has already had a serious discussion with me about my drinking. He tells me….with everything he's witnessed, along with various tests and speaking with Curtis, at the rate that I consume alcohol, I will be dead by the time I'm forty. *"You need to stop."*

After another two weeks in the hospital, I regain enough strength to get around on my own. I'm no longer seeing formal dining rooms or Ponderosa living rooms. I find out the hospital keeps its own supply of IV bags, and I'm released from the hospital. However…I don't take my doctors advice to heart. Dead by forty…? Yeah…right. Once back at home, my drinking picks up right where it left off.

I have more visits to the local ER for the rest of the year, one time, because I was seeing aliens. They were really cute. They have the appearance of a garden gnome crossed with a Smurf. They can walk through the walls of our house. I play hide-and-seek with them all through the house and outside. Curtis can't see them, but they *are* there. I grab a camera and take pictures. I tell Curtis, *"When I get these developed, you will see."* One thing that's odd is that my alien friends have babies hidden in our goose down pillows, and I need to find them. I grab a butcher knife and get our pillows. I guess Curtis can finally see everything I'm saying is true because he convinces me to take the pillows out on the front porch because it's going to make a mess. For some reason, he locks the door behind me once I'm out. I proceed to cut open the pillows looking for the alien babies. Feathers are all over the place. Before too long, an ambulance is pulling up to the curb in front of our house. Paramedics are walking slowly toward the porch trying to convince me to put the knife down so they can talk to me. I can do that. No problem. They ask what I'm doing, so I tell them about my alien friends and the babies. Some of the aliens are out on the porch with me, and I point them out, *"But they don't have names."* I tell the paramedics. Curtis has now ventured out onto the porch, and one of the paramedics speaks with him for a moment, then they ask me if I would like to take a ride with them. They convince me to lay down on the stretcher they have brought out. They strap me tightly to the stretcher and load me into the back of the ambulance. The whole time some of my gnome Smurf alien friends are at the foot of the stretcher, and I keep telling the paramedics, *"They are right there... Can't you see them? Right there at my feet playing peekaboo."*

I also find out this year that I have telekinetic powers. One time when we are in the waiting area at the hospital, we're there for "who knows what" this time, I discover that with my thoughts alone, I can rearrange all the presents that are under the Christmas tree in the corner across the room. I carefully float them all into different places, very slowly without anyone noticing. I do the same thing with all the chess pieces on the chess board at the nurse's station. I rearrange the entire board behind their backs by slowly sliding all the pieces around on the board strictly with my mind only, all this I'm doing from the other side of the waiting area. Imagine all the things I can do with a power such as this. I want to keep this a secret but have to brag about it to Curtis just a bit. When we're ready to leave, I quietly tell the nurses, in a mischievous way as we walk by, that it was me who moved *all* their chess pieces and *all* the Christmas presents. I guess Curtis just takes this all in stride now because he waits until we get outside to tell me there was no Christmas tree or chess board. It isn't even Christmastime.

*****

To this day, I don't know what caused my illness and subsequent coma. I am certain it was related to my extensive alcohol abuse. My year with demons and ghosts and aliens wasn't enough to make me see where I was heading. We didn't keep the boys much that year either. All they knew was that Uncle Craig was sick. The *aliens* never did show up in my pictures. As close to death as I had been, once again, God still was not going to let me die.

Mr. Hyde

ℰ﹆ ﹆ℛ

I'm back working again, in retail now, as an inventory manager for a nationally known home improvement center. No more hallucinations, no more voices. We're back to having nephews on weekends occasionally but not nearly as often as in earlier days. Our life is not all bad and riddled with issues. We have a lot of wonderful times. Curtis and I are taking vacations of our own these days—island hopping throughout the Caribbean, San Juan, St. Thomas, Martinique, Barbados, the Bahamas, Cozumel, Calica in the Yucatan Peninsula, and Aruba twice. We snorkel, "snuba" dive (which is like scuba), wind surf, parasail, explore caves with torches, and investigate Mayan ruins. And we drink a lot. But we have some wonderful vacations always making sure we bring back souvenirs for the family, especially the nephews. However, in between all the good times, more health issues arise, and a very bad side of me is emerging.

Me in Aruba with island mascot Tessa.

We both drink every day, but my intake is still on the rise. We keep a half gallon bottle of vodka on the kitchen counter, but I have resorted to buying fifths of vodka separately that I hide to sneak drinks from so the bottle on the counter doesn't disappear too quickly alerting Curtis to how much I'm actually drinking. I hide bottles in the garage, in my dresser, under the mattress. Sometimes, I don't even remember where I might have hidden a bottle. That usually happens when I'm coming around and desperate for a drink.

I work from four o'clock in the morning until one in the afternoon. Curtis gets home around six o'clock in the evening. I have five hours from the time I get off work until Curtis comes home from work to drink, usually starting with two drinks from "our" bottle. A drink for me is roughly eight ounces of vodka, with about two ounces of soda, on the rocks. I need these two drinks because by the time I get home, I have started getting the shakes and feeling nauseous. These initial drinks calm my body down. After that, I will get into my hidden bottles, and I'll easily finish off a fifth by the time Curtis gets home. Once I get that first drink inside me, to calm me, I don't seem to be able to stop or want to. Actually, I *do* want to but can't. I will frequently be passed out on the couch by bedtime having drank myself into oblivion. Sometimes, I get up in the mornings for work to find myself bruised and sore in spots, quite possibly from having fallen or running into a doorway somewhere, but I can't remember. Many, many mornings, I look in the mirror at a face with spider veins on its cheeks and red, saggy, bloodshot eyes and tell that face, *"Not today. Not today."* By the end of my shift, I am having the shakes, and the cycle starts again. I go to the liquor store to make sure I have enough vodka then go home, have my two from our bottle to calm me, and the race is on. Over and over and another, *"Not today"*…every day….every day.

At times, we argue. Not very often but we both drink every day, me to an extreme, so when we do argue, it usually becomes full-blown. Curtis most times remains calm, but it seems I have my mother and father buried inside me, so I'm the one who becomes full-blown.

It's not easy being with someone who thinks he's right all the time and knows everything. I like to be right sometimes and think that I might know a little. On the flip side, it's probably not easy being with me these days, but I don't pay too much attention to that thought. The problem is that in my attempts to be right, I can fly into a drunken rage. One weekend morning, we are both drinking, actually drunk by noon, when an argument starts over something stupid, it usually is, but it escalates on both sides. It is very verbal. Cuss words are coming out of my mouth at a rate that it seems I have just turned into my father. No…it doesn't seem like it…I *have* become my father with the vile language I use. Curtis exacerbates the situation in his own way to the point that I lash out physically and slightly injure him by accident and the police are called. When they come to the house, Curtis asks them not to arrest me, but they explain that once they're called to a domestic dispute, the aggressor will be removed, and they put the cuffs on me. They advise Curtis that since we have both been drinking, it wouldn't be wise for him to come to the jail to bail me out, they might have to arrest him for public intoxication. I'm taken downtown and booked on domestic violence charges. Later that evening, a bail bonds woman arrives to get me out. When all the paperwork is done and I'm ready to go, she hands me an envelope from Curtis. Inside is twenty dollars for a cab and a note that reads, *"Meet me at the bar."* Aren't we a classic pair.

Domestic violence of any degree, even accidental, is not treated lightly by the courts. It takes some talking from my public defender, and I get sentenced to a schedule of family/anger counseling, probation, and Alcoholics Anonymous. Once again, I get to try AA…just long enough to get my sheet signed.

I get even worse. Arguments are still few and far between, but during future drunken disputes, I take my rage out on the furniture instead. Over the course of time, I end up busting to pieces and replacing three sets of coffee tables and end tables and putting a hole in the wall when I throw a phone across the room. I am always deeply ashamed in the mornings, when I'm dried out a bit, looking in the mirror telling my horrid reflection, *"Not today…Not today."* I used to be a happy drunk, but now I have turned into the proverbial Dr. Jekyll and Mr. Hyde, and I don't like what I see. I have very deep anger issues that now expose themselves through my drinking, but I can't not take that first drink when my shakes eventually start, even without the shakes I "can't not" take that first drink.

New health issues have started to arise. I'm having excruciating abdominal pains accompanied by bouts of extreme nausea. The pain and nausea are so intense I have to keep drinking water just to have something to throw up. Most times, I have to gag myself with my finger to start the vomiting when the dry heaves get really bad. I stay on the bathroom floor, near the toilet, doubled up in a fetal position in extreme pain. Curtis usually has to take me to the ER where I will be put on IV's and pumped full of fluids, blood will be drawn, I'll be shot up with painkillers and given only ice to suck on.

My first time in the ER, for this condition, my blood results come back, and I'm told my pancreas is severely inflamed and my pancreatic enzyme levels are extremely high. None of that means anything to me. I just know that the pain was so bad I would almost rather be dead. I'm asked about my drinking, and I tell my doctor that I have a couple drinks a day. So it's more like a couple bottles, but as far as I'm concerned, they don't need to know that. They keep me for five days of bed rest, fluids, pain meds, and Librium for alcohol withdrawal, but I tell them again I only have a couple a day… after work. Although, I'm glad I have this Librium because I'm not experiencing the shakes and nausea that I normally get. They take me for some CT scans, and when those come back, my doctor shows them to me and has a serious talk with me about alcohol.

The scans are of my pancreas and are actually kind of pretty. What I see are shiny, glistening crystal-like formations. My doctor explains to me that I have chronic pancreatitis. My pancreas becomes so inflamed it pushes on my other organs causing the excruciating pain, and what I see as crystal-like formations is the slow progression of the calcification of my pancreas. He politely tells me that a large percentage of chronic pancreatitis is caused by long term alcohol abuse and that I should seriously consider stopping my drinking or this could very well kill me.

*****

I don't listen to my doctors. I know better than them. I spend the next few years in and out of the ER about every four or five months, almost like clockwork. Excruciating pain, ER, shot for pain and nausea, and IV fluids. I am sent home with pain pills, five days bed rest, and clear liquid diet. I know what that doesn't mean, but I ignore that also. Since the pain is gone, I stick to *my* clear liquid vodka diet while I'm on my five-day vacation, knowing it will be about four to five months before I go through this again.

*****

Rehab

ဘာ   ၈၃

My life is completely spinning out of control, has been for some time. I can't stop drinking once I start, but I have to drink because that's what takes the shakes and the painful dry heaves away. I drink myself into oblivion, passing out on the couch most nights, and sometimes, I come to having soiled myself due to my inability to function at all to make it to the bathroom. So much embarrassment and shame. Every day telling myself, *"Not today, not today, not today. No more."* The same insane cycle repeating day in and day out.

I'm getting sick halfway through my shifts at work and always hit the liquor store when I get off buying just enough for the evening because I'm *"stopping tomorrow."* When I get to the store and buy my two bottles, I have to take a few quick swigs straight from the bottle in the parking lot to try to combat my body's revolting. I have to do this about three or four times because I puke up the first two or three swigs. I just need to hold enough down to let it absorb into my system and calm my body. I always park around the side of the building so no one witnesses this pitiful display.

At home, I'm a continued mess. One time, I spend a drunk afternoon, on my day off, in a tree trying to cut branches, fall out, and dislocate my shoulder. I'm in excruciating pain and have to call Curtis at work to take me to the ER. My shoulder slides back into place, with the assistance of muscle relaxers, and I'm sent home with a suggestion from the doctor that I don't drink so much.

Curtis's company is now sending him on business trips on occasion. There are times I think Curtis would rather be on his business trips than at home dealing with me. I think he's pretty fed up with me. During one of his trips out of town, I break my foot and have to call his father to take me to the ER. I have no idea how I broke it, but I make up what I think is a plausible story. I'm fitted with a "boot" and sent home with another suggestion from the doctor that I consider not drinking so much.

Curtis and I are arguing more. My rage comes out, and it's difficult to hold it back. I get physical again but very briefly, and when I see what I'm doing, that I've kind of snapped, I can't deal with this anymore. I head down the hall to the bathroom, take my bottle of pain pills, and empty it down my throat knowing it will work itself in with the alcohol. I just want to be done with me, and I lay back on the bed. Curtis calls 911. Police and ambulance arrive, but I refuse to leave. I tell the officer that has come into the bedroom that I just want to lay here and die. He tells me I can't because suicide is against the law. The stretcher can't get around the corner and down the hall, so they carry me out to the living room, strap me in the stretcher, and cart me off to the hospital. They pump my stomach, keep me overnight for observation, and release me in the morning.

Curtis picks me up, takes me home, and goes off to work. I go to the liquor store. That night in my drunkenness, Curtis tells me that I scare him. In my shame, I ask him to take me to the well-known treatment facility in the neighboring city. I am ready to change my life. Curtis takes me there, leaves me with the staff, and heads home.

I'm ready to change until the final step of the intake process when two men put on latex gloves and come toward me to do a body cavity search. I draw the line there and tell them, *"I'm not staying."* I call Curtis in tears and beg him to come pick me up.

Over the course of the next year, nothing changes. I just get worse. Curtis has switched to drinking beer. He says he doesn't want to see himself become the person that I've become.

Mr. Hyde is starting to show his ugly face at work. I'm drinking over a fifth to a half gallon of vodka a day. So much that there's no such thing as sleeping it off. I'm showing up to work at four o'clock in the morning still slightly under the influence. I'm yelling and cussing because no one else is doing their job right and it's making mine more difficult. By eight o'clock in the morning, I have the shakes so badly that I have to hold my arm to try to write my reports legibly, but it doesn't work. By ten o'clock, I'm sick with dry heaves, and my shift won't end until one o'clock. I'm miserable beyond belief every day, but I can't stop. I need the liquor store after work to stop the shakes and throwing up, but once it's in my system, I can't stop, and my days repeat themselves with increasing madness.

It's after one of these weeks of madness that I realize I desperately need help. It's late Friday night, my week is done. Curtis has already gone to bed. As usual, I'm drunk on the couch, and I haven't been able to stop drinking since I got home at one thirty this afternoon. I'm drinking and drinking, and it's doing nothing. I can't even pass out. I can't deal with this insanity anymore. I am feeling completely soul-less, indescribably empty inside. I wake Curtis up and beg him to take me back to that treatment facility. I desperately want help this time. It's the beginning of March 2003. I will be forty in two months.

*****

The treatment center takes me…barely. I'm registering a .35 blood alcohol level. One of the attendants says I am *"dancing with death."* They won't take anyone as a patient if they are over a .35 because it is not a medical facility. Curtis stays with me through the intake process this time.

Due to the extent of my alcohol abuse and my degree of intoxication at admissions, they say they really need to keep me for a month. I agree to whatever they want to do. I'm worn out inside, and I just need help.

I'm put on medications, Librium being the primary for alcohol withdrawals, and I'm given a partner who will accompany me throughout the day, for my first week, in case I have an alcoholic seizure. The guy who is picked to be my partner turns out to be the same guy who will also be my roommate, his name is Chad.

Chad is twenty-four, and this is his third time in this treatment facility. I'm surprised to find that many of the other patients have been in treatment multiple times. With Chad having been here a few times already, the staff is familiar with him and his antics, which are funny. We end up getting along very well…very well.

This program is very structured—bedtimes, lights out, awake times, rise and shine in line for breakfast by a certain time. Rooms must be cleaned, shower dried off, and army corners on the bed. There are group classes throughout the day. Some of them are group counseling, physical education, alcohol awareness, and twelve-step classes. There is personal time with your own counselor. Many times in the evenings, a speaker comes in and talks for an hour about his or her life as an active alcoholic or addict and how life is now…clean and sober. I like these talks. I'm able to relate to a lot of what they say.

I love mealtimes. There is always so much food, and it's all so good. I have one problem, though. The Librium has been great. No nausea or cravings but it doesn't quite stop the shakes. It's difficult trying to get my eating utensil from my plate to my mouth without shaking all the food off. I have to use both hands holding my utensil to get the food to my mouth, but my trembling is so bad that sometimes, even that doesn't work and mealtimes can get frustrating. But I do realize that this is all of my own doing. However, by the end of the first week, my body is settling down, and I'm able to devour my food.

Curtis comes and visits on weekend visitation day. He brings extra money for me for the vending machines and extra cigarettes. Before I know it, the month has gone by, and I am feeling better than I ever have in my entire adult life. I have an exit session with my counselor. I will have to do a month of evening intensive outpatient treatment classes (IOP) to complete my treatment program. I'm really good with this because I feel like I'm on top of the world. I tell my counselor that, *"I am going to be one of the success stories of this treatment facility."* But I also tell her that, as great as I feel, I'm kind of scared of the world outside this facility. I've never really been sober in my entire adult life, but I do feel great, and I'm going to make it.

I resume my job as inventory manager. Work had allowed me the month off. That was hugely embarrassing but humbling, when my human resource manager had to come to the treatment center to do my short-term disability paperwork with me. Although, this was all kept private between me, HR, and only the store manager. In a short period of time, my work ethics, behavior and attitude, and job performance had changed so drastically for the better that I received a very nice raise.

Coming out of treatment, I had taken a long look at myself in the mirror and saw this 180-pound body of vodka blubber with an almost 35-inch waist. I had turned into what my mother had always said I was…fat ass, big butt, worthless good for nothing," and I really hadn't "amounted to anything." But I am sober now. I am so disgusted with what I see in the mirror that I make it a priority to join a gym.

I have finished all my IOP classes. I'm back at the gym, and within three months, I'm down to the 140 pounds and 29-inch waist that I was familiar with ten years ago. I'm also starting to get my six-pack abs back. I have to buy all new clothes, and I am feeling incredible.

I have gotten into the routine of up at 3:00 a.m. for work, get off at 1:00 p.m., turn left out of work to the gym, extensive, intensive workout, then go home, Monday through Friday. I used to turn right out of work to the liquor store then home and get drunk. I love my new routine and my new life. I feel so healthy now, except for the cigarettes. One day, maybe they will go also. In September, we even take a sober vacation, our second trip to Aruba for Curtis's birthday. It's fantastic experiencing the island and the island casinos sober.

For nine months, I'm livin' the dream. The sober dream. Absolutely loving life until one day…I had become so self-assured during these past nine months on my cloud nine that one day, I take a right turn after work instead of the left turn I had become so accustomed to. I'm just curious. I buy two miniature bottles of a green apple vodka, take them to my car, and "toss them back." It burned going down, but…oooh, that green apple flavor and the warmth that immediately enveloped my body was very intense and felt so good. So familiar. I sit there for a minute, behind the steering wheel, relishing the moment and telling myself, *"I'm much better than I was before treatment."* Then I start the car and head home not uttering a word about it to Curtis. I do the same thing the next day after work. Right instead of left. Green apple, only two miniatures. Toss 'em back along with my mental utterances of *"I'm much better than I was before treatment."* I do this the next day…and the next…and the next. For a week, after work, I'm buying two miniatures, tossing 'em back and telling myself… *"I'm much better than I was before treatment."*

The following week, since I'm much better than I was before treatment, I decide to get a half pint after work…and that really starts the ball rolling. That Friday, I'm involved in a little fender bender in which the other driver takes off. I head home shaken up, scared, not knowing what to do because I'm already under the influence. Not knowing how I'm going to explain this I call Curtis. He suggests calling the police to at least have a report taken. I do that. However, being really paranoid, and I don't have any vodka in the house, I decide I have enough time to run down the road to the liquor store and be back before the police can get here. I buy a fifth and take a few quick gulps before heading back. When I turn onto our street, I see a police car already in the driveway. I pull in get out of the car and start telling him about the fender bender and the other car that drove off. Saying he can smell alcohol on me, he tells me I'm under arrest for DUI. I find that absurd, being in my own driveway, and start to walk away. He says it's because he witnessed me driving in the street before I pulled into the driveway. I continue to walk away threatening to call an attorney. He grabs me and slams me onto the hood of the police cruiser. I vehemently refuse to be arrested, and I start to put up a very strong-willed resistance. I am unyielding and refuse to be placed in the squad car. A backup arrives, and between the two of them, being beaten in the leg with a nightstick and pepper sprayed four times, they are finally able to get me in the back seat of the squad car, and I'm taken to jail.

After they wash me up, I had gotten bloodied, and they rinse the burning pepper spray out of my eyes. I am booked for DUI and resisting arrest. They place me in a cell with a few other guys. I take a seat on the concrete slab bench, pull my legs up and cross them yoga style, close my eyes, and tell myself, *"I'm a lot better than I was before treatment."*

*****

309

This is the beginning of my rapid downward spiral into a hell, greater than the one I was living before treatment.

*****

Curtis bails me out with my money. I really have nothing to say except for an apology and some lame excuses. My drinking has already taken off, where it left off, just over nine months ago. I'm functioning at work, for the moment, but not experiencing any of the shakes or nausea, so I figure I'm okay.

Shortly after jail, I run into my old roommate, Chad, at the liquor store. He has relapsed also. Curtis is out of state on business, so Chad spends the weekend with me partying with various substances…until Curtis returns early from his trip.

For the next nine months, I'm out there like a raging wildfire. I have become that hurricane that was just on the horizon but has now made landfall. I have many drunk good days, but they are greatly overshadowed by the random days of drunken fits of rage, overshadowed by more visits to the ER for pancreatitis. One time, I go into a rage at a nurse for not tending to *my* needs. It didn't matter that there were others in the ER. I was in pain! That's all that mattered to me.

End of July 2004, we take a trip to Minnesota. Curtis and I had been to Minnesota once before, in 1995, for my younger brother's funeral, the one who was taken away when we were little. He was only thirty. I was a very proper, slightly drunk, pallbearer. I'm not comfortable around my family, but this time, we're going back mostly because my grandma is up there. I promise I won't drink for the week we are there. I keep that promise. I don't go through any obvious physical withdrawals, but for the entire week, I have such incredible cravings I feel like I will go crazy and can't wait until this trip is over.

When we get back home, I start drinking like my body, and my mind need to make up for lost time. I don't know how I'm making it through work, but by the end of my first week back, Mr. Hyde has come out to play, and he's like hell on wheels and ready to do battle with anyone because no one is doing their job right and it's making my job harder. I'm cussing everyone out. After the store opens, our human resource manager is notified of my behavior, which prompts him to ask me to do a voluntary drug screen. Generally on Fridays, I leave early so this request then prompted me to…leave early. It's about 10:00 a.m. I go to the liquor store, go home, and continue drinking.

I haven't been able to stop by the time Curtis comes home. My body or my mind, or both, won't let me stop. I'm coming completely unglued inside, totally unraveling. I want to stop, but I can't. I'm stumbling all over the house, falling, bumping into everything. My body, my mind, my soul, every fiber of my being feels like it's being ripped to shreds, like I'm on the brink of total insanity. Noiseless things shrieking in my head, shrieking but no real sound. I want everything to stop!

Once again, I go to Curtis begging for help. Begging and pleading with him to take me back to the treatment center. It's like something supernatural is whispering inside my head, among all the cacophony chaos, saying, *"It's life or death now. Live or die. You choose."* And somehow, there's still a sane part of my mind saying, *"I want to live."*

When we get to the treatment center, they won't take me. They administer the breathalyzer, and I won't register meaning my blood alcohol content is over .40. They tell Curtis to either take me to the ER or, if he can get me to drink water and get me down to a .35, they can admit me. I beg and plead to no end…but they won't take me.

Curtis doesn't take me to the ER knowing they will just detox me and release me in the morning. Instead, he goes to the liquor store and buys me a bottle knowing that I will probably fight tooth and nail, get the car myself, and drive drunk to the liquor store. I proceed to drink even more into the night with voices battling inside my head. Every fiber of my being feeling shredded more and more until I really can't take it anymore. I take the bottle and pour the rest of it down the sink saying, *"I give up!"*

The sun is starting to come up on Saturday morning. Curtis goes to the store and buys a ton of Gatorade, which I proceed to drink and drink and drink. By Saturday evening, they are able to admit me into the treatment center again. I am registering just at .35.

I get the same counselor I had the last time, and she says she's going to kick my butt. But she never does.

Something happened this weekend. My obsession to drink has been completely lifted from me. Something strange has taken place inside me that I can't explain, a feeling beyond description. They keep me for two weeks. When I'm released, this time, my counselor says she doesn't recommend IOP. She tells me that even though she can see and feels there's something different in me, I was *"dancing with death"* again this time when I came in and she will pray that this new life that is taking hold of me will continue to grow. I'm holding back tears, and I tell her, *"It's not the world out there I'm afraid of this time…It's me, that scares me."*

*****

On many occasions, I have talked about my last drunk weekend and getting sober. I always jokingly say… *"God mistook my pleas for help as a prayer."* But God doesn't make mistakes. Does He? Besides, isn't that what prayer is… a plea for help? It will still be a few more years before I realize that God had *everything* to do with my getting sober.

Sober Me

I'm fired from my job when I get out of rehab this time. But I am totally good with that. I have time to focus and center myself on my sobriety. I truly, truly believe I have a new lease on life. I hit the gym hard again. I've been told, "Muscles don't forget," and it's true. It doesn't take long to get back into shape, to get my abs ripped again. I'm hitting AA meetings every chance I get, and in between, I'm putting out resumes, and within a month, I have a job in manufacturing. The same plant that laid me off seven years ago when it went through a buyout. I love it. Twelve-hour shifts. Four days one week, three the next. It is four and three. I always have some week days off, and every other weekend is a three-day weekend. I am truly loving my life. But after a year of sobriety and a year on the job, I start experiencing incredible abdominal pains again, and I have to have major pancreatic surgery. Due to my many years of extensive alcohol abuse, my pancreatic duct has been calcified, along with half of my pancreas, creating pancreatic pseudocysts. My doctor tells me, *"If you hadn't gotten sober when you did, you most likely would not have lived this past year to see this surgery."*

The surgery takes a few hours and, as I recall it being told to me, entailed the surgical team having to scoop out some of my organs to remove the cysts and having to use some of my intestine to create a new pancreatic duct. It is by far the most painful experience ever for me. Morphine drips every fifteen minutes for two days as my internal organs feel like they are re-situating themselves, moving back into place. I will only be in the hospital for a week, but I am greatly concerned about the seven-inch incision down the center of my abdomen that has been closed with staples. I worked hard to get this washboard stomach back and worried about scars. I end up healing very well and the faint scarring that is left actually enhances the work I've done on my abs. My doctor does warn me that this was not a common surgery and most people that do have it end up becoming "porkers" due to weight gain. Ummm…No…I don't think so…Not going to happen…Not me!!! But I do have to take synthetic enzymes for life since my pancreas no longer produces certain enzymes needed for proper digestion.

Along with Alcoholics Anonymous, I have included physical fitness as part of my recovery, my new sober life. I keep a very strict gym schedule that I rarely alter. Every morning on my days off, up at 3:00 a.m., at the gym by 4:00 a.m.

After three years of sobriety (I never thought I would be able to say that), I take a gamble on something I have been very curious about doing…flipping houses. I've done my own research and study-ing and even solicited the help of a family friend, who is a realtor. I have scouted around and kept my eyes on a few foreclosures. One in particular: a three-bedroom, one-and-a-half bath, thirteen-hundred square foot brick rancher. The foreclosure price is so low. It has been off the market for a while, for no apparent reason that I can see, but something tells me to keep an eye on it. Even though this is my deal, I include Curtis because I value his input. Before I know it, the house is back on the market, and I have to take that leap of faith. I get a realtor to show it to me. It's pretty shabby inside, actually it's a complete nightmare, but I figure I can slap a coat of paint on it and have it on the market in a month and reap the rewards. So I take that leap and procure a loan on my own and become the proud owner of a foreclosed property.

After going through the house room by room, inch by inch, I make a list of all supplies I should need. Then I take advantage of twelve months no interest, no payment, with my credit card from the home improvement place I used to work for. I charge about sixteen thousand dollars worth of supplies and get to work. I'm ripping out carpets, sanding walls, redoing countertops, and painting. What I thought would take a month to do has become a meticulous labor of love. The more I get into this, the more beautifully transformed this house is becoming.

Now on my days off, I'm at the gym by 3:00 a.m. and working on the house by 6:00 a.m. until 5:00 p.m. It takes me six months on my days off to complete what I originally thought would take a month, including landscaping. I have taken many pictures of the house in transition, before, during, and after. When I walk through the house admiring it's new look, I jokingly ask God, *"What have you done to me?"* I am in awe at the work that has been done. I didn't know I could do anything like this. I'm not sure what I'm believing, so as I gaze upward, I say again, *"Seriously, God…What have you done to me?"* I feel a warmth take over inside me, not a physical warmth…a more peaceful presence type of warmth that envelops me inside but also kind of filling the room. My eyes start to tear up. I'm not understanding any of what's happening. I'm overwhelmed with emotion. I cannot begin to really explain what I'm feeling. I just get on my knees and start praying. *"God…thank you for what you are doing in me."* I don't know what He is doing in me, but I know He's doing something.

I don't know anything about "For Sale by Owner," so I obtain the services of another realtor friend to put the house on the market. It only has two showings, but in less than a month, a single mother of two young boys falls absolutely in love with the house. Even at the closing, in my attorney's office (I had to get a real estate attorney), she can't stop raving about how beautiful the house is. I am very humbled by her compliments.

Even with helping her out on the down payment, I still come out with a very sizeable profit for my first "flip." Even my realtor said the Realty Gods were looking down on me. However, oddly enough, that didn't seem as important as I thought it would be. It was incredible, but what had become more important is that I have played a part in making the life of a young single mother more fulfilling and happier by helping her to provide a home for her two children.

I bank my hefty profit, then Curtis and I celebrate with a very nice dinner out. The next day, I go to my real estate attorney and begin the paperwork to form C & C Properties LLC, then I start hunting for my next property. I've been bit by "The Bug."

*****

Curtis would later confess to me that he really didn't believe that I could go through with this project to completion. I had been slowly paying off my school loan in LA for the past ten years. Curtis now jokes, *"It took ten years to pay off a school loan and ten months to pay off a thirty-year mortgage."* He was impressed. I am in awe.

A Whole New World

ॐ   ॐ

It's May 2009. I've recently sold my second house that I was flipping. It is my own little birthday present to myself. It was also a foreclosure in shambles. Like my first house, this too went from a "rags to riches" look. When this one is finished, I'm asking God again, *"What have you done to me?"* and I'm now in the habit of praying and thanking God for all He is doing in me. I still don't really know where my beliefs lie, but yet I'm talking to God. I have a talent I didn't know about that has been revealed to me and put to use again. Next to acting, rehabbing these homes has been the most fulfilling thing I've ever done. This house was a tougher sell, though, because I had a really picky buyer. After some hard headed negotiating through our realtors, I still come out of it with a very sizeable profit again. Happy birthday to me.

Things are going so well that I even start up a second business. C & C Properties LLC doing business as "Walter's World of Gifts." I have a website. It's also on Facebook. A huge catalogue of fantastic home decor merchandise. This one takes a lot of work as well, just in a different way—door-to-door distribution of catalogues, mailing lists. I do some fairly decent business. I am having an incredible time in my life of sobriety. I have my regular job and starting two successful businesses.

*****

Curtis and I have had sixteen years together. They are mostly good years but some not so good. In my sobriety, I have done a lot of growing up. I have become a lot more responsible and realize I don't need to have someone in my life to feel whole or give me self-worth.

I have become I-N-D-E- P-E-N-D-E-N-T. Still working full time, I have started two of my own side businesses. I made a good profit on both houses I have flipped, and Walter's World of Gifts is seeing a fair share of business. I'm at the gym for four hours in the mornings, three to four days a week. I'm staying in top shape. My life has taken a different direction, for the good, and Curtis in his own direction. During the course of learning to maintain my sobriety, learning to live my life on a daily basis without the need for alcohol, Curtis and I have completely switched to opposite sides of the fence.

Many times, when I'm getting up early for work or the gym, I'm finding his car parked in the garage crooked. I'm noticing things that are making me concerned: late nights, crooked car. But I have to keep on my path...I have to. Alcohol had nearly taken my life a few times, and I don't want to go back to that. I have to talk with my friends in AA to help me keep my focus on my sobriety, or I put myself at risk. One late night, I get the inevitable call around two-thirty in the morning from the police station. Yes...we have ended up on complete opposite sides of the fence now. The tables have turned. I'm very saddened that he is going through this, and I'm not quite sure how to deal with it, but I'm very thankful for my sobriety so I am able to be of help. I'm getting just a small sample of life as he used to see it. It actually feels a little awkward. One evening after a discussion and some eye-opening divulgements, things have culmi-nated between us to a point where I felt it necessary to tell him, *"I can't do this anymore...I can't live like this."*

*****

I don't fully realize yet that God is leading me down a path in a direction more in tune with Him.

*****

I'm praying every day mostly because that's what is suggested in AA and, if it's helping me to stay sober, then I do it. I believe in God but still get confused about it a lot. Curtis and I officially "call it quits," but I'm not ready to move out of "our" house just yet. After all, we looked and found it together. Granted, Curtis pays the mortgage and major house bills, he has a far greater income than me, and that's just the way it had been for years. My income, though much, much smaller, did contribute to a lot of the lesser essentials such as groceries, yard improvements, some furniture, other than what I had broken in drunken fits years earlier, portions of vacations…and alcohol. At least the alcohol is over for me, but I'm just not ready to move out. Not ready to move into the spare bedroom either and give up the use of the master bath. So we live as we always had, only as friends.

I still ask Curtis to go with me when I'm looking for my next investment property, I value his input. His point of view is always important. I end up purchasing another foreclosed home that summer. It is a three-bedroom, two-bath, brick rancher. It's an incredible mess just like the others, but this time, I am actually able to hire a contractor to work on this house using some of the profits from my previous two houses. I can go to work and have someone working on the house while I'm gone. I will have this house finished and on the market in just a little over a month versus the six months it took me on the others doing most of the work myself.

Every day, when I see the progress on the house, I am amazed at what is taking place in my life, and I say a prayer thanking God for all He is doing in my life.

My loan officer has to come over to check the house before she can release more money to me when I need it. She always tells me that this house is definitely my best and will be my most profitable.

By the end of summer, the house is finished and on the market. The economy isn't making a quick turnaround, so I'm not getting a lot of looks, which turns out to be a blessing.

Things are getting too awkward at home with the two of us still living together. I need me to be gone for the sake of my own sobriety and sanity. I'm not thinking of drinking, but I'm aware of what can happen to a recovering alcoholic when he stays in a situation that's not healthy for him. Also Curtis needs me to be gone for himself. It will help in the long run in order for us to remain the friends we are.

We talk. I jokingly remind him that *"We're stuck with each other no matter what"* since I'm godfather to Cody and Jonathan and (honorary) godfather to Billy and considered uncle to all the boys and also considered part of the family. Curtis knows all this to be true, and we're both kind of happy with that.

I go to my bank to see about having the property taken out of my company's name and transferred to my name. I have the house appraised. Again, like the other houses, it appraises at a good twenty thousand above what I invested. Would have been more if the economy hadn't crashed when it did. We do an easy refinance and title transfer, and early in the month of November, the house is now mine. Unfortunately, the profit I would have pocketed has turned to equity. But at the age of forty-six, I now have my very own house to live in. This will also be the last house for C & C Properties.

As long as I still have use of our pickup, I have to buy a lot of new furniture. While Curtis is overseas on a business trip, I move some things from our home into my house. It makes the transition easier, and I'm really only taking a few things that I had bought for us leaving Curtis with the majority.

On New Year's Eve, December 31, 2009, I will have a very sober very wonderful first night in my first home.

I say a prayer thanking God for this beautiful home and for all that He has done for me. On January 4, 2010, I quit smoking.

Oddly…Curtis, at some point prior to our breaking up, had deposited five thousand dollars into the C & C Properties account without my knowledge. I have no idea why. My little business was going so well with the first two houses that I didn't need it, nor did I ask for it. It stayed there after I moved out. We never really discussed it. Privately, I kind of considered it to be palimony. However, I do keep Curtis on my bank accounts. He's the only one I trust to handle things in case anything were to happen to me. Hopefully, that day will not come any time soon.

Left Behind

⁊   ⹃

I have been sober for five years now, living in my new house. I still go to AA meetings regularly. I always get there early and will usually go to the thrift store a few doors down to browse before the meeting starts. There's a used book section on one end of this vast store. I always start at the other end and don't even pay attention to the books when I get to that side. As I'm wandering around, one day, I notice a small paperback novel on the floor, far away from where the books are. I've been in here many, many times and have never seen a book on this end.

I used to be an avid reader when I was a teenager—Stephen King, Peter Staub, anything scary. I would stay up into the middle of the night's reading. But I haven't really read in years. I pick this book up and turn it over to the front cover. *Left Behind* is the title. I have never heard of it. I read the back cover. It takes a fictitious family through the "rapture," as described in the book of Revelation in the Bible. It's fiction based on the prophecies of Revelation. Sounds interesting, I thought. I have actually read Revelation a couple times, in my distant past, out of curiosity, and had been fascinated, confused, and scared by it. Twenty-five cents is what this book costs. What the heck. Little…oooh, so little…do I know the journey I am about to take.

To this day, I fully believe God, through whomever was in there before me, made certain that book would be right in my walking path so I would stumble upon it.

I learned that this is a sixteen-book series. I live the book of Revelation through this fictitious family. Before I'm done with that first twenty-five-cent book, I'm at the nearest bookstore to make sure the next book in the series is available to buy. Sometimes, if there's only one copy left on the shelf of even the next one, I'll buy it also so I won't be left without.

It takes me over a year and nearly $250 to finish the series. God has me entranced with the thoughts of what might be in store for my future depending on how I live my life.

Money's tight for me, so this isn't always easy, but it's like an addiction. I'm eagerly reading each book in the series, sometimes staying up into the middle of the night like I used to do as a teenager. I even look things up in the Bible that they would refer to in the books. I am living, along with these fictional characters, the rapture of the church, the rise of the antichrist, the seven years of tribulation, the plagues, the mark of the beast, the torture of Christians, people being saved and coming to Christ, the battle in the Valley of Megiddo (Armageddon), leading up to the second coming of Christ. The emotions this series generates in me I could never completely describe. My heart and soul are literally being opened up. I'm scared and horrified at the descriptive torture of Christians knowing that my brain can't begin to imagine what it will really be like. I cry with joy when people get saved. I sometimes kneel at the edge of my bed in tears and say the prayer, the sinner's prayer, accepting Christ in my life. I'm a very compassionate, empathetic, and emotional person to begin with, but these books bring me to tears of gratitude and joy because I can honestly feel God's love and forgiveness in my heart.

Tim Lahaye and Jerry B. Jenkins are the authors of these books. When I finish the *Left Behind* series, I'm left feeling filled up but empty at the same time. Thirsty and hungry for more, I end up reading just about every book they write. I start reading my Bible more. Even my AA literature, I would normally read on my lunch breaks at work, is now replaced with more spiritual Christian reading.

*****

These books have an incredible impact on me. I don't realize yet that this is going to be the beginning of profound changes in my life, a true spiritual awakening. This is just a start, a slow process, not a burning bush, just the beginning.

*****

The Audition

ℰ ℭ

Before the *Left Behind* books, my faith in God was really based on what I had been experiencing through AA. A "higher power" could be anything you wanted. I have always believed in God but never truly "believed" yet. I pray in the morning, and I pray at night as is suggested in AA. I really don't know where my faith is.

I'm sober and prayer, early on, is more of a ritual. I'm afraid that if I stop, I might eventually get drunk again. My faith and beliefs are completely different now. These days I am actually relying on God, through Jesus Christ, to lead me through my day. Not quite whole heartedly yet but I do sometimes find myself saying little prayers of thanks during the day. I still struggle with certain issues in my life. I have become much more God conscious. I have much more confidence in myself but still so many insecurities.

Sometime in the fall of 2010, I don't know how I find out, either Facebook, some chance e-mail, maybe I overheard someone. I find out there is an audition for a musical with a very well-known local theater company. The musical is *Little Women: A Little Musical.*

It has been about twenty-two years since I have done anything in the acting world. I have always loved the stage. Inside, I am dying with excitement at the thought of being back on stage, but then those old nasty doubts about myself start to surface in the back of my mind. I push them aside, get online, and look up *Little Women* because I'm not really familiar with the story. I order the script online and rent the movie. It's a heartwarming story. I love the time period the story takes place in. I'm forty-seven now, so roles in the show are limited. The casting call says cold readings (reading from the script), so I don't have to prepare a monologue. I do, however, need a song.

It has been so long. I only have about a couple weeks before auditions, so I need to choose something I'm familiar with and within my singing range, and I have to have sheet music for the accompanist. You are not allowed to sing to recorded music, and it has to be a song from a musical. I mull around with a few songs in my head and finally settle on *Edelweiss* from my favorite musical *The Sound of Music*. Remember I had auditioned for that show in LA in my early twenties.

Now I need to rehearse with a piano. I'm at a loss because I'm such a homebody that I don't really know a lot of people, especially anyone musically inclined. I don't even know if I have any talent anymore, but something inside me is pushing me forward, telling me to take that "leap of faith" like I did with that first house I invested in.

I find out that an acquaintance of mine in AA teaches piano. Extremely nervous, I approach her and ask if she would be willing to help me. She very happily agrees to work with me. I start to get more anxious and nervous. With my job and just everyday life, there is only time for about three one-hour sessions.

I'm afraid. I haven't sung in front of anyone in years. My mother's voice creeps into the back of my mind telling me I'm tone deaf, can't sing. My past accomplishments remind me differently. My friend tells me I sound wonderful. Of course, I think she's just being nice. However…I am sober now. I've never done anything like this sober. I'm remembering that in Hollywood, every audition, every casting call, anytime on location or on set or any workshop I was involved in, I was under the influence of "something." I am petrified inside. I have turned to prayer and many conversations with God since I first heard of the audition.

The day of the audition is here. It's a work day, so I am going to rush to the Civic Center straight from work. The whole drive I'm talking to God, just asking Him to be with me. I'm not asking for any specific part. I'm reminding Him (like He needs that) that I've never done anything sober and with a clear head. *"Dear God, my Father, please help me through this. If I have any talent left or if I ever did, help me to show it. Lord, I'm going to be in front of a theater full of strangers auditioning. Please guide my thoughts, guide my words, guide my actions. Please grant me boldness and courage to just be me. Dear Lord, just be with me and help me through this. In Jesus name, thank you, God, thank you, Jesus."* That was basically how my prayer and conversation with God went.

I get to the Civic Center and head into the theater scared, but my mind is constantly talking to God. I'm calming down and starting to meet people. Conversation is starting to come out of my mouth naturally. It is very odd because people scare me. Ha ha. A lot of people here, but I'm starting to feel comfortable, kind of like I belong here. I'm so excited inside right now that I can't describe it, being in a theater again—the thrill and being sober. Inside my head, I am thanking God over and over. I fill out my audition sheets, take a seat in the theater, and the auditions commence.

Throughout the evening, the director and her assistants shuffle through our paperwork, calling names for people to read, pairing us up in different combinations. I'm called to read a few times for a secondary role. I'm told by others my readings were good, but then we say that to everyone. However, I have seen some very talented people. Eventually, the singing portion of the auditions start. I'm hearing some beautiful voices. I'm one of the last to sing. There has been so many good people before me that I'm starting to feel a little inferior. Once I hand my sheet music to the accompanist, I have to shove those thoughts aside, real fast, and a quick *"Please be with me Lord"* races through my mind. I sing. Get the light applause, as we did for everyone. The director informs me that they had recently done *The Sound of Music* and where was I for that. They seemed to really like my audition piece *Edelweiss*. I'm feeling pretty good now. It's been a long evening, and auditions are over. We are told we will be informed if we are asked to be called back. I am so thrilled inside. I'm driving home tired but thanking God over and over for the opportunity and for being with me. No matter what the outcome, God walked through that audition with me showing me that I could do it sober with a clear head. Before bed, I kneel and pray again.

The next day, I find out I made callbacks. I am ecstatic beyond description! OH...MY...GOSH!!! Thank you God. Thank you

God. Thank you God. I do have some talent. I'm realizing this for the first time as a sober person. God is still revealing so much to me.

Call backs are exciting. Another long evening of reading over and over with different people being paired up again. I am so thrilled to just be there. We are told, at the end of the evening, that if we aren't cast in a part that we wanted, it has nothing to do with our talent. We were called back *because* of our talent. The cast will be posted online.

It takes a couple days for them to post the cast. I look down the cast list. I was not cast in the part I was called back for. I was cast as part of the chorus/ensemble/townspeople. You know what…I was elated! I was thanking God with tears in my eyes. This was all beyond anything I expected. I was originally just wanting to be able to make it through an audition clean and sober. The opportunity to be back on stage was an incredible bonus. God just won't stop showing me His wondrous ways. My life just keeps getting better.

My Return to the Stage

ଛ ଔ

I work twelve-hour shifts, so I learned to adjust my daily routine to make time for rehearsals. That was not difficult because I am thrilled to be back in "the biz." Granted, it's amateur civic theater productions, but that doesn't matter because the theater is just plain exciting! Right after work, I rush straight to the rehearsal studio for long rehearsal schedules. I'm just part of the ensemble, but we still have dance numbers and a lot of music to learn. We have a lot of work to do in just a few short months before the show opens. Besides, we won't even be able to move into the actual theater to rehearse with the orchestra and get familiar with the stage until a week before opening. Even the entire set is built off site and transported to the theater the last week. I think this must be a little what a Broadway touring show goes through. How exciting that would be.

Since getting sober, I've been able to attend a couple Broadway musicals here each touring season. I am always completely entranced, watching these actors play out these stories in music and dance, drawing us into their world on stage. I'm usually left teary-eyed at the end of the show because I'm filled with so much internalized excitement. There is always such a powerful closing number and the rousing curtain calls with standing ovations. I get a little envious because of my own unfulfilled dreams, wishing it was me up there on stage.

It's opening night, and it *is* going to be me back on stage in the chorus as a townsperson but part of a whole production. It's extremely exhilarating. All the hustle and bustle of wardrobe and makeup is done. Aside from all the cast rehearsals, I've rehearsed musical numbers at home by myself. I've rehearsed dance moves at home with my broom. I'm ready. After all these years, those old, old, familiar butterflies in my stomach are back. Nice to know they hadn't completely given up on me. They were just lying in remission, butterfly hibernation, laying in wait.

The orchestra starts with the intro music. Over the intercom in the dressing rooms we're given final notice for *"Places everyone."* There's the normal banter among everyone to "break a leg." Curtains open, lights up, and we dance out on stage for the opening number. Butterflies are now gone. I am in absolute heaven. We had been told earlier that opening night was sold out. My wonderful dance partner, Stephanie, and I have to enter through the audience down to the stage, and I can see at a glance that the theater is full to capacity. My ex, Curtis, is in the audience somewhere. Aside from seeing me in "The Beastmaster" and "Back to School", he has only ever heard me talk of my acting days. He has never seen me perform live. I am also excited about that.

The first half of the show goes without a hitch and its intermission. Back in the dressing rooms, I'm just soaking it all in. I'm on cloud nine. I know I'm beaming inside. Proud to be part of such a wonderful production. All the main actors are doing a brilliant job.

Wardrobe changes, makeup touched up, last call for places, orchestra, curtains up, and we go into the second act. Before I know it, the show has come to its emotional ending, and it's time for curtain call. We are all in our places to take our bows. When the lights come up, the audience rises to their feet in a standing ovation. I can see some wiping their eyes. I am fighting back tears of excitement, jubilation, and joy—tears of pure gratitude! I am thanking God so loud in my head for allowing me to be a part of this. I am overwhelmed with emotion.

After the show, we (the cast) go out to the lobby to greet the audience. Curtis comes up to me and tells me he has never seen me look happier and says, *"I believe you are exactly where you need to be."* I love him dearly as my friend, so those words mean a great deal to me.

I am realizing that my dreams of stardom and fame so long ago are not what my heart was really about. Just to entertain, to be a part of something that brings out emotions in an audience, to draw them into the life we were portraying on stage, and to have the audience leave feeling fulfilled and entertained. That is where my talents are best suited. I didn't need to be a famous star to be content.

*****

It seems that my drug- and alcohol-induced Hollywood days are a lifetime ago, somebody else's lifetime ago. An entirely different person exists today. God has, and is, doing something truly wonderful in my life.

*****

Me and Stephanie (my stage wife) singing and dancing our way around the stage.
Opening night. *Little Women A Little Musical*, Spring 2011

Me and Stephanie in *Little Women a Little Musical*, Spring 2011

Me and Stephanie in *Little Women A Little Musical*, Spring 2011

Time for Reflection

℅ ℂ

The show finishes its two-week run and closes around the end of March. My life returns to its normal routine. Some people from work have seen the show, and I get compliments on how wonderful the show was.

During this time, I'm still working on *Walter's World of Gifts*, halfheartedly, really. It has just become more of a fun hobby. Although I do have to maintain the website which costs money.

Before too long, things start to take a turn, and I end up having to get rid of my little gift store. I won't be able to afford to keep the website up.

April 27, 2011, the tornado super outbreak occurs all over Alabama and around Huntsville. One of the tornados narrowly misses my neighborhood but tears a path through communities just over the hill from me. Homes all around where I live are untouched by tornados, but many of their trees are uprooted from the high winds. Huge pine trees and oak trees are down all over. One house around the corner from me had a tree split their home in two. All of North Alabama is without power for a week.

My property was unscathed. But not my
neighbor around the corner.

Transformers down all over.

Long lines for what little bit of food we can get.

It's during this time that I notice a small lump on my neck just under my jawline. I mess with it a bit, but I'm not too concerned. I'm sure it will go away. My whole life, I've never really been sick other than childhood illnesses or what was caused by my alcohol abuse. I've never even had the flu as an adult. I just brush this off.

Nothing to do at home without power, so I spend a lot of that week hanging out at the AA facility. Low on gas so I spend half a day waiting in the gas lines. Gas stations have to fire up generators so gas pumps can function. Fights break out in these gas lines. Police are on the scene trying to control chaos. Cars wrapped around the block at the station I'm at. Tempers are flaring. Some gas stations can't open. Others are out of gas. Store shelves are empty as we are all running out of food. It's fascinating watching human behavior under circumstances such as these. We are under a dusk till dawn curfew.

By the end of the first week in May, all power is restored to our part of the state. I am also noticing that the lump on my neck is getting larger. A voice inside my head says, *"You're almost forty-eight. Not everything just goes away."* This is Friday, May 6. I work Monday and Tuesday, so I go to my regular doctor on Wednesday, the eleventh.

My doctor looks me over. He has been my doctor for years and has seen me through my alcohol abuse and pancreatitis, so I trust him. He feels the lump in my neck, tells me he believes it to be a cyst, and instructs me not to play with it or it could get worse. *"We'll see how it looks in a couple weeks,"* he says. I get up and start to leave, and at the last minute, he says, *"Let me take a look in your mouth."* He asks me how long I've had that white spot under my tongue on the floor of my mouth. I tell him, *"Two maybe three years. Always mean to ask my dentist about it but always forget. Besides, it doesn't bother me."* He immediately has an appointment set up for me to see an ENT specialist the next day. I don't have a clue as to what's going on except that this lump looks pretty ugly.

I go to see this specialist. He examines me. When he's done, he asks me to come back the next day, Friday, for a biopsy. he tells me he's ninety-nine percent certain I have cancer. My mind is blank except for the fact that I work Friday through Sunday and can't afford to be off work. I ask him if I can come in on Monday. He looks me square in the face, directly into my eyes, and tells me, *"Craig, this is a matter of life and death. You need to make yourself available!"* All this is not quite registering, but I tell him I'll come in.

I make it in the next morning. He takes a needle, sticks me under my tongue, and injects a numbing agent. Then he takes a tiny clipper and cuts a small chunk out of the floor of my mouth. This is a "we need results ASAP" biopsy. It is shipped off STAT over the weekend. He has me scheduled to come back on Monday.

I work the weekend. I have mentioned all this to my supervisor in case I need to start taking time off, but I shrug this off also because I don't "get" stuff. This "C" word really doesn't mean much to me. It's kind of like…"yeah, right."

*****

It's Monday, May 16, my birthday. I'm forty-eight years old today.

I'm sitting in my doctor's office, no major concerns. Everything is okay. My doctor comes in and turns out he is an ENT oncologist. There is no beating around the bush. My doctor flat out tells me I have cancer: head and neck cancer. The main tumor in the floor of my mouth is the size of an apricot seed. I never really noticed. It never bothered me. One of the main causes of head and neck cancer is alcohol and cigarettes. With my history, we're basically going with that as being the cause. He sets me up for a rush PET scan the next day at the cancer institute here. A strict protein diet for the night I'm not allowed to workout forty-eight hours prior to scan. I haven't been to the gym, since I worked all weekend, and not this morning because of this appointment, so I'm good there.

He explains that there is a panel of oncologists that will discuss my case. Some teams recommend chemo, radiation, and surgery. He tells me how disfiguring the surgery would be but that his group is usually against surgery. They will decide the route to take when my results come back. I just listen, blank faced. My mind a little numb. Still none of this is completely registering in my brain. I still say everything is all right.

I drive home and sit in my car for a while thinking and reflecting. I call Curtis to tell him what's going on and to remind him that he still has power of attorney over me and that he is still on my bank accounts…just in case. Again, hopefully, that day will not come anytime soon. I still pray every day. My normal prayers are for everyone else and for me to do His will and I'm just asking Him to be with me. He knows the outcome, but I just need Him to please be with me.

The next day, I'm at the cancer institute. I had a high protein diet the night before and had to skip the gym, per instructions for PET scan. They shoot me up with radioactive glucose, and I have to relax in an easy chair in a private room for about an hour so it can work its way through my system. I go through the scan. It's harmless and I actually doze off a little. Afterward, I have to go to another room to have a mesh plaster mold made of my upper chest and head. I will get my PET results in a couple days. My appointment will be with the doctor who will be my radiation oncologist.

The Results

℘   ℜ

I meet with my radiation oncologist. He explains that I am a late stage four cancer and the cancer has spread through all the lymph nodes in my neck. The only reason I can be treated is because it has not quite reached my brain yet. I mention that my regular doctor initially wanted to wait a couple weeks then had a last-minute thought to look in my mouth. My oncologist said if we had waited those two weeks, there's a good chance it would have made its way to my brain and they would have given me only eighteen months to live.

I strongly believe it was a "God thing" that prompted my doctor to look in my mouth. I truly, truly believe that was God at work.

My radiation oncologist tells me that my tumor looks more viral to him and he's going to have a DNA test done on the biopsy taken. I'm not sure what all that means, but he then proceeds to tell me the treatment plan they have come up with.

I will go into surgery on Monday. I will be scoped down my throat to have a feeding tube placed in my stomach for nine months. I will have aggressive radiation treatments Monday through Friday. It will be like an atomic bomb going off in my mouth. I will lose all my taste buds during treatment and will not be able to eat, but in time, they will come back. My saliva glands will be killed off and will not come back completely. I will get sores inside my mouth that will be extremely painful. The muscles in my jaw will atrophy, and it will be difficult to even open my mouth. I will lose my ability to talk. I will have to keep myself fed through my tube, medications through my tube. If I don't maintain a certain weight, I will have to be hospitalized. Chemotherapy is going to be twice a week. I will be getting sick. He tells me that my cancer has the worst and most grueling treatments of all cancers.

I don't know what my brain is registering, except fear. I'm fighting back tears, not self-pity tears but tears of fear and uncertainty. I will not cry. He tells me he can see I'm getting all glassy eyed. He's going to let his nurse come in and talk to me. Before my doctor leaves the room, I look at him directly in his eyes, and while fighting back tears, I tell him, *"I will be eating by Thanksgiving!"* None of this nine month feeding tube. No! No! No! Not going to happen! It is almost the end of May. My doctor leaves. His nurse comes in, looks at me, and gives me a hug. I tell her, *"I am not going to cry!"* She says, *"It's okay."* But I still won't.

I don't remember all that happens next, but I do get scheduled for surgery on Monday, the twenty-third.

I have been sober for almost seven years and smoke free for almost a year and a half. I'm walking out to my car, my head spinning, my mind racing and reeling in so many directions. I feel like I have just been slammed into a brick wall. In earlier days, I would have gone straight for the bottle in a situation like this but not a single thought of a drink comes to mind. I could, however, go for a cigarette. But even that thought is not strong enough and passes quickly.

I sit in my car in the parking lot of the hospital for about half an hour. I don't know what I'm thinking about, if I'm even thinking. I eventually start my car and decide to head home. I come to a stoplight. I'm sitting there waiting, and all of a sudden, I softly say out loud, *"Thank you, God, thank you, Jesus, for getting me sober so I can go through this with a clear mind."* Then I remember that if I hadn't gotten sober when I did, I wouldn't even be alive. Then I start laughing. I just had this bombshell dropped on me, and I'm thanking God. That is incredible. I know that He's with me. I just know it. I don't know what's going to happen, but He is here.

I get home, and still sitting in my car, I call Curtis first to remind him he's in charge if something happens. I sit in my car a little longer and allow myself to cry a little, just a little. Yes, I'm scared but nothing gets me down—nothing. And I won't let this. I go inside and call my family. I talk to my father, leave a message for my brother, and talk to my sister. A couple weeks later, my sister sends me a prayer shawl lovingly crocheted by her women's group in church. It made me cry that people I don't know did this for me. I later tell her it's the best gift I have ever gotten. I reach my mother, but she doesn't want to talk to me about it. It's too emotional for her. She says, *"I love you,"* then we hang up. I won't be talking to my mother throughout all this, but that's okay.

I have to take off work Monday for surgery. I'm there first thing in the morning. I get prepped, taken in, and I say a silent prayer just asking God and Jesus to be with me, I'm put under. When I come around, I find out they couldn't get the tube in due to scar tissue from my pancreatic surgery. Instead, they will have to cut me open, from the outside, along the scar line from my pancreas surgery to get to my stomach, but they have to wait until Friday. I'm becoming aware that time is of the essence, and they need to get this done because I've already been placed on the treatment schedule. The cancer is that close to my brain.

Except for surgery day, I am still hitting the gym hard. This is not going to get me down or put me down.

I have to take Friday off also for surgery. It's the same thing: bring me in, prep me, say a silent prayer, and put me under. This time, when I wake up, I have a foot-long tube protruding from my stomach. I'm supposed to stay in the hospital all weekend, but I'm doing so well I get to go home by noon Saturday. On Monday, I start treatments.

Treatment

৪০ ৫২

In a matter of three weeks, I've gone from possible cyst to PET scan to finding out it's stage 4 cancer through surgery and into treatment.

Home health care has come by to drop off cases of canned nutrition to feed through my tube, wraps to hold my tube against my body under my cloths, and syringes for flushing my tube, all sorts of supplies. They will drop by once a week to make sure I have everything I need. I also think I will be able to keep going to the gym. It won't take long to realize that will be impossible.

My first day of treatment, I go into work for half a day then to the hospital for two hours of chemo. Blood work, visit with the my chemo oncologist, then into the very cold chemo room where I get hooked up to IV's and the poisonous chemo drugs start running through my veins. There are about ten other chairs in the room with chemo patients receiving their treatments. It's so cold in the chemo room they cover us with heated blankets that come out of a blanket oven. They are a godsend…so toasty warm. After my two hours of chemo, I head down to radiation. My molded mask is waiting for me. I lay on the table, they lay my mask over my head and chest and clamp me down to the table. There's a hole in the mouth area of the mask where they stick a large tube in my mouth to push my tongue back, so aside from lymph nodes, there can be a focus on the main tumor as the machine goes around my head. As the technician leaves, I can hear the thick, lead door to the radiation room closing. I'm all alone in here, me and the observation cameras. The humming of the machine starts, and in my head, I start talking to God. Kind of jokingly, I say, *"Lord, if the rapture of your church takes place while I'm in here and I get left behind, will you send someone to find me?"* My mind remains still for a moment just listening to the humming and beeps of the machine as it rotates around my head. Then my mind, as if already preparing for death, just blurts out, *"God, thank you for forgiving me of my sins."* Immediately a quiet, calm voice comes into my head and says, *"You always were."* Suddenly, my body, my heart, my soul…every fiber of my being are filled with such a peace I cannot describe. That was not my voice. My voice would never tell me something like that. My eyes start to well up, and a couple tears start to roll down the side of my face underneath my mask. I have to refocus my thinking because if I start to get all stuffed up I won't be able to breathe being clamped down with a tube pushing my tongue to the back of my mouth. But that "voice" not of my own thoughts.

On Friday, two days after my first treatment, the effects of chemo start to hit me. I'm nauseous the entire drive home from the hospital, I rush into the house and barely make it to the bathroom before being sick. With all the abdominal pressure from vomiting and the feeding tube stitched to my outer skin, that hurt. This will be my routine for the next three and a half months.

When my body settles down, I realize I need to eat. I refuse to use my feeding tube yet. It's in me waiting for the days when I'm no longer able to eat by mouth. I will force myself to eat regularly until I have absolutely no other choice. That doesn't take long. By the end of two weeks, my taste buds are pretty much radiated away—gone. Saliva glands are disappearing. I force myself to keep eating for another week. By then, everything I put in my mouth is so tasteless it's literally nauseating. It's indescribable how food can become so utterly tasteless that it makes me sick. Since taste and smell are connected, I can no longer smell anything either. By week four, I have what seems like a thousand canker sores in my mouth. I have to use an oral rinse that hurts like heck. My neck is all red and burnt from radiation, and I'm now starting to lose my ability to speak. On days I don't have chemo, I go to my car, when I'm at work, to feed my tube.

Chemo and radiation every day is draining my body of energy. I'm losing weight. I quickly go from 155 pounds down to almost 115. I'm fitting into a boys size sixteen husky pants. I get up at 3:30 a.m. before work to pour a couple cans of nutrition down my tube, liquid medications down my tube, flush my tube, and try to shower without getting tube area wet. I keep plastic shopping bags in my car because sometimes I get sick on the way to work and there goes part of my nutrition. Every day, my doctors see me and tell me how "awesome" my treatment is going, but as grueling as they are, they tell me I should consider taking off work. They say my going to work every day is unheard of. I tell them I'm okay. Colleagues at work tell me I look like the walking dead and don't know how I'm making it through the day. My head keeps telling me, *"I have a mortgage to pay that short-term disability won't take care of."* Besides, I'm leaving work four hours early each day.

I meet a lot of other cancer patients. I watch and sometimes talk with them during our chemo. The chemo room is very cold. Thank God for the heated blankets, and we have television. Some patients have eight hours of chemo. One person has chemo drugs that leaves them incredibly, painfully sensitive to cold. My doctors say my treatments are more grueling than any other cancer treatment, but I often wonder how some of these other people are making it through theirs that seem so much worse than mine. One day, I have a bad reaction to one of my chemo drugs, and I feel like I'm dying. My heart starts racing, I hear it pounding in my head. My chest gets really tight. I start to feel very hot and faint. As hard as I try, I'm barely able to whisper, *"I think something's wrong."* I'm suddenly surrounded by staff and doctors. I'm immediately unhooked, and my system gets flushed and treatment suspended that day, even radiation. The rest of my treatments will continue on schedule with that particular drug taken off my menu.

I'm also meeting new patients downstairs in radiation. One guy around forty is just diagnosed with lung cancer, married, two young children at home. He needs to run out for a cigarette before his treatment. I am so grateful to God and Jesus for taking cigarettes out of my life. If I hadn't stopped smoking a year and a half earlier, I don't know if cancer would have scared me enough to stop. When I'm clamped down and left alone, I start praying for him and all the other patients I have met. I have that tube placed in my mouth, and it's difficult to keep from tearing up when I recall their stories during my prayers. Every morning in prayer, I ask God to help me to do His will and to just help me through the day. During radiation treatment, I'm praying for the other patients or just chatting with God. I have never talked with God so much before.

During all this, something is happening inside me. I have faith but not sure where it's all coming from. I don't know what the outcome of my cancer is going to be. I'm not afraid to die physically, but during all my talks with God, I'm becoming more acutely aware and concerned about my eternity. The possibility of my eternal death becomes very real, and that frightens me. I'm having flashbacks to the horrifying "frightmares" I had during my coma in 1997: the woman with the body of a serpent and a crown on her head and the demons that were tearing me apart, pulling me to hell. I want eternity in Heaven. I want to be with Jesus when I die. This is when I start seriously thinking about church.

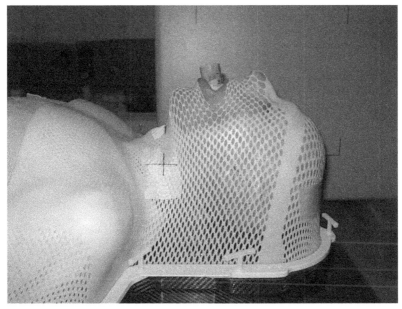

After I'm clamped down and there's no way for me to get out, I ask God, "If the rapture of your church takes place and I'm left behind, will you send someone to find me?"

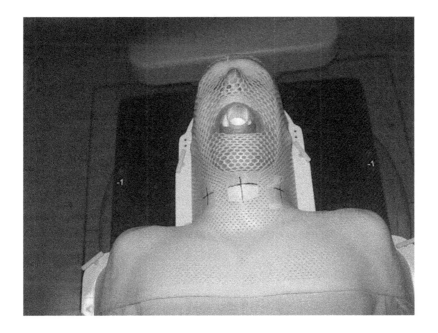

Back to Church

છ૭   ૦ર૪

Medical bills have started coming in. There are high co-pays for all the specialists I see. With the high costs of treatments, it doesn't take long to meet my deductibles and maximum out of pocket. It's paying them that's rough and all the medications I have to purchase. I realize I'm not going to be able to afford the website for "Walter's World of Gifts," so I'm financially forced to take it down. I'm grateful I have a full load of vacation time for all these days I leave early from work. However, I start to feel very overwhelmed by the bills.

Emotionally, mentally, I think I'm strong, but my doctors have warned that it's not good in my very weakened condition to let myself become overwhelmed by anything. It would be so easy because I'm very tired, but I'm told it could lead to dangerous depression.

I'm sitting on the couch, and I just start to pray something like this: *"Lord God, for whatever reasons, You have seen me through so much. You got me through my childhood. You were with me through all my years of drug and alcohol abuse. Lord, for whatever reason, You brought me through my suicide attempts. You got me sober. You carried me through my pancreatic surgery. Lord, You took cigarettes from my life. You have given me so much. I know you are with me. You have kept me alive for a reason. Lord God, I know You will carry me through this. Lord, please help me with my bills, and please, please take this load from me. In Jesus name, I pray. Thank you, God. Thank you, Jesus. Amen."*

I never worried about those bills again. Those worries and concerns were just taken from my mind. Somehow, everything seemed to get paid. God did provide. All I did was have faith, say my regular prayers every day thanking God and thanking Jesus, getting to my treatments, always praying for the others, putting one foot in front of the other and just trusting in God. There is a kind of peace inside of me that says everything is okay. There is also something else inside of me, nudging, pulling, I'm wanting to go to church. I'm feeling a need to go to church. There's a desire to fill some emptiness in me, an unexplainable desire, a longing deep inside I have never had.

I remember "The Rock" church from when I was a hopeless drunk, when I went there thinking someone would lay their hands on me and cure me of my drinking. For whatever purpose, that "voice" inside, that is not me, was leading me back to this church.

Every other weekend, I was off work. I cherished those weekends because it gave my body a much-needed rest from all the weeklong treatments. I still had to make sure I got nourishment and medications down my tube, but I could do it at a more leisurely pace, unlike workdays that were rushed in the morning, again for lunch so I can get to treatments and dinnertime if I wasn't sick. However, my Sundays off have now become much more important. I have a greater agenda: seeking Christ and getting to know Jesus. Now on my Sundays off, I do my feeding routine: shower, wrap my feeding tube to my body, dress, and head to church. If anyone had told me just a few short years ago that I would have feelings like this, I would have laughed at them.

Aside from that day as a drunk seeking immediate healing and my brother's funeral, I have not set foot in church in probably twenty years. My first time at The Rock, I feel awkward, uncomfortable. Everyone is so friendly, overflowing with joy and happiness. I can feel the sincerity in their warm handshakes and greetings. I know I should be here. I'm supposed to be here. I know I have asked Jesus into my life before, but walking into this house of God among all these Spirit-filled people, I feel like I'm bogged down under a multitude of sins that are as transparent as everything seemed when I was a child ashamed of that "bad little boy" and I don't belong. I'm not worthy. But that "voice" again tells me to stay and just keep going, almost as if I'm being led by my hand. I think I have that "fake it 'til you make it" smile on my face, but that's okay because I know I have to be here.

I walk into the sanctuary, looking nice and neat, my feeding tube wrapped up discreetly under my shirt. I have my Bible with me, the one I received during confirmation when I was thirteen, the one I had forgotten about for decades, the one Judi found and sent to me. It's like my "Linus blanket." I'm by myself. I feel like everyone is looking at me. I feel out of place. A part of me is wanting to sneak back out and head home where everything is familiar. But that "voice" again…I find a seat.

There is a band with a choir playing Christian rock music. I have never heard of this, a rock beat with Christian lyrics. It's wonderful. There is an incredibly diverse congregation. An astounding mixture of young, middle-aged and seniors of all races, all singing to this rock music. I have never seen anything like this. It's beautiful. Words to the songs are displayed on the big screens. God inspired lyrics with a rock beat… in church. I can feel the excitement and pure joy from the people around me. Some with arms raised praising Jesus. I feel a kind of love exuding from everyone that I've never experienced before—an aura, an energy that fills the entire sanctuary. I can't really describe what I feel. I am becoming overwhelmed with emotion. I can't explain any of this, but I'm feeling so happy inside. I try to hold it back but my eyes start to well up with tears. Someone near me notices and hands me a box of tissues (there are boxes of tissues all around). I apologize but she gives me a big hug and squeezes my hand. I know I belong here.

The pastor takes to the stage and finishes up the song with the band.

I don't recall what the sermon that morning was about. I remember the morning being very emotional, touched spiritually, my heart and my soul. I can feel God's love—the love of Jesus, deep down. I go through quite a few tissues during the service. During prayer at the end of the service, the pastor asks everyone to keep their eyes closed, don't look around. He starts to talk about specific trials that any one of us might be experiencing that we might need help with and prayer for and asks that we raise our hand. After each specific issue, he says to raise your hand. If you want Jesus in your life, raise your hand. I am very hesitant. I should raise my hand for each thing he mentioned, but I don't believe everyone has their eyes closed. I don't want to draw attention to myself, but that "voice," that darn "voice" is telling me to be bold. I do have this yearning for Jesus in my life. I have asked Him into my life in the past but still needed something more. Admitting openly, instead of privately kneeling at my bedside, that I want Jesus in my life. Humble myself before God. I raise my hand with tears in my eyes. Pastor is whispering in the microphone, as he's acknowledging each hand raised, *"Yes, yes, yes, yes..."* Then he invites us all with raised hands, not to be embarrassed but to please come to the altar for prayer. I am torn inside, but my feet seem to be moving before I know that I'm moving. I go to the altar. Crying, as if all my multitudes of sins are melting away, I pray with the other pastors there and in front of the entire congregation. This is when I truly receive Christ into my life.

I continue to go to church on my Sundays off, always browsing the bookstore in the church. I'm so excited about my church that I purchase some books and music CD's, recorded by the band and choir of The Rock, to give as Christmas presents. I continue my long arduous treatments, always praying for the other patients. In mid-September 2011, everything comes to a halt. My treatments are finished. There is another PET scan. I see my doctors for the results. I am down to a withering 115 pounds. I can't talk. My jaw muscles have atrophied from the radiation, and I can barely open my mouth. I'm tired. I'm weak. One of my doctors comes in, looks at me with a kind of fascinated expression, and says, *"Craig, you were on our 'not so very good' list. Your recovery has been almost 'miraculous.' You had an extremely grueling three months of very aggressive treatment and how you came through it is almost unheard of. Your cancer is gone."* He also said he believes that my being in such good physical condition played a large part in my making it through so well. I fight back tears and save them for when I get to my car. There I say a prayer of thanks to God and Jesus for staying with me. I *know* it was a miracle. This was definitely God at work. No other explanation.

I still have many follow up visits. Radiation has atrophied my jaw muscles, and I can barely open my mouth, so I will have to wear a contraption in my mouth three times a day to stretch my mouth open and exercise my jaw. Because my taste buds are starting to come to life before they should, I have my feeding tube taken out at the end of September five months earlier than projected. Doctors, once again, are saying, *"This is unheard of."* I couldn't taste a lot yet, but I *was* eating by Thanksgiving…as I told my doctor I would.

*****

I take some required classes at church and become a member of The Rock. In April 2012, I am baptized in the Holy Spirit by submersion into God's church at The Rock. I am born again. I'm almost fort-nine.

*****

The Other Diagnosis

I have learned that there are two main causes for head and neck cancer. One is alcohol/cigarettes. I definitely had plenty of that. When one of my doctors mentioned my tumor looked more viral, he had a DNA test ran on the biopsied sample. It came back positive for HPV (human papillomavirus), the other main cause of head and neck cancer. HPV is most commonly related to women and cervical cancer. They have Pap smears to detect it. There is no test for men. I had never heard of HPV related to men before, so I was completely caught off guard. I didn't even realize it to be a sexually transmitted disease (STD). Turns out to be the most commonly transmitted STD.

I am a little bit in shock. Knowing that I led an extremely promiscuous life in my younger years, on top of my smoking, drinking and drugging, I asked my doctor if this was something I have passed on. He informed me that ninety percent of the population has HPV and doesn't realize it. I could have been born with it or contracted it and, more than likely, passed it on.

Since my diagnoses, I learned that if an HPV infection is going to become cancerous, it takes many years. I have also been hearing a lot on the news, the CDC reporting an increase in HPV-related cancer among men, and they suggest that young boys also get the vaccination along with young girls, so of course, I relayed my diagnosis to my sister since she has two teen boys.

My cancer I took in stride, realizing that the way I lived my life for so many years was probably the cause of my current situation. It boils down to all the choices I had made. I once again thank God that He got me sober and off cigarettes so I could see all this through with a clear mind.

One More Show

ℰ ℛ

After my treatments are all finished and my feeding tube is removed, my taste buds slowly coming back to life and some of my saliva glands returning. My voice has come back and that mouth contraption has my jaw mobility practically back to normal. I'm back at the gym working hard, lots of protein drinks and healthy eating, getting myself back to my solid, healthy, lean, muscular 155 pounds. I notice the theater group I got involved in is having another audition: *It's a Wonderful Life*, another faith-based show. I have always loved that movie classic with Jimmy Stewart.

I love being on stage, so I decide I want to give this one a shot also. I'm glad it's not a musical because my singing voice is not back. In fact, my dry mouth is so bad, from lack of saliva glands, that I have to chew gum all the time to help create saliva.

It will be a cold reading audition, so I order a script online again and familiarize myself with characters within my age range. I talk with God, always thanking Him for the healing and everything He has been doing in my life. I don't ask Him for anything in the show. He knows my heart. Just going through the audition process is so exciting, and I'm just so grateful to be around for this opportunity, no matter what happens.

Audition days roll around. Audition papers filled out. The buzz and chatter in the theater of new actors meeting more seasoned actors. Actors that previously worked together getting re-acquainted. The excitement in the air and the nerves of some getting ready for the audition. Always exhilarating.

I am asked to read for various roles. That's usually a good start. When I'm asked to read for Mr. Welch, I look over the script, and I think, *This will be so natural.*

In the movie, Mr. Welch punches out George Bailey, in a bar, for yelling at his wife on the phone. That's the extent of that character in the movie. On stage, it's a larger role. The punching scene and then in the scene where George is never born and we cross paths again but Mr. Welch and his cronies are extremely, happily, drunk. During the audition, the anger and stage punch comes out so naturally, and of course, playing drunk is a piece of cake. The audition goes well. I got called back and ultimately cast as Mr. Welch.

It's generally a "no, no" on stage to have gum in your mouth unless the character actually calls for it. However, unbeknownst to anyone, especially the director, for the two months of rehearsals and all the performances I have to have a piece of gum under my tongue all the time to help create saliva; otherwise, I will never make it through my lines without choking on my words due to radiation dry mouth. The shows are sell outs, and once again, I'm elated to be a part of a production that leaves an audience completely enthralled. One night, the stage punch is all too real when I actually make contact with George's nose. Luckily, he isn't hurt. I do get many audience compliments on how realistic my drunk scene is. If they only knew the experiences I had to draw from.

Again, I thank God for allowing me to be a part of another production.

*****

It's a Wonderful Life, 2011

It's a Wonderful Life, 2011

Is It Satan at Work

    ℘   ℃

I s it just life happening? I have heard something to the effect that when you receive Christ, Satan works harder on you and puts a lot of obstacles in your path in areas he knows you're so vulnerable to help destroy your faith. One of my biggest vulnerabilities is finances. I'm born again. I'm a member of my church and also being of service by being an usher. I guess I'm prime material for Satan to try to dig his claws in deeper.

    I finish paying my medical bills from cancer by the end of the year 2011. I have half of my nice little nest egg left in the bank. I'm ready to start catching up, getting ahead again. In January 2012, a reckless driver totals my car that's paid off. I'm okay but now I'm making car payments again that are difficult to afford. I'm still recovering from cancer treatments and starting to stress again about finances. I tell God, *"Lord, you saw me through my cancer finances and all. Please help me through this also."*

In the middle of that year, we are having torrential rains. I'm experiencing some serious flooding in the crawl space under my house. there is six inches of water with nowhere to go. I'm sump pumping hundreds of gallons from under the house worried about foundation issues and the rains keep coming. When the weather stops for a while and things start to dry out, I have some estimates done and have to spend a good deal of money to have a French drain put in the backyard. I am reeling again about my finances as I watch my bank account dwindle some more, once more asking God to be with me through this.

As soon as my body allowed, I was back at the gym and regained the forty pounds of muscle that had been eaten away. I hadn't let cancer get me down physically. Hopefully, I will put on even a little more. During all this, I ended up injuring my right shoulder, and toward the end of 2012, I have shoulder surgery for a torn rotator cuff, labral tear and bicep tear. More specialist co-pays, deductibles, and max out of pocket. By now, I'm laughing at this past year. My bank account has dwindled even further from these three major setbacks on top of regular day-to-day, month-to-month expenses. My faith has faltered through the year, but I never completely lose faith and again ask God to help me through this. I'm also always thanking God because I know He has not left me and He does see me through this.

January 2013, my house is broken into. Very little gets taken thanks to my alarm system, but there was still damage done to the house. The entire back door was busted down and needed replacing. There were holes in the living room where the TV was torn from the wall. I had to meet my deductible before insurance would pay so everything came out of pocket to repair and replace. When all was said and done, I only got one hundred dollars from insurance. It hurt to start the year out like this again.

By midyear, the effects from all the radiation treatments are starting to manifest. Since my saliva glands will never fully return, I have severe dry mouth issues and experiencing dry brittle teeth that are starting to crack and break. An infection in my lower jaw has the left side of my face swollen. I have to see an oral specialist now. I'm told I will have to have some teeth extracted after the infection is under control. However, the radiation has done so much damage to my jawbone that I will have to go through three months of hyperbaric treatments to help the healing after the extractions. Without this, I'm at risk of losing my lower jaw bone. I'm now leaving work for three hours a day, five days a week. I'm put in a hyperbaric chamber, compressed to the equivalent of thirty-three feet below sea level (they call these "dives") and infused with one hundred percent oxygen for ninety minutes. Hmm… cancer…the gift that keeps on giving.

My first dive doesn't go too well. Before I'm completely down, the pressure in my right ear is so great they have to decompress me and I have a tube put in that ear. Future dives go better. Once I get through all the ear popping of the initial compressing, the ninety minutes is fairly relaxing. The biggest pain is that now I have major dental bills on top of major medical. Aside from the extractions, I also need to have crowns on most of my upper teeth.

In 2014, I'm playing financial catchup. The year is going smoothly. I've had a couple crowns done on my top teeth. The significant radiation damage was to my lower jaw where most of the extractions were done and about to have partials made. This is in August. Unfortunately, my dentist notices I still have exposed bone at an extraction area and sends me back to my oral surgeon. He discovers necrotic (dead) bone tissue (osteonecrosis), and my jaw bone is infected. All of this still being caused by the aggressive radiation. He sends me straight over to the hospital where I have a PICC line inserted in the main artery in my upper left arm going straight into my heart. I will now be on a permanent antibiotic IV every six hours for the next three and a half months.

Home health care will monitor me once a week and teach me how to do my IV's. They will draw blood and change bandaging. I will go through 126 syringes a week, 28 IV bags of amoxicillin a week, and change my IV tubes twice a day. I will have to wake up extra early every day for my morning IV, bring a portable IV poll to work every day and IV myself twice during my twelve-hour shift, make sure I get one last IV in before bed. It's rough but better than leaving work every day for hyperbaric and definitely better than going through cancer treatments. After three and a half months of this, I will have to be on an oral antibiotic for another year.

Bills keep piling up, but I'm still praying all the time, asking God and Jesus to just see me through all this. It's funny that my cancer is gone, but yet it just keeps on giving. I refuse to give up the gym. I keep my tubes wrapped up around my arm. I do as much as I possibly can safely, without causing too much stress to the area where the line is inserted in my left arm. I can say this, hyperbaric and this IV "thing" is a walk in the park compared to chemo and radiation, so I'm not really complaining. The ongoing bills aren't a walk in the park, though. However, I'm not even stressing too much there either. I have to keep remembering how much God and Jesus have seen me through so far, and I know They are not going anywhere.

*****

In all, I will go through four years of lower teeth extractions and hyperbaric treatments to save my dying lower jaw. During my fourth year, which will be the year following my first mission trip, I will receive some devastating news.

*****

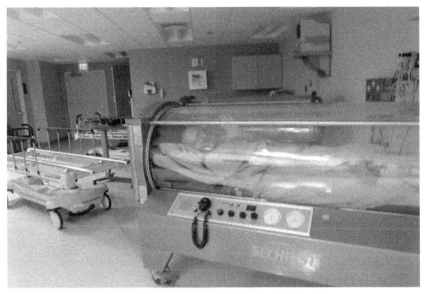

Another day, another nap in my hyperbaric tank.

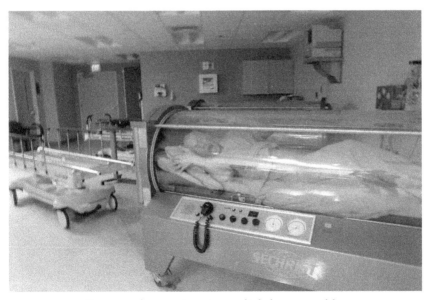

I try to take my situation as lightly as possible.

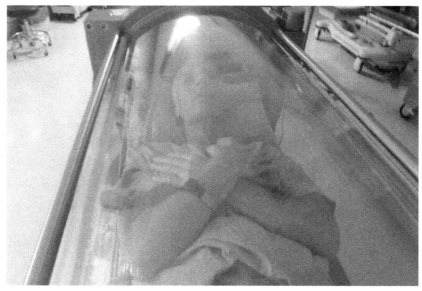

Even though I plan to be cremated, I am a bit morbidly
curious as to how I might look in a coffin.

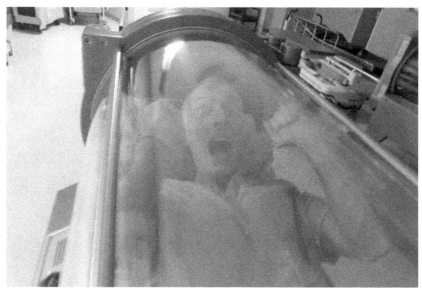

Now I've had enough and just want to get out!

My Father Passes

ℰ   ℭ

Since cancer, each year has brought about some very unfavorable situations. It's wearing me down, but I try to keep my focus on God and Jesus, and I haven't missed church through any of it.

2015 actually starts out calm. Unlike the previous three years, it looks like this one will go a little smoother. My goal is to finish up the minor dental work that needs to be done: upper crowns and upper and lower partials. With all these holes in my mouth, I really haven't been able to chew my food completely. Sometimes almost choking trying to swallow partially chewed food. I keep telling myself that soon I will be eating like a normal person again.

In early May, my brother calls to inform me that our father has passed away. I really couldn't afford it, but I head off to Minnesota anyway and throw it on a credit card. I'm still not close with my family, but I'm compelled to go. Of course, I stay with Judi, my "foster mom". That's the only place I feel comfortable.

It is so good to see Judi after so many years. Aaron is living there also to help out, Tim will stop by later. It is really great to see them also. And Danny…? Well, all I can say is that I'm told he could really use a lot of prayer at this point in his life. It's sad that he will not come over to just say hello.

I eventually head to my father's house to help, if I can, with any funeral preparations. I am sad for my stepmom. I can't imagine what she's going through. My father passed away in his sleep right next to her. I am not comfortable in the house. I walk through, and I'm flooded with bad memories, and I'm deeply saddened. I peek in the bedroom that used to be mine. The very vivid memory comes back and my mind replays it as if I'm looking down upon it, and I'm watching my dad pounding me with his fists as I fight back, my stepmom in the doorway screaming at me. I have never spent another night in this house.

My brother, sister, and stepsister show up. They are all almost like strangers to me. Eventually, my sister's boys and my brother's daughter will make it to the house. I am not comfortable around any of them either. I don't know them. I have seen them less than a handful of times in their lives, but I remind myself that this is not about me. I know how to act and be the proper family member. It's really awkward when my stepbrother shows up. I never liked him when we were younger.

I get compliments on how healthy and in shape I am. My sister expected someone more frail looking after cancer, not 155 pounds of lean hard muscle that I am now. I do show off my six-pack abs and am very proud. I had been raised believing I was all those names I had been called. I work hard to stay in shape, and seeing that my family is all overweight almost gives me a feeling of vindication, and I know that's so wrong.

My sister makes a comment about me and my stepbrother having something in common. It turns out that "something" is recovery. All of a sudden, it's like we became best buds. A huge connection was made that only people in recovery could possibly understand. We couldn't stop talking. He has about four or five more years of sobriety than me, but he confesses to me that he has some problems.

We end up spending a lot of time together. I help him shop for clothes for the funeral. He can't stop condemning certain members of his family. I keep reminding him that we're here for his mom. It's not about us. He's grateful for my company and our talks. I find myself feeling more comfortable around him than I am around anyone else. I always include him in my prayers now asking God to help him mend his family. My stepmom will tell me at the funeral that, *"Your dad would be really proud to see the two of you getting along."* I can feel my eyes wanting to tear up a bit.

At the church, before family friends start showing up, our immediate family is gathered by the minister for instructions on how the funeral will proceed. We all take our turns viewing the open casket on display with my father inside. I take a long close look. I touch his cold, waxy hands folded so perfectly across his waist. I have so many thoughts going through my mind. Mostly, I'm in silent prayer talking to God: *God, our Father. You know we weren't close. Lord, I have forgiven him but with all these thoughts in my head how do I know if I have "truly" forgiven him. God, I hope my dad's with you.*

I stand back and off to the side in a darker corner out of the way, watching other mourners file by the casket to pay their respects. I'm thinking about the trip I made home, when I was twenty-five, to confront my father about all the abuse. My father and I never became close, but because of that trip, we were able to form some semblance of a relationship. We were able to communicate. Eventually, my brother and sister come and stand near me. After a little silence, I quietly mention, *"I'm not saddened so much by dad's death. What I am truly saddened about is the family that should have been. Could have been. The family that never was."* As I stand there in the shadows looking at my father's body, my heart and soul do mourn for that family, for that little boy, me, that only knew a brutal angry father. The wake after the funeral is at my brother's house. Lots of good food. It is a very pleasant gathering.

During a more private conversation with my brother, I tell him that I had read the back of the funeral bulletin. When I read all the comments and memories that the family had about how wonderful Dad was, I tell my brother that, *"It seemed like I was reading about a complete stranger."*

My brother tells me that, *"Dad had changed over the years."*

I tell him, *"I'm glad I wasn't here for that memory session. I have absolutely no good memories. I just remember a brutal, angry man."* Yes, it was a pleasant gathering, but I couldn't wait to get home to Judi's house.

My mother knew I was going to be in town and had called to see if she could have lunch with me before I fly back home. I panic inside like I'm a little kid again. I have forgiven my mom also, but I am definitely not comfortable around her. I love her because she is my mom and God commands it. The invitation was not extended to my brother or sister, so I made sure to ask if they were going to join us. She said I could ask them if I wanted. I think she wanted it to be just me and her, but I couldn't do that. I asked my sister if she would come to lunch with us, and she said she would.

It's a ninety-minute drive for my mom for an hour or so lunch. I feel a little guilty that she's driving so far. My sister, myself, and my mom meet at a nice little restaurant. It's a pleasant enough get-to-gether. Having my sister there was good to keep conversation going; otherwise, I wouldn't know what to talk about if it were just me and my mom. To this day, I have no idea if my mother ever listened to that tape I made so many years ago.

After the meal and some more small talk, my mother asks, *"When will I see you again?"* I took a deep breath and a sigh. It is time to just blurt out the truth. *"Probably never"* is my quiet reply. She says, *"You're not going to come back to just visit family?"*

My reply was, *"I have no reason to ever come back to Minnesota."* I don't have it in me to say that there are nothing but bad memories here. Truth be told, my only real reason to come back would be for Judi Stevens and her family, if needed.

We say our goodbyes and give hugs in the parking lot, and my mother slips me a couple hundred dollar bills. I gratefully accept, once again feeling a little guilty. After my mother drives off, I ask my sister if I was too harsh. She tells me, *"You had to tell her the truth."* I'm glad my sister came to lunch. A little more time is spent with the family, and the next day, I have to leave. My trip back to Alabama is a somber one of reflection. But I can't wait to get home.

More Miracles

℀   ℀

For a while now, in my prayers, I've been asking God what else can I be doing. I'm really not doing much. I've joined the church. I'm ushering but I can only do that every other weekend due to my work schedule. And even then, usher teams are scheduled to usher every other month. When praying, I'm thanking God for so, so many blessings. *"Lord, God, You've taken alcohol out of my life and got me sober. You pulled me through my pancreatic crisis. You've seen to it that I have a house. You have taken cigarettes out of my life. You've taken cancer out of my body. You wouldn't let suicide attempts take me. You pulled me from an unhealthy relationship. You didn't want me in. So much You have done in my life. God, there are so many people suffering in this world. What else can I be doing? Being of service as an usher doesn't seem like enough. What else can I do?"*

Matthew West has a song called "Do Something." When I first heard the song then saw the video and story behind it, I knew I wanted to go somewhere on a mission trip. I would include that in my prayers, asking God if there is some place I could go to help others around the world.

A couple months later, there's a notice in the church bulletin about a mission trip to Teupasenti, Honduras. We would be assisting the organization Children's Cup and in other areas helping orphans. I went online and found out that Honduras is one of the poorest countries in the Western Hemisphere. It is also the number one murder capital of the world.

I halfheartedly respond to that notice and send a short e-mail expressing interest knowing full well I wouldn't be able to go. No one is going to get in touch with me about it anyway. Besides, I would need a total of sixteen-hundred dollars, which I definitely don't have, unless I tap into my 401K, which I'm definitely not going to do. I'm still paying off medical bills.

A couple weeks later, around June 1, I finished at the gym one morning, and there's a voice mail on my phone. It's from Pastor Dad responding to my e-mail, he heads most of the mission trips. My brain froze. I never expected this. I thought, *I'm just going to ignore this. I don't have money to go on the trip anyway.* To my astonishment, Pastor Dad calls again around midday. I ignore the call again. He leaves another message about the mission trip. I know he must be mistaken, and I really don't want to confess that I don't have any money.

That evening, just as I sit down to dinner, my phone rings. I look at it, and it's Pastor Dad. I ignore the call and continue eating. While eating, that "voice" keeps nagging me inside my head, yes, *that* "voice" saying, *"Call him back. You need to call him back."* I swear *that* "voice" won't be quiet all through my dinner.

After dinner, I reluctantly pick up the phone and call Pastor Dad. He was very happy to hear back from me. He tells me about the trip. It sounds wonderful doing a lot of God's work and working with the children. It sounded exciting, something I would love to do but then comes the money part. Eight hundred dollars is needed by July 1 to guarantee a seat on the plane and another eight hundred by August 1 for ground expenses, transportation, and such while we are there.

Embarrassed, I had to tell Pastor Dad that I don't have any money for the trip and apologized for sending the e-mail, knowing I didn't have the money. Pastor Dad tells me that many people have to raise the money to go on these trips. I tell him I'll see what I can do and that I will be able to make it to the first mission trip meeting that was scheduled for Sunday. My real thoughts were, *Who is ever going to donate money to me for a mission trip? Why would anyone believe this?* I'm extremely skeptical, but in my prayers, that night, I thank God for all the calls from Pastor Dad and for making me call him back and confess to God that I had no idea where this was going or what to do and that it's all in His hands. *"Lord, lead me and guide me down the path you have chosen for me."*

The next day at work, I let the story out about the mission trip. It spreads through the plant. People ask me about it, and I tell them what we will be doing and how much it's going to cost. I never ask for any money from anyone. I tell my friend Anesha, from Jamaica, about all my serious doubts. Anesha, being the strong Christian woman she is, continually tells me, with her cute Jamaican accent, *"Oh, ye of little faith. Craig, God will make this happen!"* I have faith, but still…I need eight hundred dollars in a month, sixteen hundred in two months. Things like this just don't happen, not to me. Someone tells me about GoFundMe.com. So that night, I set up an account with a goal of two thousand dollars, because they charge a fee, and I tell the story about the mission trip. Facebook post I did about the trip: This is from our church bulletin.

HONDURAS MISSIONS TRIP

> *Save your vacation for a mission trip to Honduras, Joe, in Valle de Angeles, will be continuing construction on the school/church/home compound being built there. Pastor Danny, in Teupasenti, will be working with Children's Cup to finish the facility for the children there. There is a need for laborers with a knowledge of construction, and just those that want to help. There will be opportunities for evangelism, and working with the disadvantaged children in both areas. This will be much more rewarding than a vacation, it will be a life lesson.*

I don't know what else to say except that God touched many people's hearts because little by little, money starts coming in. People at work handing over one dollars, two dollars, five dollars. All of this adding up. People I barely know from the gym, Donna, and Luke donate money. I also recognize Luke from church and by only mentioning the trip. He says, *"Put me and my wife down for two hundred dollars. Put my mom down for two hundred dollars also, she likes this sort of thing."* I have never met his mother, but she actually donates four hundred dollars. Money was coming in on GoFundMe. Every night, I'm posting "thank yous" on Facebook and attaching a Christian rock/pop/country video to my posts and reminding everyone that this is for the children in Honduras, letting everyone know where we stand on reaching the goal. I am actually getting more personal donations than I'm getting online for GoFundMe, but I will post everything I receive. At only three weeks in, I tell everyone that the trip is a long ways away but we are only two hundred and two dollars shy of our goal, and I thank everyone for all they are doing.

My Facebook post:

> *Alright everyone…!!! The Mission Trip total board is on the rise again. sometimes leaps & bounds, sometimes hops & skips. Tonight our total is up to $1,798.00. Only $202.00 to go to reach the goal!!! Again…thank you for every bit you give. The children in Teupasenti, Honduras are waiting for the help we will be giving.*

The next morning, I wake up and check online before going to work to find that a complete stranger left a message saying, *"Pack your bags and go take care of those wonderful children."* along with a donation of two hundred and two dollars. His message and donation made my eyes well up with tears. Tears of immense gratitude toward this complete stranger. This was his actual message:

$202.00
DC Bowman
> *Now get to packing and serve those children. Show them the love and mercy God shows us. Know we are praying for your, and their, safety. God is using you and you are answering the call. "Be thou faithful unto death, and I will give thee a crown of Life." Revelation 2:10*

I am so thankful to everyone. My prayers every night are filled with abounding thanks to God for touching so many people for me. In three weeks time, I have reached the goal of two thousand dollars. In four weeks, by July 1, I have donations totalling $2,650. I only needed $1,600. I am going on my first mission trip to Honduras. For whatever reasons, God is seeing to that.

A post of mine on Facebook:

> *Hey you guys. This journey just keeps getting more and more incredible. Far far greater than my early expectations because I really had no clue what would take place. My Church Mission Trip donations goal was $2,000.00. I lacked in faith that it could even come close to being realized. God has truly placed something in so many hearts that, through all of you, donations have risen to $2,650.00 and I have been told there is still more coming.*

As quickly as all this was happening, I still had my doubts that it would be possible. I knew it was truly God at work. I expressed it in my nightly Facebook posts. I was completely in awe at the miracle taking place before my eyes but still doubts floated around inside my brain. God really needs to smack me upside the head a little more often. Anesha was right. God *would* make this happen. After all this, I tell Anesha of another dream, *"I would really love to do a mission trip to African countries where so many children are dying from the dirty water and help build clean water wells, but those trips are really expensive, and I don't know how I would ever get that much money."*

She just shoots me a stern look, a glare of disbelief, and says, *"Oh, ye of little faith, Craig, do you not see what all just happened."*

Another Facebook post:

> *This trip was meant to be, for whatever reasons. And, through all of your generous donations, it has*

been made possible and you are all part of this journey. It will only get better through all the smiles, hugs, laughter and tears when we get there. I truly look forward to being able to share pictures and stories with everyone. It is still a month and a half away. Never thought this money would come so quickly. If anyone has any doubts…this is truly God at work!!!

******

My eyes are watering as I write this. Tears of gratitude. It is amazing how soon I could forget the miracle that had just taken place and think God could not do one even bigger. God wants me in Honduras, why not Africa one day.

More Obstacles

℘   ☙

I now have the money, and then some, to go on my first mission trip. I'm very excited, but in July, I injure my shoulder and my knee, more than likely due to the strenuous four-hour workouts I do on my days off, three to four days a week. Chest press alone, I'm pressing 320 pounds, four sets of fifteen. The biceps, triceps, back, and shoulders, 800 ab reps, of various types, in sets of fifty. I hate working lower body but push myself anyway, plus a full hour of high paced cardio and a half hour workout in the sauna. It's no wonder that scans show I have a torn meniscus in my right knee and a labral tear in my left shoulder. I also have another tooth on my lower jaw that has broken. My oral surgeon says it needs to come out, along with another tooth, but I will need four weeks of hyperbaric treatments again before the extraction and another six weeks after to help insure healing.

I'm starting to panic a little inside. We leave on the Honduras mission trip in a month. We work it out, so I can start hyperbaric immediately, pause for the trip, oral surgery as soon as I get back and pick up the hyperbaric until finished. My knee and shoulder need prompt attention also, so we schedule knee surgery two weeks after oral then schedule shoulder surgery two weeks after the knee.

My head is reeling thinking about the expense, medical on top of dental. In the back of my mind, I wonder again if this is Satan at work trying to bring me down, so in the forefront of my mind, I remind myself of all that God has done for me and continues to do. How the money for this mission trip miraculously came to be and with extra money donated that will be able to be used to help with the visits to specialists in order for me to still be able to make this trip. I mention this to some of my personal donors, and it's okay with them that their contributions are used in this way to help me make the trip. I see that God is working, and I fully believe He intends for me to be in Honduras for whatever His reasons. I keep thanking God for where I am in life and for continually seeing me through.

With my work schedule, I'm only able to make a couple of the mission trip meetings on Sundays, but I notice that one of the guys in the meetings, Danny, who is a friend of mine outside of church, is a part of this mission team. Our church is so large I didn't know he was a congregant. I'm glad because I'm not always comfortable around unfamiliar people and now I know one person. I get the list of special items to bring and packing suggestions for a trip of this nature. I won't be able to make it to our final meeting before the trip, so I schedule a separate meeting with Pastor Dad for a morning on a day off after hyperbaric treatment.

It is almost two weeks until we leave. I get to Pastor Dad's office, and we discuss the excitement surrounding the trip. I am still in such amazement that I will be going. He mentions that when we all get to Tegucigalpa, the capital city, we will be splitting into two groups, each group heading to a different destination. The group I'm in will be heading to Teupasenti. Most of the week there I will be doing a lot of construction type work, painting, digging, etc. I'm becoming a little disappointed inside because I really wanted to be going to where all the children were. Children to be loved on, hugged, and shown that they're important. My mind also keeps telling "my mind" to just *"Shut up! Stop whining!"* that I am going where God wants me to go. The purpose of the trip is doing God's work no matter where I am. A light spiritual slap upside the head is what that was. Just the fact that I am going is what matters.

A week before the trip, I get all my medical issues taken care of. This is my last week of hyperbaric until I get back. I get a cortisone shot in my shoulder and my knee that will take away the pain for the duration of the trip. I finish buying items that I need and get my packing done. On a mission trip, you only need the bare essentials. Clothes can be washed by hand and hung to dry, so you don't pack a lot of clothes. Everything you need for a week can be put into a carry-on or a very small checked bag. Curtis is going to keep an eye on the house and feed the cats while I'm gone.

*****

I have been on many extravagant vacations in my life—fancy four and five star hotels, cruise ships—San Juan, St. Thomas, Martinique, Barbados, Aruba twice, the Bahamas, Mayan ruins in Cozumel and in Calica. But this will be an entirely different kind of trip. I am about to embark on a spiritual vacation. I am going to discover that this will be a "Beyond life changing" experience.

My First Mission Trip

ℰꝏ   ℭℛ

P eople at work have been excited for me all summer. I've been like a little kid waiting for Christmas morning to finally arrive. Well, it's finally here. Just the thought of going to a foreign country is exciting, let alone the fact that we are going there to do mission work. According to the Internet, Honduras is the third poorest country in the Western Hemisphere and is considered the "murder capital" of the world. Honduras is also home to the second most dangerous city in the world. This trip should be very exciting.

We're all at the airport by 5:00 a.m., Saturday. I have been packed for two days waiting with anticipation. It felt like today would never get here. We fly from Huntsville to Atlanta, then it's over a three and a half hours flight to Tegucigalpa, the capital of Honduras. I love flying.

Honduras coastline.

Flying into the capital city of Tegucigalpa.

Honduras is beautiful from the sky. Once we are inland, it's mountains as far as the eye can see.

We are met at the airport by Pastor Danny, who is American, with Children's Cup, and his church, Casa de Oración Familiar (Family House of Prayer), is in Tegucigalpa. He will be with us in Teupasenti. He is also fluent in Spanish with the Honduran dialect. An added plus on this trip is that my friend Danny (not Pastor Danny) will be my roommate when we get to Teupasenti.

We spend Saturday night in Tegucigalpa and go to services at Pastor Danny's church Sunday morning before heading to Teupasenti. We are given such an incredibly warm and gracious welcome by Pastor Danny's congregation. I only remember a little Spanish from high school and don't understand most of what is being said, but you can definitely feel it in all the hugs we are given. They are all so overflowing with gratitude for the help we are bringing to their people in Honduras. I am so moved by the outpouring of love and appreciation that I'm fighting back tears, and inside, I'm thinking, *It's you I should be thanking for having us here.* After the wonderful service, which Pastor Danny simultaneously translated, we receive more hugs and goodbyes and head out to Teupasenti.

It's a two-hour drive, so Danny (my friend) and I decide to ride it out in the back of Pastor Danny's pickup. It's a rough, bumpy ride through the mountains, but we enjoy the gorgeous mountain scenery. We see some of the poverty in Tegucigalpa before we head out of the city, but we are seeing a lot more as we pass little villages on the way to Teupasenti. We pass a lot of sugar cane fields, coffee fields, and banana plantations. It's all so beautiful. Even all the little shacks made from salvaged corrugated metal, being used as make-shift homes, are beautiful in the sense that they look like pictures out of a *National Geographic* magazine come to life. I am just in awe that I am here, and I'm taking pictures with every turn of the bend on this mountain road. I want to capture everything I possibly can.

Restaurant security in the capital city Tegucigalpa.

Bottom L–R: Mark, Me, Danny.
Top L–R: Josh, Pastor Danny.
Overlooking capital of Honduras, Tegucigalpa.
Melissa doesn't like to be in pictures.

When we arrive in Teupasenti, we settle into our very small but rather quaint hotel. Our room is a cozy, probably ten feet by ten feet and two wooden frames with mattresses. It has a very small bathroom with a shower and no hot water. All this is okay because I am still just amazed that I am here.

After we've quickly settled in, we head out to the church where we will be working. We were told there will be a lot of work to do. We are the team that will lay the groundwork, start all the digging, for the park that is going to be built next to the church for the children. There's also a lot of work to be done on the upstairs addition to the church.

When we get there, we are warmly and enthusiastically greeted by many of the villages people and a throng of beautiful children. Everyone is asked to gather around and an explanation, in Spanish and English, is given as to what is about to take place on the land we are standing on. How this area will be transformed into a park.

*****

My days start out before the sun rises. I'm an early riser any-way, so I still wake up at 4:00 a.m. I lay in bed contemplating my being here, the people we have met, the beautiful children, the work we are going to accomplish, and the money that was miraculously raised for me to be here. I lay in bed with tears in my eyes thanking God for allowing me to be here, for extending this opportunity to me. I tell Him, *"I know I haven't done anything to deserve this, but I know You must have me here for a reason. I know there is a purpose for all that has happened."* I'm not talking to Him anymore, but in my head, I wonder why I am here. As soon as I wondered that, to myself, that "voice" comes into my head again. It has been a while, but that "voice" says, *"You will see."* I silently sob a little more, feeling totally and completely humbled. I wipe my eyes, get on my knees next to my bed, and say my morning prayer.

After a cold morning shower, there is no hot water, I dress and go outside. Mark and Josh are in the next room. The walls are very thin with a gap between the wall and ceiling so just about any noise can be heard in the adjoining rooms. I tried to be quiet, but Mark has heard me get up, so he dresses and comes out. We go downstairs, and it seems Melissa is an early riser also. She has heard us, dresses, and comes outside.

This is a remote village nestled way back in the mountains, two hours from the capital city, dirt village roads. No one is up anywhere except for us, it seems. It is so quiet that even our whispered conver-sation can be heard by the lightest sleeper. One of the guys who helps run this small hotel has heard us and comes out. We have decided we want to take a morning walk around the village as the sun comes up. With his little bit (very little) of English and our little bit (muy poquito) of Spanish and lots of hand gestures, he unlocks the gate for us and we're told to just be careful.

Teupasenti is absolutely beautiful in the predawn hours and at sunrise. We walk all over taking pictures. We also know we have to be back by 6:00 a.m. because that's when breakfast, Honduran home-made by the hotel owners, will be ready. When we get back, everyone else is up and ready, and breakfast is about to be served. We eat at little tables on the walkway outside of our rooms. Wonderful food. We tell everyone about our walk and decide we want to do this every morning. No one else wants to join. That's a little too early for them.

After breakfast, we have devotional time with Pastor Danny. A reading from the Bible followed by an explanation of the reading and then a short discussion. I feel a little out of place because every-one else seems so well versed in the Bible. But that "voice" tells me, *"You're okay."* I fight back tears, we pray and head out.

*****

Our hotel in Teupasenti

My friend Danny and I shared this room.

Outside: Me, Danny, Josh, and Marks rooms
upstairs. Laundry hangs out to dry.

Everyone else: Pastor Danny, Melissan David, and Deborra are downstairs. This is also where we eat. Josh (seated) and Mark.

*****

Most of the time, we walk through Teupasenti to the church. Our start time is 7:00 a.m. When we get there, a group of men from the village is always already there to help. I find out that some of the younger men in the group, the older teenagers, will receive roughly seven dollars a day. That is equal to 163 Lempiras in Honduras. Seven dollars a day is hard for me to fathom, but I'm told that it's very good for down here. I had also been told that six out of ten families live on less than a dollar twenty-five a day. That is truly difficult to comprehend.

Another observation is that of one little boy in particular who showed up by himself around 7:00 a.m. before any of the other children start showing up around 7:30 and 8:00 a.m. His name is Mauricio, he's four years old and has the run of the village streets from early morning.

I first meet Mauricio when I'm busy digging trenches for the wall that will go up (there is no such thing as a backhoe). We dig and dig and dig. I am basically knee deep in the trench shoveling rock hard clumps of dirt onto a pile when Mauricio squats down in front of me trying to tell me he wants to help. We don't have to speak the same language because the moment we make eye contact it's like I can see into his four-year-old mind and heart. We look into each other. He holds out his hands. I give him a small clump of dirt, and he gets the biggest little smile on his face and throws that little clump onto the pile of dirt. He wanted more and more little clumps. From that moment on, Mauricio, my little man, was there every morning, 7:00 sharp. He became my shadow and helper for the rest of our mission trip. He calls me *"Gringo Craig."*

Morning devotional room.

Me and Mauricio

That becomes my name for all the children, and there are a lot of them. It seems I almost always have children around me. By the end of our trip, Mark has given me the nickname "Pied Piper." I was always taking pictures with my tablet. Kids would climb trees yelling, *"Gringo Craig, Gringo Craig,"* and waving their hands, so I would take their picture. Then they hurry down to see how they look and right back up they go again for more pictures. Up and down, up and down, I'm all about the kids. I didn't have a childhood, so I think my heart just stayed that age. Sometimes, I'm not sure whether I worked hard at all on the park or played more with the children.

My shadow, my little man, Mauricio.

There is another boy that catches my attention. He seems to hang out in the background kind of shy and quiet. I'm reminded of myself when I was little, always shying away, not sure of the big people. I feel a little bad for him. I don't see him smiling at all. I go over to him, kneel down, and make a sad face. Then, with my fingers at the sides of my mouth, I move my mouth into a smile. He just looks at me. I tell him, *"Mi nombre es* (My name is) *Gringo Craig."* That makes him laugh. So then I ask him, *"Su nombre?"* (Your name?)

He tells me, *"Carlos,"* then starts talking away nonstop, and I don't understand a thing. I can only put together simple sentences, and I know many single words but never fluent. I have to tell Carlos, *"No comprendo. Mi Espanol es muy poquito."* (I don't understand. My

Spanish is very little.) That was okay with him because he just kept talking, and I kept trying to pick out little words I knew to get the gist of what he might be saying. I am able to ask him, *"Cuantos anos tienes?"* (How old are you?)

He says, *"Tengo nueve anos. Mi cumpleanos es en Septiembre."* (I'm nine. My birthday's in September.)

That's next month. I don't know what else to try to say, so I just wave my arm and say *"Venga."* (Let's go.) to get him to come and play. Carlos keeps talking and glancing at me as if hoping I'm understanding, but most of the time, I have to look at him real deep, trying to understand but shrug my head saying, *"No comprendo,"* and go on playing. That's the one thing all the children understand is playing. There is no language barrier there, especially when it came to playing tag. I was always the one to be tagged. From that moment on, Carlos became my big buddy.

*****

Carlos, my big buddy.

Carlos in the trenches.

Mis monos (my monkey's) in Teupasenti.

*****

There is so much to be done. With the help of some of the men in need of work, in Teupasenti, we dig a lot of trenches. The dirt is so dry and hard to break up that we work in pairs, one of us using a spiked pole, about five feet tall, to break the ground while the other digs. As the trenches and support holes for the base of the wall are being completed, we busy ourselves preparing gravel and sand and water for cement. There are no cement trucks. Cement is made from scratch in a big mound on the ground. The cinder blocks for the foundation of the walls, and any of the building that takes place here are also made by hand down the road. Much the same way as cement, then molded and sun dried and sun baked.

On the second level addition to the church, all the new cinder block walls need to be plastered and painted. Plaster is also made from scratch, similar to making cement but the gravel and sand is sifted through a screen so the very finest particles are separated then mixed in a bucket with water to the right consistency. My friend Danny is pretty much in charge up there since he is a painter by trade.

During the day, if I'm not playing with the children, I am busy with everyone else digging trenches, mixing cement or plaster, or helping Danny and his crew upstairs. I think I'm mostly playing with the children and taking pictures, someone has to document, but I still get my hands dirty and get sweaty, and I do help get a lot done.

In the evenings, after wonderful homemade Honduras dinners at our hotel, Pastor Danny accompanies us to the village square for ice cream from the little corner adobe store. It seems that most of the village gathers in the square in the evenings to socialize. It's a wonderful, warm communal feeling watching and listening to everyone gathered. We are greeted with many kind handshakes or hugs and lots of "gracias" and many other warm words of gratitude and appreciation that I don't understand but is translated through their gentle tones and warm embraces.

For us, the village square is also the only place we can connect to Wi-Fi from the little police station. This is where I post my nightly mission updates and pictures to Facebook. I quickly get a large following. I love that so many people are taking an interest in what we are doing down here through my Facebook page.

Every day, we start out early. Melissa, Mark, and I make a ritual of our morning walks. Every morning, I wake reminiscing of the glorious day before and pondering, with anticipation, the day that lies ahead, continually thanking God, with tears in my eyes, for allowing me to be a part of this incredible experience. When I just stand still, stand back, and soak it all in, my heart is flooded with emotion. I feel so totally overjoyed and completely blessed to be here working side by side with all these beautiful people and surrounded by all these wonderful children.

Before we left on this missions trip, we were asked, only if we wanted, to write up some type of a testimony. We might be on a Christian radio station. I am not versed in the Bible, but with so many miracles that I have witnessed in my life, I decided I would put together something. I'm not a writer and didn't know exactly how to put anything down on paper, so I did a lot of praying and asking God for help to let me write what He wants me to speak on, not that I was expecting to be on the radio but just in case. Actually, the thought of it made me incredibly nervous, but I put a day aside to do this.

A couple days into our week in Teupasenti, Melissa went on the air and so did Josh. I was too busy working, or maybe playing with the kids, that I didn't know about it until they came back. Pastor Danny asked if I would like to go tomorrow. My heart starts pounding, but that "voice" comes into my head calming me, and as if nudging me, I distinctly heard, *"This is what I want you to do."* And instantly, I say, *"Yes,"* without even really realizing I said it.

The next day, Pastor Danny takes me to the radio station. Melissa and I have become relatively close friends, and she comes along to help ease my fears. I wasn't hearing that "voice" today. It is up to me today, and God is just letting me be. I do say many prayers asking Jesus to be with me and guide me and hold my hand through this.

Before I know it, the station producer is counting down—three, two, silent one—and we are on the air. There is a brief introduction about our church group being here and what we are doing then a short intro for me by Pastor Danny, and without thought, words are flowing out of me with Pastor Danny translating for the radio audience.

Pastor Danny later posted this to Facebook:

Daniel Dyer with Craig Walter.
August 19, 2015 ·
On Christian radio in Teupasenti with Craig Walter from The Rock FWC. Incredible man with an incredible testimony. The whole radio station is in tears. (Facebook posting from Pastor Danny)

*****

*****

Tomorrow, we are going to minister at the men's prison in Danli. We wake up early as usual in the morning. Mark, Melissa, and I never miss our predawn walks. These days, we head to the village square first for a quick Wi-Fi fix to send off any early morning messages to family or friends back home, more Facebook posts for me, then on to our picture taking explorations of Teupasenti. We are seeing, and I am documenting to Facebook, so much. It is so beautiful in its own impoverished way, like walking through the pages of a *National Geographic* magazine. Sometimes, I feel like I should have been a photojournalist.

After our walk, breakfast, and morning devotional with Pastor Danny, we load up and head out on our bumpy mountainous drive to Danli. It will take about an hour. Although it gets a little rough on our behinds, my friend Danny and I always sit in the back of Pastor Danny's pickup to take in the scenery and grab some good pictures.

I've never been inside a prison, let alone a foreign prison. I've only been a guest in jails in my earlier years. When we arrive, we join up with our other team that's been with another ministry and are told to leave any cameras, phones, tablets, and all electronic devices in our vehicles. The prison in Danli doesn't resemble anything like U.S. prisons you see in the news, in movies, or on TV. The guards escort us into the main prison area, which is outside, and there appear to be rows of single story cells, many with clothes lines stretched in between and prison laundry hung to dry. Prisoners are just milling about, some braiding leather strips attached to hooks, of some sort, making them into belts that can be sold outside of prison at souvenir stands, I believe. It is their way to make money from inside prison. We work our way down the outdoor corridor, ducking under or walking around hanging laundry, nodding and saying hello (hola, hola.) to the men in the yard, until we get to, what seems to be, the prison community room that doubles as a chapel.

There's already a Honduran pastor, a friend of Pastor Danny's, inside along with a small band consisting of a drummer, guitar player, and keyboard player. Shortly, prisoners start wandering in, some with their Bibles. The band starts playing Christian rock music. I recognize much of the music. It's what I listen to on K-LOVE and WAYFM, my two favorite Christian rock stations, but the lyrics are Spanish. This is so cool. Before long, the chapel is full, probably about a hundred guys, with only room left outside for the men to pear in through the glassless barred window openings and standing in the doorway.

It's incredible watching and listening to these prisoners singing with so much joy and unashamed, professing their faith through their singing, many with hands raised in praise singing so loudly from their soul. I not only hear but also feel the fire burning bright inside them. I am so moved. These prisoners who are locked up but, by the same token, being so free, freer than even me. I am still so locked up inside myself. I have come to Christ, I have been saved, but I have spent so much of my life afraid of what others think of me that I keep my own fire locked up inside. I'm reserved and shy, but I have this burning fire that I hold as prisoner because of my own fears. I am moved to tears that I fight to hold back because I don't want to be seen crying. I have tears of joy because I know I am so blessed to be here experiencing this. I have tears of shame that I don't let myself be free. Watching these men, I just want to hug them all and absorb what they have. I am actually jealous of their boldness in faith that I also feel within me but too timid to show. Through all my emotions, I'm feeling I am also thanking God for allowing me to be here, thanking Him from the bottom of my soul. And He knows how deep that gratitude is.

When all the singing is done, Pastor Danny and the other pastor take the stage. Pastor Danny in English, while the other Pastor translates, introduces our whole mission group to the prisoners and then starts to introduce the person who is going to speak to them today. The introduction is nice. Some young man that's going to give an incredible testimony they will all love to hear. Everything Pastor Danny is saying about this guy has me intrigued...up to the point when he calls me to the stage and introduces Craig Walter from The Rock Family Worship Center. Oh...my...gosh!!! This was not expected. Fear and panic have just hit but with a quick *"Lord, help me. Jesus, I need you."* in my head, I walk up anyway. Fortunately, I still had my notes in my pants pocket from yesterday. God, that "voice" is not talking to me right now. I get no silent voices in my head. The voice I do get is Pastor Danny whispering in my ear, *"Your testimony and what you have to say is what these prisoners, these men, will be able to relate to."* My eyes are still moist from all the praise and worship as I take center stage and look out at all these men looking back at me with anticipation. Oh my gosh…what an incredible…I'm almost speechless as I look out at all their faces. I am so…so…immensely humbled at this very moment. I say a quick silent *Jesus* in my head.

With the other pastor translating, I start by telling them how truly humbled and absolutely privileged I feel to be here with them to be asked to talk to them. I also tell them how I was even jealous of them during their praise and worship. My words to them just started flowing, and I really didn't need to refer to my notes for this. I felt like I belonged here with them.

*****

This is the actual outline of my testimony I gave on Christian radio and to the prisoners at the prison in Danli. I was able to elaborate from this outline when I spoke. The very last sentence was actually an adlib since I didn't know previously that I was going to speak at the prison.

> *My being here is a miracle in itself in many ways. 2 months ago I had absolutely no money to make this trip. God touched many people's hearts and money was donated from all over, friends, family and strangers, so that I could be here and be able to be of some service to the people of Honduras.*
>
> *11 years ago in 2004 at the age of 41, I got sober. I am now 52. I had been drinking/smoking since 19 and an everyday drinker since I was 25. The last 10 yrs of my drinking I drank nearly a ½ gallon of vodka a day. I nearly drank myself to death. I had become completely mentally, physically, emotionally & spiritually bankrupt. My last drunk weekend in Aug 2004 I remember begging, pleading, praying for help. My obsession to drink after 22 yrs was taken away. A year later I had major surgery on my pancreas. Alcohol destroyed nearly ½*

of it. Dr.'s said if I hadn't gotten sober when I did, I wouldn't have lived that last year. It wasn't until yrs later I realized it was God at work. God wasn't done with me yet.

I had been smoking over a pack of cigarettes a day for 28 yrs and in 2010 God took cigarettes out of my life. God was still not done with me yet. By taking alcohol & cigarettes away I believe He was preparing me for my next ordeal.

In 2011 I was diagnosed late stage 4 cancer. Very aggressive radiation & chemo every day. Feeding tube in stomach. I wasn't scared to die physically but the very possibility of my eternal death became real. I never really went to church but I knew of The Rock and started going. I talked with God everyday during treatments. Just talked. Did a lot of praying for the other cancer patients I met. I went to work every day (Dr.'s don't know how). One Sunday at church, after an emotional service for me. I went to the altar for prayer, feeding tube wrapped neatly under my shirt so no one could see, and that is when I really allowed Jesus Christ into my life. By the end of 2011 I was done with treatments and my cancer was gone. My Dr.'s said I had been on their "Not so good" list and to them my recovery was "almost miraculous". I believe it "was" miraculous. I got baptized at The Rock in 2012.

My being here today, being able to share my story with you, tells me that God is still not done with me yet.

Just by you being here listening to me, regardless of what you did to be here, means that God's not done with you yet either.

*****

I speak to these men for at least a good half hour. At times, I am fighting back tears of my own, tears that express my extreme gratitude to God for the blessings in life I have. By the time I'm finished, I see a number of men wiping away tears of their own. I do not see prisoners. I just see men, not unlike myself, that made bad choices in their lives. I feel so blessed to be a part of this.

Aside from some sniffling, the room remains quiet as I take my seat. Pastor Danny and the other pastor lead us all in prayer and an altar call for anyone who wants to receive Jesus Christ. Many of the men work their way forward to the front for prayer. There are so many with hands raised to receive Christ that can't make it to the front. Many are in tears. I am deeply moved witnessing this. The Holy Spirit fills this room, and I can feel God's presence in this prison.

Some of the people on our team go to these men and lay their hands on them and pray with them. Although I don't feel worthy enough to be a conduit such as this, I am compelled to do the same, to at least lay my hands on their shoulders while the pastors are praying, just letting them know that I care. I pray silently in my head for each man I touch. I may not know what to pray, but God knows my heart, and because of my faith and belief in Jesus, I believe God's Spirit flows through me. Again, I am moved to tears. Afterward, I receive many hugs from these same men, and I am told that that's just what these men need...sometimes just a hand on the shoulder.

When we are finished at the prison, we head back to Teupasenti where the children are and our part of the work that needs to be finished. Toward the end of our trip, after I get to play so much more with all the kids, I find out that Children's Cup is setting up a sponsorship program for all the children. There are just many loose ends that need to be tied up before it goes online. Immediately, before I even know what sponsorship entails...because it really doesn't matter, I inform Pastor Danny that I would love to sponsor Carlos and Mauricio. Pastor Danny puts the word out that I have "dibs" on these two boys.

On our last day, we have some very emotional goodbyes with everyone. This has been an incredible life-changing experience for me. I am very fortunate to have been a part of this mission trip. I don't know that I could ever do a five-star vacation again and feel good about it.

After we get back to the states, I have my surgeries: oral, knee, and shoulder. I finish my hyperbaric treatments, which also helps the healing from my surgeries. I get a partial denture, and I settle back into my regular routine. I heal quickly and don't need any physical therapy. I just take it real slow at the gym for a little while. Life is good.

I have also started my own little campaign with Children's Cup to ensure that I will be able to Sponsor Carlos and Mauricio. For almost four months, I am relentless in my e-mails and phone calls to Rebekah, one of the Children's Cup representatives. We even become friends on Facebook so she can see all the pictures of the children in Honduras. She's working real hard on my behalf. Then on December 17, I receive this e-mail:

> Rebekah R <xxxxxxxxx@childrenscup.org>
> To
> Craigawalter
> 12/17/15 at 4:41 p.m.
>
> Hi Craig!
> *Boy do I have great news for you today!! We have both of your little guys, Carlos and Mauricio, registered and ready for sponsorship:) I have connected them to your account and will print the booklets and mail them out tomorrow! YAY!! Oh I did want to let you know that the little boy you know as "Mauricio" is actually Denis Mauricio. Same picture as the one you sent us and Pastor Danny confirmed.*

My post to Facebook:
December 17, 2015.

I am extremely blessed, privileged & honored!! As of today I am officially sponsoring my little buddy, Carlos & my little man, Mauricio in Teupasenti, Honduras. God saw to it, through all of you, that I was on that mission trip for a reason. I am certain this is just the beginning. Thank you all for your prayers and assistance!!

I receive a great many responses to this including one from Pastor Danny.

Daniel Dyer *They couldn't be in better hands! Congratulations Craig.*

What a great early Christmas present!

New Year's News

ℰ   ℭ

After the beginning of the New Year, I start to have oral issues again. More teeth are coming loose. I'm becoming very frustrated. I thought after last year, it was all under control. I know what this means: more extractions, more hyperbaric, more money. Cancer was five years ago, and I'm still dealing with the after effects. As I keep saying, *"Cancer, the gift that keeps giving."* I always say this lightheartedly because I am so very aware that it nearly took my life, but by God's mercy and grace, I am still here…alive. But it still gets frustrating.

I go see my oral surgeon. We're getting to know each other fairly well. He does mission work, in his field, in Central America also. We have some nice little chats. This visit is different. He takes his scans, does his looking in my mouth, and informs me that there is not much more he can do. With each extraction I've had, the jawbone keeps dying and moving on to the next tooth on either side. He says we can keep this going, extraction and hyperbaric, but we are not accomplishing anything. I only have seven teeth left on my bottom jaw. My radiation was from my lower jaw down through my neck, so my upper jaw is fine. Thank God. He wants to send me to someone more specialized in osteonecrosis of this type. There's a top doctor at Vanderbilt in Nashville and another at Kirklin Clinic in Birmingham. Huntsville is in between both, but I opt for Birmingham since I'm more familiar with that area. We set up an appointment for the end of January, a little over a week away.

When I get to the Kirklin Clinic, my doctor reviews my history and does his own looking and asking of questions. I'm given an injection then taken to have bone scans done. It's a two-part process that

399

takes about three hours. There are the initial scans then more scans after the injection has had time to make it into my jawbone.

It takes a while for my doctor to get the results, and when I'm called back in, I am given the devastating news. He informs me that due to the radiation treatments for my cancer, the vascular system that supplies blood and oxygen to my jawbone is no longer supplying the amounts required. My jawbone is slowly dying. I will need surgery to remove part of my jawbone. He proceeds to explain what would take place.

I will have a feeding tube for about three months. (No! Not this again. Cut me open. Canned nutrition feeding sessions again. It took me so long to get my abs back.) This is what's running through my mind.

One of the two main arteries from my left arm will be removed, connected to the carotid artery in my neck, and worked into the jaw area to create a new vascular system.

Part of my jaw will be cut out and, possibly, replaced with titanium and a flap of skin from the underside of my left wrist will be used to create new gum tissue.

This surgery will take many hours. My head is reeling. It's not cancer but…my gosh.

Lord, God, what's happening. My mind is thinking dollar signs. Every year, it is another thing. I can't keep doing this anymore. But my first question is, *"Will I be disfigured?"* He assures me that any scarring on my neck and arm will be very minimal and faint. Okay, I feel a little better, but not a lot. He showed me the scans and explained what we were looking at as he rotated my scanned head skeleton around and inside out on the computer. I've known my bone was dying but thought everything was getting better, until this past month. I quickly resign myself to the fact that this needs to be done. We talk some more. He gives me a bunch of papers to take home to read that gives a more in-depth explanation of this procedure. I am to come back n two weeks for more scans, questions if I have any, and we will set the surgery date.

On my ninety-minute drive home, I'm fighting back tears. I've seen pictures of people that have had to have jaw bones removed. It is absolutely not pretty. I'm asking God to help me accept this and listening to my Christian rock stations, WAYFM and KLOVE. All this music helps to calm me. I remember my friend Melissa is part of a ministry team through our church, The Bridge Ministry. They do a service for the homeless on Sunday's, at the homeless center First Stop, and serve them lunch after. I had volunteered with the homeless at Thanksgiving. I think I will stop by there to help when I'm done ushering at church Sunday.

Even after my usual morning prayers, I'm still feeling a little down on Sunday when I go to church. I can't stand it when I'm feeling even a little bit of self-pity. I don't remember feeling that going through cancer, but I'm having a tough time with this one. During our group usher prayer, I do ask them to pray for me. That was not easy. After my church service ends, I go to First Stop and sit with the homeless through their service and help with lunch.

My Facebook posting later in the afternoon:

Craig Walter
January 31 · Huntsville

Recently my doctors told me that radiation from my cancer treatments has done irreparable damage. Vascular system killed off, lower jawbone is dying. Parts of jaw will be cut out replaced with grafted tissue, an artery from left arm removed to replace dead vascular system in jaw. Feeding tube for a little while. This has all been a bit scary. Shallow fears. Will I be disfigured (they say no) finances, the EXTREME inconvenience in my life. I went to church this morning as usual and afterwards went to First Stop, a center for homeless where they also do a little service and lunch on Sundays. My friend Melissa, who was on the Honduras Mission Trip with me, dedicates a lot of her time there. I was also able to help at Thanksgiving serving the homeless.

The lady who led the service today had me nearly in tears.

Then we served lunch. All I had to do was serve the lasagna, that Melissa had been up since 5:30am preparing. All the homeless and much less fortunate people coming through to get lunch with their very heartfelt "thank you's" sometimes timid "bless you" most hoping there will be enough for them to get seconds. My heart just floods. I should be thanking them. It is truly a privilege to be able to serve them. God reminding me that no matter how bad my situation may be there are always others in less fortunate positions in life. I am usually aware of that but sometimes get caught up in, what I would call, my own misfortunes and need a spiritual knock upside the head. Things can always be worse. On the drive home Chris Tomlin's "How Great Is Our God" followed by his song "Good Good Father" came on the radio. What a beautiful morning it has been.

Two weeks later, I go back to the Kirklin Clinic for more scans. I'm in my doctor's office discussing the surgery. We're ready to schedule when my scans come down. I take a deep breath and, silently in my head, say, *"Lord God, my Father…Jesus…just be with me."*

My doctor is not talking. He pulls up my scans from two weeks ago on the other computer. He's looking at them side by side. With some hesitation in his voice and almost sounding perplexed, he says, *"We don't need to do surgery anymore."* He keeps looking at my scans and rotating them. I know he has the right scans because that's definitely the silhouette of my big nose on that skull.

Now I'm confused. *"How can that be?"* I ask.

After a few moments of silence, all he could come up with, for lack of anything else to say, was *"Good oral hygiene?"* I tell him I've always had good oral hygiene, even taking all the rinses my other doctor had prescribed. He just tells me that something has happened over the past two weeks, some unforeseen healing. We don't need to do surgery. He continues to explain to me that while we're where we're at, I should have the last of my teeth extracted all at one time, to be safe, and do another three months of hyperbaric. When I'm finished healing, I would be able to get a full denture. I'm in disbelief, and he admits that he doesn't really understand it. I mention, *"I know I have had a lot of people praying for me."* He didn't have anything to say about that. I drove home with tears of gratitude, talking to God out loud, thanking Him. I even called a friend.

My Facebook post when I got home:

Craig Walter
February 8 ·Huntsville

Any skeptics where the power of prayer is concerned...?? Please read all of this. Two weeks ago I was given the horrifying news from a top specialist that due to radiation damage from cancer treatments I was going to have to have part of my jawbone removed, be on a feeding tube for a while, an artery removed from left arm & transplanted to my carotid artery & into my jawbone & skin graft taken to replace gum & bone tissue. I never asked for prayer before nor prayed for my own... healing. Even going through cancer I only prayed for the healing of the other patients. Even so, my doctors said that I was on their "not so good list" being late stage 4 to cancer free they said my recovery was near miraculous. I did ask for prayer this time and I know A LOT of people through groups at my church The Rock, and from friends, were praying for healing.

I just got back from Birmingham's Kirklin Clinic again having had more scans done. Before my results came back my Dr. asked if I had read the material he gave me about the surgery & if there were questions. Basically we were ready to finalize

& schedule. My scans came down, he looked at them with some disbelief, compared them to the scan 2 weeks ago, after a couple of minutes he told me that surgery did not seem necessary anymore. The scan today showed healing that was not expected. Could not have been foreseen. I asked him how could that be and he really didn't have an explanation. I will still lose the remaining lower teeth and go through more hyperbaric treatments and get some form of a denture but something happened these last 2 weeks that completely changed the course of action against this radiation damage. That something I truly believe to be "The Power Of Prayer" I am not going to have a feeding tube or jawbone removed or artery transplanted. I called a friend on the way home to share the good news, she said "I guess it's one of those unexplained phenomenons" I told her "it's called prayer" she said "yeah, well..." Now...What Do You All Think???

*****

Immediately following this Facebook post, I was flooded with replies of "Prayer works," "Amen," "Praise God," "To God be the Glory," "Sending more prayers." To me, there is absolutely no disputing the power of prayer and the healing powers of God through Jesus Christ.

Who I Am

꽃

First and foremost, as the lyrics go in the song "Hello My Name Is" by Matthew West, I am a "Child of the One True King. I've been saved, I've been changed, and I have been set free." I am a child of God.

For a good part of my life, I had a deep set belief that I was who my mother and father said I was: good for nothing, fat a_ _, not worth the f_ _ _ing trouble, worthless, less than, ugly, and on and on. I couldn't escape that. I had absolutely no positive self-image, no self-confidence, and no self-worth or self-respect. I was broken as a child, broken as a young adult. Even today, those painful words still linger in the far recesses of my mind. Fading memories that won't go away, but just seem to want to stay. However, I have learned and come to believe and know that I do have merit, talent, beauty, and worth. I am a very compassionate, caring, and loving person. I believe I am who God says I am.

I am me.

That, in itself, is a truly beautiful and wonderful thing.

I remember when I was certain acting was going to be my life. I loved acting. I loved being on stage. I loved being and bringing someone else to life, entertaining the audience. I wanted to do that in movies. I wanted fame. I wanted fortune. Through all the characters I would portray, I was going to gain the type of recognition that let everyone know "I am somebody", not the "nobody" I grew up believing I was. I wanted to be a star. God didn't see it that way, though. I wanted everything, but for all the wrong reasons. I had no idea the insane roller-coaster ride of crazy, bad choices God was going to allow me to take before I would realize this.

When I look back at my life, I don't understand my childhood—why all the abuse, anger, and rage. But I also realize I don't need to understand. I never would be able to. It just was for whatever reason, something that had to be. Growing up and into my adult life, I witness boys and men's interactions with their parents. I observe and listen to how a son's love and respect is showered upon his mother. I watch the close bond fathers and sons share. I am unable to comprehend how any of that must feel.

My parents were responsible for my upbringing. They played their role in molding the young adult I had become, full of self-loathing and absolutely no self-respect. I had come to blame them for the disaster my life had become. My upbringing did influence my decision-making as a young adult. But ultimately...I realize today... as an adult...my choices had become my own regardless of how I was raised. I am accountable.

When I left Minnesota for LA... Hollywood to be exact...to pursue my dream of acting and stardom and Oscars...to escape my past, I became rebellious inside to a certain extent. I was going to live life, experience life, see things, do everything, and bury my past. Instead of burying my past, I found something. Actually, something found me: a drug—drugs and alcohol. They showed me I didn't have to bury the past. But through them, I could forget the past and just feel good. I could feel whole. I could feel like I belonged, normal. I liked the way they made me feel. I fit in. I could feel good about myself until I came down. I felt popular until I came down. I could look in the mirror and see someone I liked... until I came down. Someone attractive... until I came down. I wasn't worthless... until I came down. Everything was right and good with the world... until I came down. Slowly these mind altering substances became a strong and powerful need. My best friend.

By the time I was twenty-five, they were an everyday occurrence.

By the time I was thirty, they were taking over my life.

By the time I was forty, they had complete control and were killing me.

None of the things I had become were ever on my bucket list. As a child, I certainly didn't dream of becoming an alcoholic or a drug user. I had much loftier goals and desires. My very sordid and unsavory lifestyle of night clubs and sex clubs was most certainly not part of the picture I had painted for my future.

For many years, my life had become a wild roller-coaster ride full of corkscrew twists and turns, exhilarating highs, upside downs, and crashing lows. Over the years, hardly a day went by that I wasn't driving under the influence of one substance or another. Today, my life is more like a Caribbean cruise…peaceful and tranquil. When a cruise ship hits rough waters, it has stabilizers to steady itself. When I hit rough waters today…God and Jesus are my stabilizers.

I found out that through God and Jesus Christ, I could feel whole, no longer broken.

I used to feel a lot of shame about my past. Drugs, nightclubs, sex clubs then I am reminded, through the lyrics in a song titled "Clean" by an amazing Christian artist Natalie Grant:

> There's nothing too dirty
> That You can't make worthy
> You wash me in mercy
> I am clean

I want to just stop wherever I am when I hear this song and cry as I try to comprehend how pure and unconditional God's love is for me. I am so undeserving, yet through Jesus, He shows me so much mercy, grace, and forgiveness. Or this song by the Christian rock group Mercy Me, "Flawless":

> Could it possibly be
> That we simply can't believe
> That this unconditional
> Kind of love would be enough
> To take a filthy wretch like this
> And wrap him up in righteousness
> But that's exactly what He did
> No matter what they say
> Or what you think you are

The day you called His name
He made you flawless

He is continually blessing me, showing me mercy and grace.

*****

Not too long ago, I was out and about running errands when a lady came up to me in a store and asked, *"Don't I know you?"*

I replied, *"You look vaguely familiar."* I really had no clue.

She asked, *"Is your name Craig?"*

Very confused, I hesitantly replied, *"Yes...but I'm not sure how I would know you."*

She went on to explain that she used to be the manager of a certain liquor store that I frequented quite often. I told her that I remember I would go there every day to buy my vodka but that I have been sober for twelve years now. I asked her how she knew my name. She replied by telling me the story about how one day they refused me service because I was already intoxicated. It seems I called their corporate office in Montgomery to complain. Someone came to Huntsville to meet with me, but I was intoxicated that day also and was banned from that store.

I apologized to her. She said it was okay because she could see by looking at me that my life has changed. She said I used to be "heavier" back then but I look to be in incredibly good shape now and have a very healthy "glow" about me. I told her that I had been a slovenly 180 pounds of vodka when I got sober. Now I'm 155 pounds of lean sober muscle, and that "glow"...is actually God doing His work in me.

I appreciate the forgotten memory being brought to light. It's a good reminder for me as to the ugly past the Lord has rescued me from.

Something happened to me that last drunk weekend that I couldn't explain. How my obsession to drink had just been lifted from me, taken away. I used to say that "God mistook my pleas for help as a prayer." But isn't that what prayers *are* most of the time anyway? Pleas for help? I didn't have to specifically say "God." He knew where I was at, and He knew I was ready. I didn't realize it at the time, but ever since, I've slowly been letting God into my life. It wasn't until I accepted Jesus as my Savior and asked Him into my life that my world really started to change and my faith grew.

I used to think that if I could live my younger years over, I would hopefully make better choices. But then, during the writing of this book, Mercy Me came out with a new song called "Dear Younger Me," and I listen to these lyrics.

Dear younger me
I cannot decide
Do I give some speech about how to get the most out of your life
Or do I go deep
And try to change
The choices that you'll make cuz they're choices that made me

I have to believe that I am the person today that God had intended all along.

Every mountain every valley
Thru each heartache you will see
Every moment brings you closer
To who you were meant to be

It took all those choices I made throughout my life, good and bad, disastrous or achieving, to be who I am today, and I am still not fully the person that God intends me to be. God is continually working in me and through me, even when I allow myself to stray off the path He has chosen for me.

Then I hear the lyrics at the end of the song.

You are holy
You are righteous
You are one of the redeemed
Set apart a brand new heart

You are free indeed

And my eyes tear up.

Yes, I do a lot of crying these days. Not "bawling" crying, just wet eyes and a few tears that just run down my cheek with a smile on my face. But it's all out of gratitude, humility, and joy. I see and feel things today that I never used to or even believed I ever would. I see and feel every day how truly blessed I am in knowing God and Jesus are with me. I rejoice inside knowing God loves me unconditionally. I'm moved to tears at times knowing I'm not deserving, but He still loves me and is always forgiving.

Sometimes, just topping the hill on my drive home from work, looking across the valley, over all the tree tops to the hills in the distance, I often just say a quiet, *"Thank you, God. Thank you, Jesus,"* and my eyes will water.

When I first went back to church, feeling so uncomfortable and awkward, I like to believe this is what God was telling me, straight from the Matthew West song "Mended."

> When you see broken beyond repair
> I see healing beyond belief
> When you see too far gone
> I see one step away from home

Even Christian artist TobyMac basically summed up my journey to date in four lines in his song "Love Broke Thru."

> I did all that I could to undo me
> But You loved me enough to pursue me
> Yeah, You drew me out of the shadows
> Made me believe that I mattered, to You

That's God. Never giving up on me.

It hasn't been easy to come to terms with, but since coming to Christ, I have learned that I am not defined by my past. Not only does my pastor help me realize this through his messages in church, but also the Christian music that I listen to every day helps to reinforce that.

Tenth Avenue North (You Are More)

You are more than the choices that you've made,
You are more than the sum of your past mistakes,
You are more than the problems you create,
You've been remade.

I had never heard of Christian rock. I didn't know there was such a thing until I was introduced to it during my fight with cancer. I have realized that it's the gospel put to a beat—a rock beat, a pop beat, a rap or country beat. It's the Bible to music. There are many times I will be at church and our pastor is reading from scripture, and suddenly, I'm thinking "there's a song about that by so and so" or that verse is used in such-n-such song. This is all I listen to. My car is always tuned to WAY-FM or KLOVE. I always show up to work in a great mood. This Christian music helps keep my mind focused on the path before me, God's will. I even wake up in the mornings singing a song in my head as if it's been playing all night.

I have to work every other weekend, and I really miss being in church on those working weekends. When I am at church, I see so many young people in their teens and twenties that I can tell are filled with a love for God and Jesus through all the joy they exude during praise and worship when they are singing along with the band and choir. I sometimes wish that what I see in them, I had had at that age. But then…who would I be today? The song "Dear Younger Me" comes to mind again. I am moved to tears of happiness for them and pray that they don't let it go. I hope I see the number of young people continue to multiply. It is such a beautiful thing.

*****

I used to wonder if there could possibly be anything special about me. I found out: "To God, *everything* about me is special." My sins are no greater than yours and yours no greater than mine. In God's eyes, sin is sin and all sin is an abomination. God loves me. He loves us all in spite of our sins. God uses flawed and sinful people throughout the Bible for good works.

Yes, I have come to Christ, but I still struggle with issues in my life. God has seen to it to take some of them from me but many I'm left to wrestle with. Some more than others. God leaves me with the choice as to whether I call on Him, through Jesus, for help or if I go it alone. Many days, I fail miserably. Every day, I fall short.

I still have my defects and flaws. I have so very much of my parents inside me. I have the potential for their anger and rage, and I pray and ask for help every day. I have resentments, jealousies, and envies. I have my desires and my attractions. Although I still struggle, my behaviors and my attitudes have changed. The more I walk in faith, the more they continue to change. I am more aware of my wanting to be obedient in my walk with Christ.

I will always stumble and fall, but I am so much more conscious of the way I'm acting and living. Many times, throughout a day, I will find myself apologizing to God for the foul words I just used because the guy in the car next to me cut me off, or the agitated thoughts directed toward someone at the gym who interrupts my "ever so important" (as if I'm all that matters) circuit training routine and jumps in on a machine in front of me, or when I come home from a long day at work and I get angry at my cats because there's a hair ball vomited up on the living room carpet, or the customer at the register in front of me is taking too long and I don't always have the patience. Quite a few choice words go through my mind on occasion. Many times, I find myself saying out loud or quietly in my head, depending on where I am, *"Sorry, God. Sorry, God. Sorry, God. I didn't mean that. Well, okay, yes, I did, but I'm still sorry."* I apologize to God when I cuss myself out for doing something stupid. I do a lot of apologizing, but I also do a lot of thanking. I am also learning to take a step back, if I'm irritated with someone, take a good look at them, and remind myself that they are no different than me—a child of God with problems of their own.

Many times, throughout a day, I will find myself just chatting with God or saying short little prayers of thanks. *"Thank you, Lord, for just being with me."* I almost always have a Christian song playing in my head.

I believe that my life is meant to honor God. God didn't place me on this earth to pursue my own happiness, my own desires. God wants me to be happy, but I am learning that only through my pursuit of Him, through Jesus, can I find real happiness. I am realizing that more and more each day.

*****

I still workout hard at the gym. Even though my doctors used the word *miraculous* in regard to my cancer healing, they also said they believe that my being in such good shape going into treatment played a large part in my "miraculous" recovery. I, most absolutely, give God all the credit. This has been all God, all along. There isn't a day that goes by without my thanking God for giving my life and my health back to me. I say *"Thank you"* with every morning prayer and always a *"Thank you"* when I'm at the gym.

I still enjoy the many compliments I get. Yes, a part of my ego plays into my staying in shape. I like to look good. But when I am complimented, it usually gives me the opportunity to turn the conversation toward God. All I do is mention that *"Just a few years ago, I was a late stage 4 cancer."* That typically blows them away, leaves them stunned. They tell me how lucky I must feel and then they want to hear the story. I share the major details and tell them God had absolutely everything to do with my survival and miraculous recovery. Sometimes, my talk of recovery, God and Jesus will start to get a little emotional, but it almost always ends up with the other person saying something to the effect of, *"You are truly an inspiration. Definitely an inspiration to me."*

I'm blessed to have a new Christian friend at the gym. His name is Jonathan, he's also a pastor. We really only met because I was wearing my "Lion of Judah" shirt one day, which prompted him to comment on it. That opened the door to periodic chats we have in the locker room or outside, about God, Jesus, church, Christian music. Whenever I'm in a spiritual, faith-based conversation, I feel so alive inside. A spiritual kind of alive that I can't fully describe. I feel close to Jesus, and again, I'm reminded of lyrics to yet another song. This one by Citizen Way, "When I'm with You."

> When I'm with You
> I feel the real me finally breaking through
> It's all because of You, Jesus

I don't do this often enough, and I generally get emotional every time I have the opportunity to talk about God and Jesus, everything that He allows me to do. It's like Jesus is standing with me listening to me share my stories of His wondrous works in my life with animated gestures and a smile on my face usually holding back a tear or two. This is when the real me starts to come out. The me God wants me to be more often.

Every morning, a part of my prayer is, *"Lord, help me to be able to help someone else find you."* When I post on social media, I almost always accompany my post with a Christian rock video. One day, I posted Mathew West's "Broken Things," and this was a comment I received:

> Holly Smith:
> *I guess God does use broken things, because he's used me. To what extent I don't know, but I know that he has. I have to tell you after your last post & listening to the song, I listened to a few other songs after that. One of them spoke deeply to me. I have believed in God, but have been unsure of my belief in Jesus for over 29 years. That wound finally healed tonight, & I can now honestly say I believe in Jesus Christ once again. This is a miracle for me, one I thought would never happen as I had so many*

doubts & fears. I wish I could remember the name of the song! In it, it says something like "you couldn't bear heaven without me so you brought heaven down to me". I was saved before. I am saved once again. And I am "Walking in the light". Thank you for helping to make that possible! I only owe you my life.

I had to reply.

Craig Walter:
You don't owe me your life. I'm just one of those "broken things" God uses. Just one of His instruments. All I do is share my story, my testimony, my ever growing faith and belief. Only through Jesus are we truly saved.

2 Corinthians 5:17; New Living Translation (NLT) 17 This means that anyone who belongs to Christ has become a new person. The old life is gone; a new life has begun!

Josh Wilson's "That Was Then This Is Now"

That was then, this is now
You're bought by the blood, saved by the Son the saints all sing about
That was lost, this is found
And it's time to say goodbye to the old you now

*****

I was homeless at one point as a teenager, almost homeless in LA in a rat-infested boarding house, lived in the back of a van for a short period of time when I moved to Huntsville, so I'm blessed to be a small part of The Bridge Ministry Team through my church that my friend Melissa had introduced me to. We hold a service for the homeless community three Sundays of each month, at a center, and serve lunch after the service. Through this ministry, I have become acquainted with many from the homeless community. I'm not sure how, but over a period of time, I have become a close friend and mentor with one of our homeless parishioners.

Calvin is thirty-seven, and for six months, he and I have built up a trust. I saw his positive side. I felt his big heart. He had some minor legal issues, and I would make sure I got him to court. Even the magistrate lady would make mention of his huge heart, and we both agreed that most people just don't take the time to sit and listen to him. Calvin is also schizophrenic, six foot seven, doesn't like to take his medication and lives in a shed on an abandoned lot.

Calvin had been to my home on quite a few occasions for dinner, when he would spend the night prior to a court date, to play basketball, or to just hang out. We would talk about many things, anything he needed or wanted to talk about—help in getting a job, getting off the street, his family, and all the wrongs he has done in his life. He liked to talk about God and the Bible. One time, he asked me, *"Which Calvin is God going to judge. The Calvin you see, or the schizophrenic Calvin that gets crazy?"* When not on his medication, he can be prone to very extreme anger and violent rages. I had witnessed a little of that, but he was never that way with me. He was always so respectful and courteous at my house to the point that I was going to consider helping him get a job through a temp agency and letting him stay with me three days a week since those days would coincide with my schedule.

When everything was looking good and positive, he was going to do his drug test and hopefully start work the next week, then I would share my idea with him...he messed up...very badly! I came home from work to find my property had been burglarized. Calvin had made it across town with some friends from tent city and an acquaintance with a truck that tore up my backyard to break into my brick storage shed taking over two thousand dollars of yard equipment. Two days later, he beat me to a bloodied, bruised mess. I can't hurt him back because it's not in me to do so. I have already called the police, so I just restrain him. He is in jail but we still keep in touch.

You see…another thing I have learned through God and Jesus, from my pastor's in church, through Christian music…is how to forgive. God not only commands this of us, but also it's the only right thing to do. If we don't forgive, God can't forgive us. I did my best friend very wrong in my past, and he forgave me. How could I not forgive Calvin. I keep a phone account open for whenever he just needs to talk to someone from jail. One time, he called to let me know he's okay and they're making sure he gets his medication. I've spoken with his public defender and the prosecutor about my concerns, not for vengeance, but for wanting what is going to get Calvin the help he needs. They are going to try to have this case moved to mental health court, which I'm happy to hear. Calvin knows I will remain a friend, just a little more cautious whenever he gets out.

After Calvin, however, my faith was beginning to falter in this area of helping others: boundary issues, trust issues, fears, and telling myself I'm much better with children, not adults. A little battle in my heart was ensuing. I shared my concerns with Melissa and she sent me this:

Galatians 6:9; New International Version (NIV)
Let us not become weary in doing good, for at the proper time we will reap a harvest if we do not give up.
"I don't believe a bit of what you poured into Calvin was wasted. Just don't tie your faith up, or your desire to serve others, with the outcome of this one circumstance. God has given you a huge heart to give and help."

I have since become a friend and mentor to others, like Quincy, who is vigilantly trying to find work. He sleeps in his car and sometimes manages to get a hotel room. We met on a Sunday service. Melissa noticed him indicating that he needed prayer and she asked me to go to him. It was awkward because I so often feel that I'm not worthy or qualified to pray over someone when I have so many issues myself. I had to push that negative aside and go over to him. I put my arm around his shoulder, held his hand, and asked what he needed prayer for. A sudden warmth came over me as I listened and started to pray with him. It felt as if Jesus, Himself, was laying his hands on our shoulders. I had to fight back tears during our prayer.

After we served lunch, I invited him to go with me to my house, I didn't tell him why, but I had left my wallet at home before my church service at The Rock and had been driving without my license or money. We spent a lot of time talking, and he couldn't stop saying how blessed he felt to have me praying for him. Afterward, he and I went shopping so he could get a new pair of shoes for an upcoming interview.

On a different Sunday service at the homeless center, I meet Rodney and his wife Angie. They needed prayer also. I put my arms around the two of them and pulled them close and prayed for their needs. It's getting easier if I just let Jesus guide me. All our prayers are in His name after all. Rodney and Angie are homeless only because things happened in life that were out of their control. Rodney is gainfully employed, but they no longer have a place to live and very few belongings. They really needed to do some laundry, mostly clothes for Rodney's job. Angie only had one pair of pants and a shirt, so we did a shopping trip then found a laundromat. God has so amazingly blessed my life that my new friends always get something extra to put in their pocket.

I also meet Diontay through a very heartfelt prayer request. He sleeps on the sidewalk outside a local charity. With all the assistance this young man needs, he has become a regular guest at my home and my church, and is constantly striving, very hard, to better himself.

Then there is also Quentin. He works at a car wash and makes sixty-five cents per vehicle plus tips, not much money in a day. At night, he gets to sleep in a small van at the back of the parking lot of the car wash. He routinely comes to my house for dinner, to do laundry and shower. We don't pray. We don't even talk about God. We tried that once, but it ended in an argument because Quentin believes all the problems today are God's fault. Quentin is not happy with, nor does he like, God. I do include him in my private prayers. I have assisted him in obtaining his birth certificate and a CDL drivers instruction manual. He has since received assistance from a trucking company that will put him through their school to be a commercial driver. They even paid for his bus ticket to get there. Once he arrived, he texted me asking if I would pray for him to get through the training. I replied, *"I didn't want to tell you at the risk of making you mad, but you have always been in my prayers."* So far, he is doing very well. I am certain he will be on the road real soon and not having to worry about sleeping in the back of a small van anymore, where to shower or do laundry. I am very happy for him. God is so good.

I look forward to my every other Sunday's off work, not only for my regular church service but also to see my friends and acquaintances in the homeless community during their service and lunch, to lend a hand, an ear, a prayer, or just a hug.

*****

I have such an amazing life today, an incredible life that only God could have orchestrated. Left up to me, I would have been dead by now. I am very happy and blessed. This is how I see it, how the Master Director that He was, He is, and He always will be in my life, took over my show.

My childhood was…it just was. I had no choice in that matter. But as I grew older and my childhood influenced my choices and decision-making into adulthood, God just gave me free reign and let me go. Even though I had knowledge of the church, I went my own direction—the drugs, the alcohol, the sex clubs, the nightclubs, and the whole sordid life I led. The very self-destructive path I followed, the suicide attempts, God allowed. But He never left. The times I could have died…should have died…meant to die…wanted to die…God wouldn't let me die. Even during my coma, when I believe I was being pulled toward the gates of hell, God didn't let go of me. God stayed with me until I was ready for Him.

It wasn't until that very last drunk weekend when I was pleading for help in every direction that, I believe, God told His angels… *"He's ready."*

God took my obsession to drink from me. He started me on a positive path and showed me I had a talent for flipping houses because He knew I was going to need one of them before too long.

He took me from an unhealthy relationship He didn't want me in. He took cigarettes from my life because, God says, *"He doesn't know that stage 4 cancer is right around the corner."* And then He told His angels, *"He doesn't know this either, but…he's coming to me."* God used my cancer as an opportunity to give me a jolt. It was a wake-up call to let me know that my time could be near. I felt that jolt and told God I was ready. He has kept me moving ever since. As I look back, I can see God's hand in my life, where I have come from to where He has brought me today.

I cry some and I laugh a lot. I have my angry moments, and I enjoy my quiet time. I make mistakes, many mistakes. Sometimes I get it right. I struggle, I pray, I overcome sometimes, and I pray some more. I always pray for others. I love God. I love Jesus. I love my church. I love all people. I especially love children because children are so special and should be treated as such.

The nephews I used to spoil are all grown now and the oldest, James, has a son of his own with his wife Heather. I adore their little Max and spoil him rotten whenever I can. I am blessed to have the title of "Gruncle" (great-uncle).

My friend Remethia, also known as simply "Meka," has a little boy Ethan who adores me, but that's because I also spoil him as much as possible and let him know how special he is.

I have a very spacious back patio with a basketball goal, the good kind, the tall kind where the post is cemented in the ground. It's the only one in the neighborhood, so I leave my backyard open for the kids in the area to come play. The only rule is…they must respect my property. For young kids, they do a fairly good job of that. I enjoy being able to provide them a place to play.

Then of course, there's "my" kids in Honduras. It is not only Carlos and Mauricio, but I also love to make them all feel special when I am there. When I really think about it…I think I do play more than I work, but making the children laugh and smile is well worth it. I want to be doing more.

I have learned to forgive my parents and to love them because they are my parents and God's children also. I have no hate nor anger toward them. My father has passed away. My mother and I don't talk, but we exchange the usual birthday and holiday cards. She also generously donates to my mission trips each year. I exchange yearly holiday cards with my stepmother also. We've barely had a relationship, but she also generously donates to my trips. I am grateful and blessed.

Another long-lost friend of mine from high school, Karen, recently found me on social media. It's been a few decades, and she was one of my very few close friends. This prompted me to take a look at some old school yearbooks. She had once written:

"I can just see it now. Me sitting in a movie theater watching one of your movies…You have a 'very special' role in life…God bless you. Love Karen."

My role in life? I didn't become the big star I wanted to be in high school, but God has blessed me in so many other ways. I continue to pray that He has more plans for me alongside Carlos, Mauricio, Honduras, and The Bridge Ministry with the homeless. There are so many people and children around the world, in extreme situations, that need help. I want to be able to do something. I want to be a part of that help. He showed me before, and I believe He will show me again. I look forward to each new day, and as long as God allows me to wake another day, as long as I have faith and believe in Jesus…and allow myself to be led by Him, I will be personally escorted down the path that was intended for me.

A few years ago, I was dying. All my doctors had me on their "not so good" list. But God has kept me here for a reason. I just don't know why entirely. Did God place Mauricio and Carlos in my life for their benefit or mine? Did God place my friend Calvin, Quentin, and the others from the homeless community in my life for their benefit or mine? Did God keep me here to be able to give my testimony to all those prisoners in Honduras, for their benefit or mine? Each person I meet, each person God places in my path…is it for their benefit or mine? Does God have me writing this book for the benefit of many or mine? My guess is "all of the above" and more.

You see…God's not done with me yet. He's only just begun!

GOD'S NOT DONE WITH ME YET

Epilogue

80 CB

My story was not unique. There are many similar stories and worse out there. Many, so sadly, are currently in the making. Of children, right now, experiencing horrifying abuses. Of young adults and adults who have already lived through it and find themselves on a path in life entirely different than what they had dreamed.

I was at the gym one morning and saw a horrific story on the news about a fourteen-year-old boy who had been locked in the basement for most of two years. Denied medical treatment and malnourished. He weighs fifty-five pounds and is fighting for his life in the hospital. The boy had been adopted, and his adoptive parents have been arrested.

There are many, many more stories like this going on all around our country, all around the world. These children become so damaged and broken. This needs to stop.

Parents…*love* your children. Biological or adopted or fostered, they are a *gift from God* to you.

This wasn't about me. This wasn't about my story. This *is* about everyone out there who needs to know there is still hope. Unending hope.

Love to you all,

Craig Walter

Craig Walter

P.S. One day—Africa.

"I always knew there was something special about you. Your smile could light up the room, but I also saw a painful darkness behind those beautiful eyes. You're a wonderful person. I love what you have written. Can't wait to read the book. I still wish I could go to Honduras with you. You have touched so many hearts there. You're going to the top. Love ya, Holly."

"Craig, you are a very humble and loving person, you have influenced more people than you may know, and I am *very* blessed that God has put you in my life! If it weren't for you, I would not be doing mission work, not to mention the inspiration you have given me in my fitness/health. God is using you in ways you may not even know, to reach so many people. I'm very proud to know you. I know God will bless you in all your efforts to serve Him. —Luke"

Judi once told me that she never stopped praying for me, that one day, I would find the Lord.

I never would have believed.

"From the day so many years ago, when Tim brought you home to us because you had nowhere to go, until today, I knew the Lord was waiting for you with open arms. He had wonderful plans for you. I prayed for you almost every day. You have come so far and accomplished so much. I remember crying the day you left us for California, I knew you weren't ready, and you would have so much to go through. I am proud of you, and I know you will walk with Jesus and sincerely love Him with all your heart. Stay true to Him, and you will never regret it. Love u bunches. —Judi"

Tim, Judi, Me, Dan, Aaron

One Sonic Society (Great Are You Lord)

All the earth will shout Your praise
Our hearts will cry, these bones will sing
Great are You, Lord
It's Your breath in our lungs
So we pour out our praise, We pour out our praise
It's Your breath in our lungs
So we pour out our praise to You only

For nearly two years of writing this book, my usually neat and clean coffee table is scattered with Post-its and anything I could find to write notes on.

The many faces of Carlos.

Nuhman, Carlos, and Ariel.

Carlos and his friend Nuhman.

Carlos was so happy when he got to play with my tablet and take pictures. He watched very carefully and learned quickly.

On a different trip. My two boys getting older. Inside the
Church Casa de Oracion Familiar in Teupasenti, Honduras.

On this other trip, outside of Carlos's home, I was able to give
Carlos his first brand new bike, along with other presents.
He calls it his Ferrari. Mauricio was very excited for him.

Mauricio with his grandmother opening
gifts I brought on a different trip.

Mauricio's home. One room, two beds.
He's the happiest little boy.

The Children's Cup church in Teupasenti.

Two of our weary fearless leaders David and Deborra.

Making cement. Just have to add water and stir. A lot.

Process for making plaster.

I love this little guy. All he wanted was hugs. Picture courtesy of Carlos.

We call him "Juan Valdez." Off to the coffee fields.

The store where we would get ice cream.

Village square.

The police station. Our WiFi connection.

Dental facility and Red Cross in Teupasenti.

Trying to make a new friend but he wasn't keen on the idea.

My more docile new friend.

Burro's freely roam the streets.

Cinder blocks are made by hand and sun dried/baked.

Honduran Lempiras

CPSIA information can be obtained
at www.ICGtesting.com
Printed in the USA
LVHW110806031218
598971LV00036B/566/P